**THE PARK
LEARNING CENTRE**
The Park, Cheltenham
Gloucestershire GL50 2RH
Telephone: 01242 714333

UNIVERSITY OF
GLOUCESTERSHIRE
at Cheltenham and Gloucester

WEEK LOAN

al

657 4/2011

The Basics of Digital Forensics
The Primer for Getting Started in Digital Forensics

John Sammons

Technical Editor

Jonathan Rajewski

ELSEVIER

AMSTERDAM • BOSTON • HEIDELBERG • LONDON
NEW YORK • OXFORD • PARIS • SAN DIEGO
SAN FRANCISCO • SINGAPORE • SYDNEY • TOKYO

SYNGRESS.

Syngress is an imprint of Elsevier

Acquiring Editor: Chris Katsaropoulos
Development Editor: Heather Scherer
Project Manager: Danielle S. Miller
Designer: Alisa Andreola

Syngress is an imprint of Elsevier
225 Wyman Street, Waltham, MA 02451, USA

Library of Congress Cataloging-in-Publication Data
Sammons, John.
  The basics of digital forensics : the primer for getting started in digital forensics / John Sammons.
    p. cm.
  ISBN 978-1-59749-661-2
  1. Computer crimes–Investigation. I. Title.
  HV8079.C65S35 2012
  363.25'968–dc23
                    2011047052

British Library Cataloguing-in-Publication Data
A catalogue record for this book is available from the British Library.

For information on all Syngress publications
visit our website at: *www.syngress.com*

Typeset by: diacriTech, Chennai, India

Printed and bound by CPI Group (UK) Ltd, Croydon, CR0 4YY

Transferred to digital print 2012

For Lora, Abby, and Rae for making me a truly
blessed and lucky man.

To my mother Juanita, and my grandmother Grace.
For the many sacrifices you made and
the example you set … I miss you.

Contents

Seal Team Six tore the hard drives from Osama bin Laden's computers. Some of Michael Jackson's final words were captured on an iPhone. Google searches for chloroform played a central role in the trial of Casey Anthony. This list could go on and on. Digital forensics is used to keep us safe, to ensure justice is done and company and taxpayer resources aren't abused. This book is your first step into the world of digital forensics. Welcome!

Digital forensics is used in a number of arenas, not just in catching identity thieves and Internet predators. For example, it's being used on the battlefields of Afghanistan to gather intelligence. The rapid exploitation of information pulled from cell phones and other devices is helping our troops identify and eliminate terrorists and insurgents.

It's being used in the multibillion-dollar world of civil litigation. Gone are the days when opposing parties exchanged boxes of paper memos, letters, and reports as part of the litigation process. Today, those documents are written in 1s and 0s rather than ink. They are stored on hard drives and backup tapes rather than in filing cabinets.

Digital forensics helps combat the massive surge in cybercrime. Identity thieves, child pornographers, and "old school" criminals are all using and leveraging technology to facilitate their illegal activities.

Finally, it's being used in the workplace to help protect both companies and government entities from the misuse of their computer systems.

INTENDED AUDIENCE

As the title suggests, this is a beginner's book. The only assumption is that you have a fundamental understanding or familiarity of computers and other digital devices. If you have a moderate or advanced understanding of digital forensics, this book may not be for you. As part of Syngress's "Basics" series, I wrote this book more as a broad introduction to the subject rather than an all-encompassing tome. I've tried to use as much "plain English" as possible, making it (hopefully) an easier read.

I'd like to emphasize that this is an introductory book that is deliberately limited in length. Given that, there is much that couldn't be covered in depth or even covered at all. Each chapter could be a book all by itself. There are many wonderful books out there that can help further your understanding. I sincerely hope you don't stop here.

ORGANIZATION OF THIS BOOK

The book is organized in a fairly straightforward way. Each chapter covers a specific type of technology and begins with a basic explanation of the technology involved. This is a necessity in order to really understand the forensic material that follows.

To help reinforce the material, the book also contains stories from the field, case examples, and Q and A with a cryptanalyst as well as a specialist in cell phone forensics.

Chapter 1 – Introduction

What exactly is digital forensics? Chapter 1 seeks to define digital forensics and examine how it's being used. From the battlefield to the boardroom to the courtroom, digital forensics is playing a bigger and bigger role.

Chapter 2 – Key Technical Concepts

Understanding how computers create and store digital information is a perquisite for the study of digital forensics. It is this understanding that enables us to answer questions like "How was that artifact created?" and "Was that generated by the computer itself, or was it a result of some user action?" We'll look at binary, how data are stored, storage media, and more.

Chapter 3 – Labs and Tools

In "Labs and Tools," we look at the digital forensic environment and hardware and software that are used on a regular basis. We will also examine standards used to accredit labs and validate tools. Those standards are explored along with quality assurance, which is the bedrock of any forensic operation. Quality assurance seeks to ensure that results generated by the forensic examination are accurate.

Chapter 4 – Collecting Evidence

How the digital evidence is handled will play a major role in getting that evidence admitted into court. Chapter 4 covers fundamental forensically sound practices that you can use to collect the evidence and establish a chain of custody.

Chapter 5 – Windows System Artifacts

The overwhelming odds are that you have a Windows-based computer on your desk, in your briefcase, or both. It's a Windows world. (No disrespect, Mac people. I'm one of you.) With over a 90% market share, it clearly represents the bulk of our work. Chapter 5 looks at many of the common Windows artifacts and how they are created.

Chapter 6 – Antiforensics

The word is out. Digital forensics is not the secret it once was. Recovering digital evidence, deleted files, and the like is now common place. It's regularly seen on such shows as NCIS and CSI. The response has been significant. They are now many tools and techniques out there that are used to hide or destroy data. These are examined in Chapter 6.

Chapter 7 – Legal

Although a "forensic" science, the legal aspects of digital forensics can't be divorced from the technical. In all but certain military/intelligence applications, the legal authority to search is a perquisite for a digital forensics examination. Chapter 7 examines the Fourth Amendment, as well as reasonable expectations of privacy, private searches, searching with and without a warrant, and the Stored Communications Act.

Chapter 8 – Internet and E-Mail

Social networks, e-mail, chat logs, and Internet history represent some of the best evidence we can find on a computer. How does this technology work? Where is this evidence located? These are just a few of the questions we'll answer in Chapter 8.

Chapter 9 – Network Forensics

We can find a network almost anywhere, from small home networks to huge corporate ones. Like computers and cell phones, we must first understand how things work. To that end, Chapter 9 begins with networking basics. Next, we start looking at how networks are attacked and what role digital forensics plays in not only the response, but how perpetrators can be traced.

Chapter 10 – Mobile Device Forensics

Small-scale mobile devices such as cell phones and GPS units are everywhere. These devices are in many respects pocket computers. They have a huge potential to store evidence. Digital forensics must be as proficient with these devices as they are desktop computers. We'll look at the underlying technology powering cell phones and GPS units as well as the potential evidence they could contain.

Chapter 11 – Looking Ahead: Challenges and Concerns

There are two "game-changing" technologies that are upon us that will have a huge impact on not only the technical aspect of digital forensics but the legal piece as well. The technology driving solid state hard drives negates much of the traditional "bread and butter" of digital forensics. That is our ability to recover deleted data. As of today, there is no answer to this problem.

Cloud computing creates another major hurdle. In the cloud, data are stored in a complex virtual environment that could physically be located anywhere in the world. This creates two problems; from a technical standpoint, there is an alarming lack of forensic tools that work in this environment. Deleted files are also nearly impossible to recover. Legally, it's a nightmare. With data potentially being scattered across the globe, the legal procedures and standards vary wildly. Although steps are being taken to mitigate this legal dilemma, the situation still persists today.

Being in its infancy, the digital forensics community still has work to do regarding how it conducts its business, especially in relation to the other more traditional disciplines. Chapter 11 will explore this issue.

Acknowledgments

Although my name may be on the cover, this book would not have been possible without the help and support of many people. First, I'd like to thank my family, particularly my wife Lora, and my two girls, Abby and Rae. Their patience, understanding, and willingness to "pick up my slack" while I wrote was invaluable. Thank you, ladies.

Next I'd like to thank Nick Drehel, Rob Attoe, Lt. Lannie Hilboldt, Chris Vance, and Nephi Allred for sharing their expertise and experiences. I have no doubt their contributions made this a better book.

My Chair, Dr. Mike Little, and my Dean, Dr. Charles Somerville, also helped make this book a reality. It would have been impossible for me to write this book and still do my "day job" without their support and assistance. Thank you, gentlemen.

I'd like to thank my Editor, Heather Scherer, and my Tech Editor, Jonathan Rajewski, for keeping me on task and on point. Danielle Miller, my Project Manager at Syngress, deserves my thanks as well for putting up with my last minute editing.

Many thanks go to Jennifer Rehme and Jonathan Sisson. Jennifer, as my GA, helped keep me afloat during the semester handling much of my grading and research for this book and other projects. Jonathan, a digital forensics student here at Marshall, created most of the graphics for this book. I have no doubt that each will be wildly successful and real contributors to the forensic science community. I wish you both nothing but continued success after graduation.

Finally, I'd like to thank Angelina Ward for giving me this opportunity.

John Sammons is an Assistant Professor at Marshall University in Huntington, West Virginia. John teaches digital forensics, electronic discovery, information security and technology in the Department of Integrated Science and Technology. He is also the founder and Director of the Appalachian Institute of Digital Evidence. AIDE is a non-profit organization that provides research and training for digital evidence professionals including attorneys, judges, law enforcement and information security practitioners in the private sector. Prior to joining the faculty at Marshall, John co-founded Second Creek Technologies, a digital forensics and electronic discovery firm. While at Second Creek, John served as the Managing Partner and CEO. John is a contract instructor for AccessData and is certified by them as both an instructor and examiner. He is a former Huntington Police officer and currently serves as an investigator for the Cabell County (WV) Prosecutors Office. As an investigator, he focuses on Internet crimes against children and child pornography. John is a member of the FBI WV Cybercrime Task Force. John routinely provides training for the legal and law enforcement communities in the areas of digital forensics and electronic discovery. He is an Associate Member of the American Academy of Forensic Sciences, the High Technology Crime Investigation Association, the Southern Criminal Justice Association, and Infragard.

Jonathan Rajewski (EnCe, CCE, CISSP, CFE, CSI, SANS Lethal Forensicator) is an Assistant Professor in the Computer & Digital Forensic program at Champlain College. Aside from his teaching responsibilities he is member of the Vermont Internet Crimes Task Force serving law enforcement and governmental entities. He is also a Director and Principle Investigator with the Senator Patrick Leahy Center for Digital Investigation. In his prior life he was a Global Senior Digital Forensic Consultant with Protiviti. He was recently honored as 2011 Digital Forensic Examiner of the Year by www.forensic4cast.com.

His high degree of professionalism, passion, and experience in the detection and prevention of white-collar crime complements his ability to teach, manage, and conduct digital forensic investigations. Jonathan has a keen ability to articulate very technical topics and present in such way that's understandable to both experienced and nontechnical audiences. Jonathan is also the author of the 2011->future Undergraduate Digital Forensic curriculum at Champlain College.

Jonathan has served many high profile confidential clients and has worked alongside many governmental and corporate teams. Jonathan holds a B.S. in Economic Crime Investigation from Hilbert College and an M.S. in Managing Innovation & Information Technology from Champlain College. Jonathan resides in Vermont with his family.

CHAPTER 1

Introduction

Information in This Chapter:

- What Is Forensic Science?
- What Is Digital Forensics?
- Uses of Digital Forensics
- Role of the Forensic Examiner in the Judicial System

"Each betrayal begins with trust."

—**"Farmhouse" by the band Phish**

INTRODUCTION

Your computer will betray you. This is a lesson that many CEO's, criminals, politicians, and ordinary citizens have learned the hard way. You are leaving a trail, albeit a digital one; it's a trail nonetheless. Like a coating of fresh snow, these 1s and 0s capture our "footprints" as we go about our daily life.

Cell phone records, ATM transactions, web searches, e-mails, and text messages are a few of the footprints we leave. As a society, our heavy use of technology means that we are literally drowning in electronically stored information. And the tide keeps rolling in. Don't believe me? Check out these numbers from the research company IDC:

- The digital universe (all the digital information in the world) will reach 1.2 million petabytes in 2010. That's up by 62% from 2009.

If you can't get your head around a petabyte, maybe this will help:

> "One petabyte is equal to: 20 million, four-drawer filing cabinets filled with text or 13.3 years of HD-TV video."
>
> **(Mozy, 2009)**

The impact of our growing digital dependence is being felt in many domains, not the least of which is the legal system. Everyday, digital evidence is finding its way into the world's courts. This is definitely not your father's litigation. Gone are the days when records were strictly paper. This new form of evidence presents some very significant challenges to our legal system. Digital evidence is considerably different from paper documents and can't be handled in the same way. Change, therefore, is inevitable. But the legal system doesn't turn on a dime. In fact, it's about as nimble as the Titanic. It's struggling now to catch-up with the blinding speed of technology.

Criminal, civil, and administrative proceedings often focus on digital evidence, which is foreign to many of the key players, including attorneys and judges. We all know folks who don't check their own e-mail or even know how to surf the Internet. Some lawyers, judges, businesspeople, and cops fit squarely into that category as well. Unfortunately for those people, this blissful ignorance is no longer an option.

Where law-abiding society goes, the bad guys will be very close behind (if not slightly ahead). They have joined us on our laptops, cell phones, iPads, and the Internet. Criminals will always follow the money and leverage any tools, including technology, that can aid in the commission of their crimes.

Although forensic science has been around for years, digital forensics is still in its infancy. It's still finding its place among the other more established forensic disciplines, such as DNA and toxicology. As a discipline, it is where DNA was many years ago. Standards and best practices are still being developed.

Digital forensics can't be done without getting under the hood and getting your hands dirty, so to speak. It all starts with the 1's and 0's. This binary language underpins not only the function of the computer but how it stores data as well. We need to understand how these 1's and 0's are converted into the text, images, and videos we routinely consume and produce on our computers.

WHAT IS FORENSIC SCIENCE?

Let's start by examining what it's not. It certainly isn't Humvees, sunglasses, and expensive suits. It isn't done without lots of paperwork, and it's never wrapped up in sixty minutes (with or without commercials). Now that we know what it isn't, let's examine what it is. Simply put, **forensics** is the application of science to solve a legal problem. In forensics, the law and science are forever integrated. Neither can be applied without paying homage to the other. The best scientific evidence in the world is worthless if it's inadmissible in a court of law.

WHAT IS DIGITAL FORENSICS?

There are many ways to define digital forensics. In *Forensic Magazine*, Ken Zatyko defined digital forensics this way:

> "The application of computer science and investigative procedures for a legal purpose involving the analysis of digital evidence after proper

search authority, chain of custody, validation with mathematics, use of validated tools, repeatability, reporting, and possible expert presentation."

(Zatyko, 2007)

Digital forensics encompasses much more than just laptop and desktop computers. Mobile devices, networks, and "cloud" systems are very much within the scope of the discipline. It also includes the analysis of images, videos, and audio (in both analog and digital format). The focus of this kind of analysis is generally authenticity, comparison, and enhancement.

USES OF DIGITAL FORENSICS

Digital forensics can be used in a variety of settings, including criminal investigations, civil litigation, intelligence, and administrative matters.

Criminal Investigations

When you mention digital forensics in the context of a criminal investigation, people tend to think first in terms of child pornography and identity theft. Although those investigations certainly focus on digital evidence, they are by no means the only two. In today's digital world, electronic evidence can be found in almost any criminal investigation conducted. Homicide, sexual assault, robbery, and burglary are just a few of the many examples of "analog" crimes that can leave digital evidence.

One of the major struggles in law enforcement is to change the paradigm of the police and get them to think of and seek out digital evidence. Everyday digital devices such as cell phones and gaming consoles can hold a treasure trove of evidence. Unfortunately, none of that evidence will ever see a courtroom if it's not first recognized and collected. As time moves on and our law enforcement agencies are replenished with "younger blood," this will become less and less of a problem.

BIND. TORTURE. KILL.

The case of Dennis Rader, better known as the BTK killer, is a great example of the critical role digital forensics can play in a criminal investigation. This case had national attention and, thanks to digital forensics, was solved thirty years later. To all that knew him before his arrest, Dennis Rader was a family man, church member, and dedicated public servant. What they didn't know was that he was also an accomplished serial killer. Dennis Rader, known as Bind, Torture, Kill (BTK), murdered ten people in Kansas from 1974 to 1991. Rader managed to avoid capture for over thirty years until technology betrayed him.

After years of silence, Rader sent a letter to the Wichita *Eagle* newspaper declaring that he was responsible for the 1986 killing of a young mother. The letter was received by the *Eagle* on March 19, 2004. After conferring with the FBI's Behavioral Analysis Unit, the police decided to attempt to communicate with BTK through the media.

In January 2005, Rader left a note for police, hidden in a cereal box, in the back of a pickup truck belonging to a Home Depot employee. In the note, he said:

> "Can I communicate with Floppy and not be traced to a computer. Be honest. Under Miscellaneous Section, 494, (Rex, it will be OK), run it for a few days in case I'm out of town-etc. I will try a floppy for a test run some time in the near future-February or March."

The police did the only thing they could. They lied. As directed, they responded (via an ad in the *Eagle*) on January 28. The ad read "Rex, it will be ok, Contact me PO Box 1st four ref.numbers at 67202."

On February 16, a manila envelope arrived at KSAS, the Fox affiliate in Wichita. Inside was a purple floppy disc from BTK. The disc contained a file named "Test A.rtf." (The .rtf extension stands for "Rich Text File"). A forensic exam of the file struck gold. The file's metadata (the data about the data) gave investigators the leads they had been waiting over thirty years for. Aside from the "Date Created" (Thursday, February 10, 2005 6:05:34 PM) and the "Date Modified" (Monday, February 14, 2005 2:47:44 PM) were the "Title" (Christ Lutheran Church) and "Last Saved By:" (Dennis).

Armed with this information, investigators quickly logged on to the Christ Lutheran Church web site. There they found that Dennis Rader was the president of the church's Congregation Council. The noose was tightening, but it wasn't tight enough. Investigators turned to DNA to make the case airtight. Detectives went on to obtain a DNA sample from Rader's daughter and compared it to DNA from BTK. The results proved that BTK was her father. On February 25, three days after the DNA sample arrived at the lab, Rader was arrested, sealing the fate of BTK. He is currently serving ten consecutive life sentences (Witchita *Eagle*).

Civil Litigation

The use of digital forensics in civil cases is big business. In 2011, the estimated total worth of the electronic discovery market is somewhere north of $780 million (Global EDD Group). As part of a process known as **Electronic Discovery (eDiscovery)**, digital forensics has become a major component of much high dollar litigation. eDiscovery "refers to any process in which electronic data is sought, located, secured, and searched with the intent of using it as evidence in a civil or criminal legal case" (TechTarget, 2005).

In a civil case, both parties are generally entitled to examine the evidence that will be used against them prior to trial. This legal process is known as "discovery." Previously, discovery was largely a paper-based exercise, with each party exchanging reports, letters, and memos; however, the introduction of digital forensics and eDiscovery has greatly changed this practice.

The proliferation of the computer has rendered that practice nearly extinct. Today, parties no longer talk about filing cabinets, ledgers, and memos; they talk about hard drives, spreadsheets, and file types. Some paper-based materials may come into play, but it's more the exception than the rule. Seeing the evidentiary landscape rapidly changing, the courts have begun to modify the rules of evidence. The rules of evidence, be they state or federal rules, govern how digital evidence can be admitted during civil litigation. The Federal Rules of Civil Procedure were changed in December 2006 to specifically address how electronically stored information is to be handled in these cases.

Digital evidence can quickly become the focal point of a case, no matter what kind of legal proceeding it's used in. The legal system and all its players are struggling to deal with this new reality.

Intelligence

Terrorists and foreign governments, the purview of our intelligence agencies, have also joined the digital age. Terrorists have been using information technology to communicate, recruit, and plan attacks. In Iraq and Afghanistan, our armed forces are exploiting intelligence collected from digital devices brought straight from the battlefield. This process is known as **DOMEX (Document and Media Exploitation)**. DOMEX is paying large dividends, providing actionable intelligence to support the soldiers on the ground (U.S. Army).

MOUSSAOUI

It's well documented that the 9-11 hijackers sought out and received flight training in order to facilitate the deadliest terrorist attack ever on U.S. soil. Digital forensics played a role in the investigation of this aspect of the attack.

On August 16, 2001, Zacarias Moussaoui was arrested by INS agents in Eagan, Minnesota, for overstaying his visa. Agents also seized a laptop and floppy disk. After obtaining a search warrant, the FBI searched these two items on September 11, 2001. During the analysis, they found evidence of a Hotmail account (pilotz123@hotmail.com) used by Moussaoui. He used this account to send e-mail to the flight school as well as other aviation organizations.

For those not familiar with Hotmail accounts, it's a free e-mail service offered by Microsoft, similar to Gmail and Yahoo!. They're quite easy to get and only require basic subscriber information. This information is essentially meaningless, because none of the information is verified. During the exam of Moussaoui's e-mail, agents were also able to analyze the Internet protocol connection logs. One of the IP addresses identified was assigned to "PC11" in a computer lab at the University of Oklahoma.

The investigation further showed that Moussaoui and the rest of the nineteen hijackers made extensive use of computers at a variety of Kinko's store locations in other cities. Agents arrived at the Kinko's in Eagan hoping to uncover evidence. They were disappointed to learn that this specific Kinko's makes a practice of erasing the drives on their rental computers every day. Now forty-four days after Moussaoui's visit, the agents felt the odds of recovering any evidence would be somewhere between slim and none. They didn't bother examining the Kinko's computer. The Eagan store isn't alone. Other locations make a routine practice of erasing or reimaging the rental computers as well. This is done periodically, some as soon as twenty-four hours, others as long as thirty days. The drives are erased to improve the performance and reliability of the computers as well as to protect the privacy of its customers (Lawler, 2002).

Administrative Matters

Digital evidence can also be valuable for incidents other than litigation and matters of national security. Violations of policy and procedure often involve some type of electronically stored information, for example, an employee operating a personal side business, using company computers while on company time. That may not constitute a violation of the law, but it may warrant an investigation by the company.

THE SECURITIES AND EXCHANGE COMMISSION (SEC)

In 2008, while the economy was in the beginning of its historic downward spiral, the Securities and Exchange Commission (SEC) should have been policing Wall Street. Instead, many of them were spending hours of their days watching pornography. Computer forensics played heavily in this administrative investigation.

In August 2007, the SEC's Office of the Inspector General (OIG) officially opened an investigation into the potential misuse of governmental computers. The OIG was alerted to a potential problem after firewall logs identified several users that had received access denials for Internet pornography. The SEC firewall was configured to block and log this kind of traffic. The logs showed that this employee attempted to visit sites such as www.thefetishvault.com, www.bondagetemple.com, www.rape-cartoons.com, and www.pornobaron.com.

On September 5, 2007, the OIG notified the Regional Director that one of his employees was the focus of an investigation regarding the misuse of their government computer. On September 19 this same employee reported that her laptop hard drive suddenly crashed. She was issued a replacement drive and went back to work. A forensic analysis of her hard drive found 592 pornographic images (in her temporary Internet files) along with evidence that she had attempted to bypass the SEC's Internet filters.

The scope of this investigation eventually expanded considerably, identifying several more employees or contractors that were viewing pornography on their governmental computers while at work.

After further investigation, the OIG found that:

- A Regional Staff Accountant received over sixteen thousand access denials for pornographic web sites in a single month.
- A Senior Counsel for the Division of Enforcement accessed pornography from his SEC laptop computer on multiple occasions. His hard drive contained 775 pornographic images.
- A Senior Attorney at Headquarters downloaded so much pornography that he literally ran out of disk space.

The report went on to list the policies that prohibited these behaviors. It says in part:

> "SECR 24-4.3 TK IIIC, provides that '[m]isuse or inappropriate personal use of government office equipment includes the creation, download, viewing, storage, copying, or transmission of materials related to gambling, weapons, terrorist activities, and any other illegal activities or activities otherwise prohibited etc' id at 3. The cover memorandum to SEC employees accompanying SECR 24-4.3 states that employees are prohibited from "accessing materials related to illegal or prohibited activities, including sexually explicit materials."

In the end, as this was not considered to be a crime, the entire matter was referred to the SEC administration for disposition (U.S. Securities and Exchange Commission).

LOCARD'S EXCHANGE PRINCIPLE

Locard's exchange principle says that in the physical world, when perpetrators enter or leave a crime scene, they will leave something behind and take something with them. Examples include DNA, latent prints, hair, and fibers (Saferstein, 2006).

The same holds true in digital forensics. Registry keys and log files can serve as the digital equivalent to hair and fiber (Carvey, 2005). Like DNA, our ability to detect and analyze these artifacts relies heavily on the technology available at the time. Look at the numerous cold cases that are being solved as a result of the significant advances in DNA science. Viewing a device or incident through the "lens" of Locard's principle can be very helpful in locating and interpreting not only physical but digital evidence as well.

SCIENTIFIC METHOD

As an emerging discipline in forensic science, digital forensics is undergoing some expected growing pains. As of today, digital forensics lacks the vast foundation and long-term track record set by forensic DNA. DNA is now considered by many to be the "gold standard" of the forensic sciences. Digital forensics simply lacks the years of development, testing, refining, and legal challenges DNA has undergone since its inception.

Plotting the course forward are several organizations that are looked on to establish the protocols, standards, and procedures that will push digital forensics ahead. The following sections provide more information on these important organizations.

ORGANIZATIONS OF NOTE

There are several organizations that make significant contributions to the discipline of digital forensics year in and year out. These organizations not only set standards and establish best practices, they provide leadership as well. Examiners should be familiar with these entities, the roles they play, and the contributions they make. As professionals, it's our responsibility to participate in one or more of these organizations.

Scientific Working Group on Digital Evidence

http://www.swgde.org/

Standards and techniques are an essential part of valid and accurate forensic science. They are its foundation, its core. Along with other federal agencies, the FBI has supported the formation and efforts of a wide range of Scientific Working Groups (SWGs) and Technical Working Groups (TWGs) (Federal Bureau of Investigation). These collaborative groups draw their members from "forensic, industrial, commercial, academic and in some cases international communities" (Federal Bureau of Investigation). Some examples include the Scientific Working Group for DNA Analysis Methods (SWGDAM) and the Scientific Working Group for Firearms and Toolmarks (SWGGUN). Digital evidence has now joined the party with the formation of SWGDE.

Formed in 1998, the **Scientific Working Group on Digital Evidence (SWGDE)** is made up of "federal government agency, state or local law enforcement agency involved in the digital and multi-media forensic profession" (Scientific Working Group on Digital Evidence).

The mission of SWGDE is as follows: "Brings together organizations actively engaged in the field of digital and multimedia evidence to foster communication and cooperation as well as ensuring quality and consistency within the forensic community" (Scientific Working Group on Digital Evidence).

American Academy of Forensic Sciences

http://www.aafs.org/

The **American Academy of Forensic Sciences (AAFS)** is considered the premier forensic organization in the world. Members of the Academy work for the National Institute of Standards and Technology (NIST) and National Academy of Sciences (NAS). The directors of most federal crime labs are members of AAFS. Members of AAFS are also active in the various Scientific Working Groups including SWGDE. The Academy plays a critical role in developing consensus standards of practice for the forensic community.

The Forensic Science Education Programs Accreditation Commission (FEPAC) was a creation of AAFS to ensure quality forensic science education and background for future forensic scientists.

The AAFS has approximately six thousand members and is divided into "eleven sections spanning the forensic enterprise." The Academy comprises "physicians, attorneys, dentists, toxicologists, physical anthropologists, document examiners, psychiatrists, physicists, engineers, criminalists, educators, digital evidence experts, and others" (American Academy of Forensic Sciences).

The Digital & Multimedia Sciences section represents digital forensics. As of November 3, 2010, the Digital Evidence section had 103 members. Despite the name, the reach of the AAFS is truly global, representing over sixty countries around the world (American Academy of Forensic Sciences).

American Society of Crime Laboratory Directors/Laboratory Accreditation Board

http://www.ascld-lab.org/index.htm

ASCLD/LAB (pronounced as-clad lab). The ASCLD is to forensic laboratories what Underwriters Labs is to household products. ASCLD/LAB is the "oldest and most well known crime/forensic laboratory accrediting body in the world." ASCLD/ LAB accredited labs are the "gold standard" in the world of forensics. A lab becomes accredited only after successfully meeting all of the standards and requirements set forth in the ASCLD/LAB accreditation manual. These requirements and standards cover every aspect of a lab's operation and must be strictly followed. Adherence to these standards must be thoroughly and completely documented (American Society of Crime Laboratory Directors/Laboratory Accreditation Board).

National Institute of Standards and Technology (NIST)

http://www.nist.gov/itl/ssd/computerforensics.cfm

National Institute of Standards and Technology (**NIST)** was founded in 1901 and is a part of the U.S. Department of Commerce. It was the first federal physical science research laboratory. Some of NIST's areas of focus include bioscience and health, chemistry, physics, math, quality, and information technology (National Institute of Standards and Technology).

NIST is heavily involved in digital forensics. Some of the programs and projects include:

- National Initiative Cyber Security Education (NICE)—A national cyber-security education program teaching sound cyber practices that will improve the country's security.
- National Software References Library—A collection of known software file signatures that can be used by examiners to quickly exclude files that have no investigative value. This would include things like operating system files. This can really reduce the time spent on an examination.
- Computer Forensic Tool Testing—Intended to develop testing methodologies and standards for forensic hardware and software.

(National Institute of Standards and Technology)

American Society for Testing and Materials (ASTM)

http://www.astm.org/Standards/E2763.htm

Another major player in the development of standards is **ASTM**. ASTM is a global organization that has developed approximately twelve thousand standards that are used to "improve product quality, enhance safety, facilitate market access and trade, and build consumer confidence." ASTM, founded in 1898, comprises about 30,000 members broken into 141 committees. The Forensics Sciences committee, known as E30, is further divided into several subcommittees. The Digital and Multimedia Evidence subcommittee is known as E30.12 (ASTM).

ROLE OF THE FORENSIC EXAMINER IN THE JUDICIAL SYSTEM

The digital forensics practitioner most often plays the role of an expert witness. What makes them different than nonexpert witnesses? Other witnesses can only testify to what they did or saw. They are generally limited to those areas and not permitted to render an opinion. Experts, by contrast, can and often do give their opinion. What makes someone an "expert?" In the legal sense, it's someone who can assist the judge or jury to understand and interpret evidence they may be unfamiliar with. To be considered an expert in a court of law, one doesn't have to possess an advanced academic degree. An expert simply must know more about a particular subject than the average lay person. Under the legal definition, a doctor, scientist, baker, or garbage collector could be qualified as an expert witness in a court of law. Individuals are qualified as experts by the court based on their training, experience, education, and so on (Saferstein, 2011).

What separates a qualified expert from a truly effective one? It is their ability to communicate with the judge and jury. They must be effective teachers. The vast majority of society lacks technical understanding to fully grasp this kind of testimony without at least some explanation. Digital forensic examiners must carry out their duties without bias. Lastly, a digital forensics examiner must go where the evidence takes them without any preconceived notions.

The CSI Effect

It seems that everyone either does or has watched one or more versions of the popular TV series *CSI*. These shows and others like it tend to convince jurors that some form of forensic science can solve any case. In other words, they now *expect* it. These unreasonable expectations can lead to incorrect verdicts. The jury could acquit a guilty defendant simply because no scientific evidence was presented, the presumption being that if the defendant was guilty, there would be some kind of scientific evidence to prove it (Saferstein, 2011).

SUMMARY

In this chapter we looked at what forensic science, particularly digital forensics, is and is not. Forensic sciences aren't the fast-paced crime-solving dramas that we watch on television, but a scientific method of collection, investigation and analysis used to solve some kind of legal problem. Digital forensics isn't limited to computers. It encompasses any kind of electronic device that can store data. These devices include cell phones, tablets, and GPS units just to name a few.

Digital forensics is applicable well beyond criminal investigations. It's used routinely in civil litigation, national and military intelligence matters as well as the private sector.

There are multiple organizations that help establish the standards and best practices used in digital forensics. These organizations include the American Academy of Forensic Sciences, the Scientific Working Group on Digital Evidence, and ASTM.

As a practitioner, communication skills are extremely important. You will spend a significant amount of time explaining your findings to police officers, attorneys, and clients. Most important, you must be able to explain these things to judges and juries. All of these stakeholders must be able to understand your methods and findings. Like all scientific evidence, digital evidence can be quite confusing and overwhelming. With this kind of testimony, it's very easy to lose people. Losing a judge or jury in a trial can have disastrous consequences such as having your findings ignored or misunderstood.

References

American Academy of Forensic Sciences. (n.d.). *About AAFS*. Retrieved February 4, 2011, from: http://www.aafs.org/about-aafs

ASTM. (n.d.). *ABOUT: ASTM*. Retrieved February 23, 2011, from: http://www.astm.org/ABOUT/aboutASTM.html

ASTM. (n.d.). *E30*. Retrieved February 23, 2011, from: http://www.astm.org/COMMIT/SUBCOMMIT/E30.htm

ASTM. (n.d.). *Overview: ABOUT: ASTM*. Retrieved February 23, 2011, from: http://www.astm.org/ABOUT/overview.html

Carvey, H. (2005, January 27). *Locard's Exchange Principle in the Digital World: Windows Incident Response*. Retrieved February 23, 2011, from: http://windowsir.blogspot.com/2005/01/locards-exchange-principle-in-digital.html

Federal Bureau of Investigation. (n.d.). *Scientific Working Groups: Federal Bureau of Investigation*. Retrieved February 19, 2011, from: http://www.fbi.gov/about-us/lab/swgs

Lawler, B. A. (2002, September 4). *Government's Response to Court's Order on Computer and Email Evidence*. Retrieved September 13, 2011, from FindLaw.com: news.findlaw.com/hdocs/docs/moussaoui/usmouss90402grsp.pdf

McKendrick, J. (2010, May 12). *Size of the Data Universe: 1.2 Zettabytes and Growing Fast: ZDNet*. Retrieved February 23, 2011, from: http://www.zdnet.com/blog/service-oriented/size-of-the-data-universe-12-zettabytes-and-growing-fast/4750

Regional Computer Forensics Laboratory. (n.d.). *RCFL: Regional Computer Forensics Laboratory*. Retrieved February 4, 2011, from: http://www.rcfl.gov/

Saferstein, R. (2006). *Criminalistics: An Introduction to Forensic Science* (College Edition). Upper Saddle River, New Jersey: Prentice Hall.

Scientific Working Group on Digital Evidence. (n.d.). *Scientific Working Group on Digital Evidence—About Us*. Retrieved February 4, 2011, from: http://www.swgde.org

Stuart, J., Nordby, J. J., & Bell, S. (2009). *Forensic Science: An Introduction to Scientific and Investigative Techniques*. February 20, 2009 (3rd ed.). Boca Raton, FL: CRC Press.

U.S. Army. (n.d.). *Document and Media Exploitation (DOMEX): 2010 Army Posture Statement.* Retrieved February 23, 2011, from: https://secureweb2.hqda.pentagon.mil/vdas_armyposture statement/2010/information_papers/Document_and_Media_Exploitation_%28DOMEX%29.asp

U.S. Department of Justice. (2009). *RCFL Annual Report for Fiscal Year 2009.* Washington, DC: U.S. Department of Justice.

Zatyko, K. (n.d.). *Commentary: Defining Digital Forensics.* Retrieved February 19, 2011, from: http://www.forensicmag.com/node/128

CHAPTER 2

Key Technical Concepts

Information in This Chapter:

- Basic Computer Operation
- Bits & Bytes
- File Extensions and File Signatures
- How Computers Store Data
- Random Access Memory
- Volatility of Data
- The Difference Between Computer Environments
- Active, Latent, and Archival Data
- The Difference Between Allocated and Unallocated Space
- Computer File Systems

INTRODUCTION

Intimate knowledge of the inner workings of a computer is critical for the digital forensics practitioner. It's this knowledge that permits us to conduct a thorough examination of the evidence and render an accurate opinion. Simply put, we can't do our job without it. Not all processes and hardware hold the same value forensically. Memory and storage play a major role in almost any examination. The processor or CPU, by contrast, plays little if any role. This chapter takes a broad look at some of the technical details of basic computing. Its focus will be on the major areas that impact an investigation. There is no substitute for the mastery of this material. Our responsibilities as an expert witness include explaining technical subject matter in a way that the average person is able to understand.

BITS, BYTES, AND NUMBERING SCHEMES

To the computer, things are pretty black and white. It's all about the 1s and 0s. Computers use a language called **binary**. In binary, there are only two possible outcomes: a 1 or a 0. Each 1 or 0 is called a bit. In mathematical terms, binary is classified as a base 2 numbering system. In comparison, we use a base 10 numeral system known as **decimal**. Decimal uses numerals 0–9. To speed things up, computers work with larger collections of bits. These larger chunks of data are called **bytes**. A byte is made up of eight bits. It looks like this: 01101001.

How do bytes relate to letters and numbers? Each letter, number, space, and special character is represented by a single byte. For example, using the ASCII character set 01000001 represents an uppercase "A," while a lowercase "a" is 01100001.

Let's do a little experiment so that you can see this in action. Open a new text document (using a plain text editor, not a word processing application like MS Word) on your computer and type the phrase "Marshall University Digital Forensics." Now, count all the letters and spaces. Next, save and close the new text file to your desktop. Right click on the file and select properties. What's the file size? It should be 26 bytes, which is also the exact number of letters and spaces.

To get a broader perspective, let's look at all of the binary necessary to represent our sample phrase "Marshall University Digital Forensics":

01001101011000010111001001110011011010000110000101100110001101100001000000101010101101110011010010111011001100101011100100111001101101010010111010001111001001000000100010011010010101100111011010010111010001100001011011000010000001000110011011111011100100110010101101110011001101101110011011010010110001101110011

At first glance, that's a little tough to read, no doubt. Fortunately, there is a shorthand that we can use to make this more readable. This shorthand is called **hexadecimal**.

Hexadecimal

Hexadecimal, or hex, is a base 16 system that is an expedient way to express binary numbers. Hex is expressed using the numerals 0–9 and the letters A–F. An uppercase "M" is expressed as 4D in hexadecimal. A lowercase "a" is 61. Quite often you will see a hexadecimal number expressed with the prefix 0x. This prefix or the suffix "h" is used to designate or identify it as a hexadecimal or base 16 number. Here is the same phrase (Marshall University Digital Forensics) expressed in hexadecimal:

4d 61 72 73 68 61 6D 6C 20 55 6E 69 76 65 72 73 69 74 79
20 44 69 67 69 74 61 6D 20 46 6F 72 65 6E 73 69 63 73

If you look closer, you'll see the number "20" repeated throughout the string. The number "20" in hex represents a space.

Binary to Text: ASCII and Unicode

So how do these 1s and 0s end up as As and Bs? Computers use encoding schemes to convert binary into something humans can read. There are two

encoding schemes we need to be concerned with, **ASCII** and **Unicode**. ASCII, the American Standard Code for Information Interchange, is the encoding scheme used for the English language. ASCII defines 128 characters, of which only 94 are actually printable. The rest are control characters used for spacing and processing. In contrast, **Unicode** is intended to represent all of the world's languages and consists of thousands of characters (Unicode Inc., 2010).

So, how is this relevant to digital forensics? In many instances, examiners must look at the data at the "bit" and "byte" level to find, extract, and interpret the evidence. This is most evident in a process called **file carving**. File carving is done to locate and mine out files from amorphous blobs of data, like the unallocated space (also known as drive-free space). The first step in the file carving process is to identify the potential file. Normally, the file is identified by the header, if it has one. Once the footer is found, the file can be extracted through a simple copy and paste as long as it is continuous. A fragmented file is far more difficult to recover (Casey, 2011). Having the ability to interpret binary and hex makes file carving possible.

FILE EXTENSIONS AND FILE SIGNATURES

Fundamentally, **files** are strings or sequences of bits and bytes. Identifying a file can be done in a couple of different ways. **File extensions** are the most common. As users, we usually identify the file type by the file extension, if the system is configured. An operating system can be set such that file extensions are hidden. File extensions are the suffixes added to the end of a computer file name, indicating its format. Examples would include .docx and .pptx (for the latest versions of Microsoft Word and PowerPoint, respectively).

For our purposes, a file extension isn't the most reliable way to identify it. The file extension is very easily changed, requiring only a mouse click and a couple of keystrokes. You can try this yourself. In Windows, simply right click on the file name and rename it, changing the extension. Let's say we change the extension of a Word file to that of an image, JPEG for example. This is easily accomplished. On a Windows machine, simply click, slight pause, click again. On a Mac, it's click + Return. What happens when we try to open that file? Nothing. It won't open. Change it back and it opens right up.

Some people will attempt to take advantage of this ability to change file extensions as a way to conceal data, hiding them in plain sight. Forensically, this approach is not very effective. Forensic tools identify files based on the header, not the file extension. Many tools will even separate out those files whose header does not match the extension, making them easily discovered. This comparison is generally known as **file signature analysis**. Figures 2.1 and 2.2 illustrate what happens when a file extension is changed.

FIGURE 2.1
Here we've changed the file extension on "Smoking Gun.docx" to .mp3. Note that the icon has changed. Graphic courtesy of Jonathan Sisson.

File Content				
Hex	Text	Filtered	Natural	
410	0B BB 02 15 ED FF D9 D8–CF BC 3C E7 E4 15 6A 86			·»··iÿÙØÏ¼çã·j·
420	6D D4 3C 09 B4 97 85 34–0D 9F 2A 19 1E 28 39 81			mÔ<·´··4··*··(9·
430	FD 8E F1 00 DB 75 24 46–6D 7A 9F 73 6D E9 11 BE			ý·ñ·Ûu\$Fmz·smé·¾
440	81 C3 E8 98 43 FD 02 3D–09 09 FE 36 0B E8 6D 6F			·Ãè·Cý·=··þ6·èmo
450	35 EB C5 F6 93 59 AF 9F–1C 71 F1 31 12 73 74 FF			5ëÅö·Y¯·qñ1·stÿ
460	8F 65 E3 36 96 2D 65 04–BB 1B 0C 1B B7 30 EC F6			·eã6·-e·»····0ìö
470	31 68 BE 70 FA 07 50 4B–07 08 8E C9 65 35 2F 02			1h¾pú·PK···Ée5/·
480	00 00 5E 07 00 00 50 4B–03 04 14 00 08 08 08 00			··^···PK········
490	F7 6E 51 3F 00 00 00 00–00 00 00 00 00 00 00 00			÷nQ?············
4a0	11 00 00 00 77 6F 72 64–2F 64 6F 63 75 6D 65 6E			····word/documen
4b0	74 2E 78 6D 6C ED 56 4D–8F 9B 30 10 BD F7 57 10			t.xmlíVM·0·½÷W·
4c0	DF B3 7C 94 AD B6 28 B0–87 92 56 95 DA 55 A4 A4			ß³|··¶(°··V·ÚU¤¤
4d0	BD 22 C7 18 B0 82 3F 64–4F 60 D3 5F 5F 3B 40 B2			½"Ç·°·?dO`Ó__;@²
4e0	2B B5 55 54 F5 D0 03 17–CF 0C E3 F7 9E 6D 2C CF			+µUTõÐ··Ï·ã÷·m,Ï
4f0	AC 1E 9F 79 EB 75 54 1B–26 45 8A C2 BB 00 79 54			¬··yëuT·&E·Â»·yT
500	10 59 32 51 A7 E8 DB EE–E3 F2 01 79 06 B0 28 71			·Y2Q§èÛî ̂áò·y·°(q

FIGURE 2.2
Here is the hexadecimal view of "Smoking Gun.mp3." Note the highlighted file header showing this is actually a Word document. Graphic courtesy of Jonathan Sisson.

STORAGE AND MEMORY

Where and how data are stored and written is one of the major fundamental concepts that must be learned. There is more that one way to write data. Today, data are generally created in three different ways: **electromagnetism**, **microscopic electrical transistors (flash)**, and **reflecting light** (CDs, DVDs, etc). Storage locations inside a computer serve different purposes. Some are for the short term, used to temporarily hold the data that the computer is using at the moment. The other is for more permanent, long-term keeping.

Magnetic Disks

Most drives in today's computers read and write data magnetically. They will render each particle either magnetized or not magnetized. If the particle is magnetized, it's read as a 1. If not, it's read as a 0. The drives themselves are usually made up of aluminum platters coated with a magnetic material. These platters spin at very high speeds. The platters spin in the neighborhood of 7,000 rpm to 15,000 rpm. The speed could even be greater for high-end drives. These heavy-duty drives are typically found in servers or professional grade workstations. From a forensic standpoint, faster drive speeds can result in faster acquisitions.

Let's look at the major parts of a standard hard drive. The platters revolve around a small rod called a spindle. The data are physically written to the platter using a read/write head attached to an actuator arm, which is powered by the actuator itself. The actuator arm moves the head across the platter(s), reading and writing data. The read/write head floats on a cushion of air. The read/write head, as it's called, is barely floating above the platter surface, at a height less than the diameter of a human hair. These devices are really pretty amazing. Figure 2.3 shows

FIGURE 2.3
The inside of a typical magnetic drive.

us the inside of a typical magnetic drive. We can clearly see the platters, actuator arm, and the read/write head.

Flash Memory

Flash memory is used in a wide range of devices. Thumb drives and memory cards provide reliable storage in a very portable package, allowing us to take more pictures and take our files on the road. Unlike other kinds of memory, flash memory retains our data even without electricity. Flash is made up of **transistors**. Each transistor is either carrying an electric charge or it isn't. When the transistor is charged, it is read as a "1"; without a charge it's read as a "0."

Flash based hard drives are starting to become more and more common. Unlike magnetic drives, flash drives are solid state, meaning that they have no moving parts. They are often referred to as an SSD or **"Solid State Drive."** They offer several significant advantages including increased speed, less susceptibility to shock, and lower power consumption.

SSDs will play a major role in computing and digital forensics going forward. Although these devices offer improved performance, they also present a major challenge to digital forensics. We'll take a deeper look at the momentous challenge presented by SSDs in Chapter 11.

Optical Storage

Optical media read and write data using a laser light along with a reflective material incorporated into optical discs. Optical discs are made of a polycarbonate base covered by a thin layer of aluminum. The disc is then coated with a clear acrylic material for protective purposes. During the manufacturing process, the disc's surface is embossed with tiny bumps. This series of bumps form one long, single, spiral track. A laser projects a highly focused beam of light onto the track. The light is reflected differently from the bumps and the spaces in between, called **"lands."** This change in reflectivity is what the system reads as binary (Brain). The most common types of optical storage media include CDs, DVDs, and Blu-ray discs (Brain).

Volatile versus Nonvolatile Memory

Memory and **storage** are two terms that are somewhat synonymous when it comes to computers. They both refer to internal places where data are kept. Memory is used for the short-term storage, while storage is more permanent. No matter what you call it, there is a significant difference between the two, especially from a forensic perspective. That difference lies in the data's volatility. Data in RAM exist only as long as power is supplied. Once the power is removed (i.e., the machine is turned off), the data start to disappear. This behavior makes this kind of memory volatile. In contrast, files saved on your hard drive remain even after the computer is powered down, making it nonvolatile (Cooper, 2004).

RAM stores all the data that are currently being worked on by the Central Processing Unit (CPU). Data are fed from the RAM to the CPU, where they are executed. Traditionally, forensic analysis of a computer focused on the hard drive, as much of the evidence can be found there. Today, we're finding that's not always the case. Some instant messaging applications, for example, don't write to the hard drive unless the logging feature is turned on. AOL Instant Messenger and MSN fall into that category. So, if logging is off (which it is by default), the only evidence will be found in RAM while the machine is running.

COMPUTING ENVIRONMENTS

Not all **computing "environments"** are created equal. There are substantial differences between them. We can encounter individual computers, networks of various sizes, or even more complex systems. These disparities will have a significant impact on your collection process, where you look for data, the tools you will use, and the level of complexity required. An accurate clarification of the environment is useful to have right from the start of an investigation, even before you respond to a scene. Environments can be broken down into four categories: stand-alone, networked, mainframe, and the cloud.

A stand-alone computer is one that is not connected to another computer. These are the easiest to deal with and investigate. Possible locations for evidence are reasonably confined. Stand-alone systems are routinely encountered in residences such as apartments and houses.

A networked computer is connected to at least one other computer and potentially many, many others. This escalates the complexity as well as the places evidence could be found. We now can see files and artifacts normally found on the local machine spread out to servers or other machines. This environment introduces a variety of variables into the equation. Even though networks are more commonly found in a business setting, they are found more and more in homes.

Unlike a stand-alone machine, a **mainframe system** centralizes all of the computing power into one location. Processors, storage, and applications can all be located and controlled from a single location.

Cloud Computing

You may not be familiar with the term "**cloud computing**," but if you use Gmail, Facebook, or Twitter, you're already using it. Cloud computing is a hot topic these days, garnering much attention from both the IT and business communities. This "new" model of computing is very similar in many respects to the mainframe systems of old. Like the mainframe, the computing resources are moved from the local machine to some other centralized place.

The cloud model presents some very interesting features that make it attractive to businesses, especially from a cost perspective. The cloud offers software along with computing infrastructure and platforms on an elastic, pay-per-use model. This affords companies the luxury of only paying for what they use.

Technology behemoths such as Microsoft, Google, and Amazon are just three of the companies that are jumping on the bandwagon offering cloud services. Cloud services include **Infrastructure as a Service (IaaS), Platform as a Service (PaaS), and Software as a Service (SaaS).** All of these are delivered over the Internet. In the cloud, customers only pay for the resources they actually use, just like the way we pay for our water and electricity.

IaaS

With IaaS, organizations outsource their hardware needs to a service provider. This would include everyday hardware needs such as servers, storage, and the like. The associated costs for running and maintaining the hardware are paid by the provider.

PaaS

Programmers develop their software to function in specific computing environments (operating system, services, etc.). PaaS gives developers the ability to rent the environment (hardware, operating systems, storage, servers, etc.) on an "as-needed" basis. PaaS provides excellent flexibility in that the operating system can be modified or upgraded frequently.

SaaS

In the cloud, SaaS provides applications on demand to customers over the Internet. These applications are hosted and maintained by the service provider.

The cloud represents a huge challenge to the digital forensic community, from both a technical and a legal standpoint. Technically, the cloud presents a very complicated, virtualized environment that frustrates if not downright negates many routine forensic procedures. Legally, it can be a jurisdictional nightmare. In the cloud, data know no bounds. The evidence can literally be in the next state or a foreign country halfway around the globe. We'll look closer at the cloud and its impact on forensics in Chapter 11.

DATA TYPES

Data can be lumped into three broad categories: active, latent, and archival. Looking at data in this way helps in clarifying their location, how they're accounted for by the file system, how they can be accessed by the user, and so on. It also helps to narrow down the cost and effort required to recover the data in question.

Active Data

Active data are the data that we use every day on our computers. The operating system "sees" and tracks these files. You can locate these files using Windows Explorer. These are the files that reside in the allocated space of the drive. These data can be acquired with standard forensic cloning techniques.

Latent Data

Data that has been deleted or partially overwritten are classified as **latent**. These files are no longer tracked by the operating system and are therefore "invisible" to the average user. Go looking for one of these files with Windows Explorer and you won't find it. A bit stream or forensic image is required to collect these data.

Archival Data

Archival data, or backups, can take many forms. External hard drives, DVDs, and backup tapes are just a few examples. Acquisition of archival data can range from simple to extremely complex. The type and age of the backup media are major factors in determining the complexity of the process.

Backup tapes can present some very big challenges, especially if they were made with software or hardware that is no longer in production. Tapes are created using specific pieces of hardware and software. These same tools will be needed to restore the data into a form that can be understood and manipulated. Where it gets really exciting is when the hardware and software are no longer in production. It could be an older version of the software is no longer available or the company is no longer in business. This is known as **legacy data**. What do you do if you no longer have and can't get access to the necessary tools to restore the data? Sometimes eBay can save the day.

FILE SYSTEMS

With all the millions or billions of files floating around inside our computers, there has to be some way to keep things neat and tidy. This indispensible function is the responsibility of the **file system**. The file system tracks the drive's free space as well as the location of each file. The free space, also known as unallocated space, is either empty or the file that previously occupied that location has been deleted.

There are many different types of file systems. Some of the most commonly encountered by forensic examiners include FAT, NTFS, and HFS+. Let's take a closer look:

> **File Allocation Table** (FAT) is the oldest of the common files system. It comes in four flavors: FAT12, FAT16, FAT32, and FATX. Although not used in the latest operating systems, it can often be found in flash media and the like.
> **The New Technology File System** (NTFS) is the system used currently by Windows 7, Vista, XP, and Windows Server. It's much more powerful than FAT and capable of performing many more functions. For example, "NTFS can automatically recover some disk-related errors, which FAT32 cannot," it provides better support for larger hard drives, and better security through permissions and encryption (Microsoft Corporation).

Hierarchical File System (HFS+) and its relatives HFS and HFSX are used in Apple products. HFS+ is the upgraded successor to HFS. This newer version offers several improvements including improved use of disk space, cross-platform compatibility, and international-friendly file names (Apple, Inc., 2004).

ALLOCATED AND UNALLOCATED SPACE

Before we get much further, it's time we talk about how the computer views the space on a hard drive. Generally speaking, the file system categorizes all of the space on the hard drive in one of two ways. The space is either **allocated** or **unallocated** (there are a few exceptions; see the side bar on Host Protected Areas). Put another way, either the space is being used or it's not. Windows can't see data in this unallocated space. To the Operating System, files located in unallocated space are essentially invisible. It's important, however, to understand that "not used" does not always mean "empty."

MORE ADVANCED

Host Protected Area (HPA) and Device Configuration Overlays (DCO)
Host Protected Areas (HPAs) and **Device Configuration Overlays** (DCOs) refer to hidden areas on a hard drive that are often difficult to detect. These areas are created by manufacturers that can be "accessed, modified, and written to by end users using specific open source and freely available tools, allowing data to be stored and/or hidden in these areas" (Gupta, Hoeschele, & Rogers, 2006). HPAs can contain diagnostic tools, an operating system for recovery purposes, and so on. It's rare that the HPA is used by suspects to conceal data.

Data Persistence

Like a telemarketer, data on a hard drive are pretty persistent. It's not as easy to get rid of as you may think. Deleted files will sit there until they're overwritten with more data. You might be asking yourself, "So how long does that take?" The answer is, it depends (which, by the way, is one of the most popular answers in digital forensics). With the massive amount of storage space available on today's hard drives, a file stands a good chance of never being overwritten. Your bachelor (or bachelorette) party pictures could remain on your hard drive for a long, long time. Just keep that in mind before you run for public office.

Remember, the file system's job is to keep track of all files and storage space. The file system keeps things nice and orderly. Think of a file system as an index in the back of a book. When looking up a particular subject, we flip through the index until we find the term we're looking for. Our handy index then gives us the page number and off we go. The file system works basically the same way. Using the book analogy again, deleting a file would be akin to removing the entry from the book's index. Although our subject is no longer referenced in the index, the page and all its content are still in the book, intact and untouched.

You may be surprised to know that when you save your file, it's not necessarily stored in one place. In fact, your spreadsheet could be scattered all over the platter(s) of your hard drive. Strange, huh? You would think as orderly as computers are, that wouldn't be the case.

The file system's job is to keep track of these separate clusters so they can be reassembled the next time you open that file. Have you ever "defragged" your hard drive? If you have, you were simply moving these disparate pieces as close together as possible. Moving them closer together speeds things up for your computer. The closer they are, the faster they can be put together and made available to you. Some crooked individuals may attempt to destroy data using the defragging process. In Chapter 6, we'll see how that may or may not be effective.

Files that are overwritten are generally considered to be unrecoverable. But all is not lost (pardon the pun). Like many rules in life, there are exceptions and this is one of those. It is possible that the new file assigned to that space won't need all of it. If that's the case, the original file is only *partially overwritten*. The piece that remains *can* be recovered and could contain information we can use. This remaining space is called **slack space**. Before we take a little closer look at slack space, we're going to have to get a little more technical. So, get your "nerd on" and follow along.

HOW MAGNETIC HARD DRIVES STORE DATA

We need to understand how the computer stores your files. Computers store your data in defined spaces called **sectors**. Think of sectors as the smallest container a computer can use to store information. Each sector holds up to 512 bytes of data as illustrated in Figure 2.4. It can hold less, but it can't hold more.

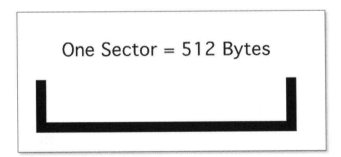

FIGURE 2.4
One sector.

While a sector is the smallest container of data, a computer's operating system only stores data as clusters. Clusters are comprised of multiple sectors. In this example our clusters contain four sectors. Each sector can hold up to 512 bytes of data, giving the clusters the storage capacity of 2048 bytes. See Figure 2.5.

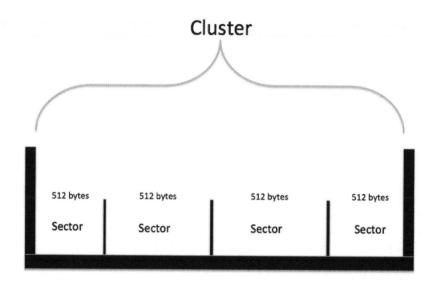

One cluster = 2048 bytes

FIGURE 2.5
A sample cluster containing four 512 byte sectors, giving it a maximum capacity of 2048 bytes.

It's important to remember that computers write data to the drive in clusters. If the file is larger than a single cluster, the system assigns it an additional cluster even though a portion of that cluster may not be used. Let's work through a little hypothetical exercise to better illustrate this concept.

Suppose we save our master criminal plan to our hard drive. We'll call it "evidence1.doc". It just so happens to be 2304 bytes in size. Since it's larger than our cluster size limit (2048 bytes) it's assigned to two separate, unallocated clusters (in this example, clusters 5245 and 5246). You'll also notice that our file only uses a portion of the first sector in the second cluster. Since the machine has to write 512 bytes at a time, it fills that leftover space with zeros. See Figure 2.6.

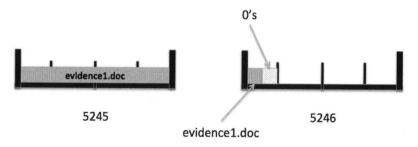

FIGURE 2.6
The file, evidence1.doc is saved to the hard drive. It's assigned to clusters 5245 and 5246. Note that the rest of cluster 5246 is left unallocated.

What about the last three sectors in cluster 5246 that weren't used? The answer is nothing. As we'll see in just a bit, this system behavior can leave some evidence behind. See Figure 2.7.

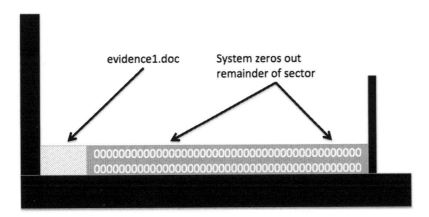

First Sector of Cluster 5246

FIGURE 2.7
The unused portion of the last sector occupied by "evidence1.doc" is filled with zeros because the computer only writes data 512 bytes at a time.

After watching Abby and McGee work their magic on NCIS, we start to have second thoughts. We decide it's probably better not to have that file on our computer. So we hit the delete key, sending the "evidence1.doc" to the recycle bin. With a sly grin we empty the recycle bin, content in the belief that "evidence1.doc" is now residing in digital oblivion. But wait, not so fast. The problem for us as bad guys is that unbeknownst to us, our incriminating file is STILL on the drive. It will remain in those two clusters until it's been overwritten by another file. Given the size of today's dives, that could take a very, very long time. Using standard forensic tools, we can recover any part of the document that hasn't been overwritten. Figure 2.8 depicts our two clusters after the recycle bin has been emptied.

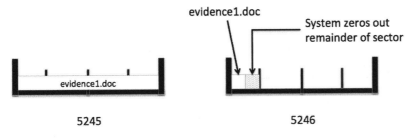

FIGURE 2.8
The file evidence1.doc has been deleted. Clusters 5245 and 5246 are now marked as unallocated (available). Notice that even though evidence1.doc has been deleted, it's still on the hard drive.

Now for some really cool forensic stuff. Even if the clusters containing our evidence are allocated to another file, all is not lost. It's still possible that we can extract a portion of the original file. Here's how it works. Two days later, we save another file to our drive. We'll call this one "evidence2.doc". It's only 768 bytes in size so it only takes one cluster to hold it. The system sees that cluster 5245 is available and decides to put it there. Remember, evidence1.doc is still sitting in the cluster even though it's been "deleted". The system writes "evidence2.doc" to the first sector and part of the second. It then does its normal thing and fills the remainder of that second sector with zeros. So what happens to the rest of evidence1.doc? When we first saved it, it took up all of cluster 5245. Our new file (evidence2.doc) has overwritten only PART of evidence1.doc. The remnants of evidence1.doc that sits in the last two sectors can be recovered! See Figure 2.9.

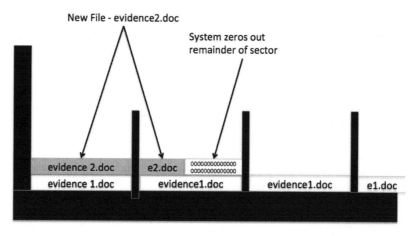

Cluster 5245

FIGURE 2.9
"evidence2.doc" is saved over "evidence1.doc," overwriting the much of the original file.

To recap, only the first 780 bytes of our original file have been overwritten. Some quick math tells us that there are still 244 bytes of our original file remaining. Those 244 remaining bytes comprise what's known as slack space. The **slack space**, depicted in Figure 2.10, is the difference between the space that is assigned and the space that is actually used.

So, out of the slack space we can recover fragments of the previous file. It may not be useful. But then again, it just might. It could be part of an incriminating spreadsheet, email or picture. These fragments could contain just enough of an email to identify the sender or the senders IP address. A partial picture of the victim could link them to the suspect. Slack space can't be accessed by the user or the operating system. As such, this evidence exists unbeknownst to all but the most tech-savvy suspects.

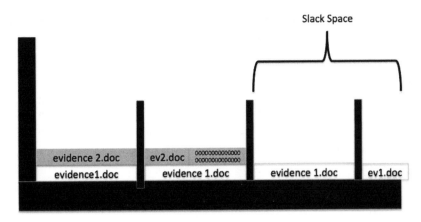

Cluster 5245

FIGURE 2.10
Note the new file, "evidence2.doc" only overwrites a portion of "evidence1.doc." The data in the remaining two sectors are still intact. This fragment of data can be recovered and could contain useful evidence.

Unfortunately, recovering evidence from slack space may very well become a thing of the past. We'll explore that bad news more in Chapter 11, "Looking Ahead: Challenges and Concerns."

SUMMARY

In Chapter 2 we took a closer look at how computers store data in different forms including magnetic, optical, flash, and others. Each of these storage methods is different and those differences have forensic implications. Computers operate with both memory and storage. While they sound similar, their intended purposes are distinctly different. Memory holds the data that the computer is actively working on at the moment. It's volatile, meaning that it holds data as long as it has power. When power is removed, the data begins to go away. The RAM in your computer is used for memory.

In contrast, storage is used for the long-term storing of data. Storage is considered non-volatile because the data remains even if the device loses power. Your hard drive is an example of storage.

A computer's file system is at the heart of how it saves and retrieves data. File systems keep track of the various pieces of data that must be found and reconstituted in order to open a file. There are multiple file systems in use today, each with their own way doing things.

Not all computing environments are the same. Some are relatively simple, others much more complex. Stand-Alone computers, networks, and the cloud were covered in this chapter.

As forensic examiners, we must have command of this material so that we can explain it to the average person. It is these "average people" that make up our juries.

References

Apple, Inc. (2004, March 5). *Technical Note TN1150 HFS Plus Volume Format.* Retrieved August 10, 2011, from: http://developer.apple.com/library/mac/#technotes/tn/tn1150.html

Casey, E. (2011). *Digital Evidence and Computer Crime: Forensic Science, Computers and the Internet.* Waltham, MA: Academic Press.

Casey, E. (2009). *Handbook of Digital Forensics and Investigation.* Burlington, MA: Academic Press.

Cooper, B. (2004, August). *What Is the Difference Between Memory and Storage?* Retrieved August 10, 2011, from: http://searchstorage.techtarget.com/answer/What-is-the-difference-between-memory-and-storage

Dale, N. (2009). *Computer Science Illuminated, Fourth Edition.* Sudbury, MA: Jones and Bartlett.

Gupta, M. R., Hoeschele, M. D., & Rogers, M. K. (2006). Hidden Disk Areas: HPA and DCO. *International Journal of Digital Evidence, 5* (1).

Microsoft Corporation. (n.d.). *Comparing NTFS and FAT File Systems.* Retrieved August 10, 2011, from: http://windows.microsoft.com/en-US/windows-vista/Comparing-NTFS-and-FAT-file-systems

SearchStorage.com. (2000, December). *Optical Media.* Retrieved August 10, 2011, from: http://searchstorage.techtarget.com/definition/optical-media

Unicode Inc. (2010, September 17). *What Is Unicode?* Retrieved August 10, 2011, from: http://www.unicode.org/standard/WhatIsUnicode.html

CHAPTER 3

Labs and Tools

Information in This Chapter:
- The Role and Organization of Forensic Laboratories
- The Purpose of Policies & Procedures in Forensic Laboratories
- The Role of Quality Assurance in Forensics
- Digital Forensic Hardware and Software
- Accreditation versus Certification

INTRODUCTION

In this chapter we will explore the different types of laboratory setups as well as the hardware and software tools in common use. We'll also take a look at Standard Operating Procedures and Quality Assurance, two critical components of an effective digital forensic lab. Obtaining and maintaining laboratory accreditation, although time-consuming and expensive, greatly improves a lab's performance and the quality of its findings. Examiner certification ensures that the skill of the labs meets a minimum level. At the end of the day, these elements come together to ensure that only valid and reliable results are produced and that justice is served.

FORENSIC LABORATORIES

Forensic labs are scattered throughout the United States and closely follow the jurisdictional lines of law enforcement (local, county, state, and federal) (James & Nordby, 2009). The majority of these facilities are run by a law enforcement agency. The FBI's crime laboratory in Quantico, Virginia, has the distinction of being the largest lab in the world (Saferstein, 2006).

Not all computer forensic examinations are conducted in what would be considered a traditional laboratory setting. Many agencies conduct them locally at their departments if they have the necessary equipment and trained personnel on hand.

Digital forensics isn't cheap, so not every agency can afford to train and equip their own examiners. One way to meet this ever-growing demand is the **Regional Computer Forensic Laboratory (RCFL)** program started by the FBI. The RCFL program runs sixteen facilities throughout the United States. They provide digital forensic services and training to all levels of law enforcement. Each RCFL is staffed and managed by a partnership of local, state, and federal law enforcement agencies.

The RCFL program is a great success, and making a significant dent in the backlog of digital forensic examinations across the country. During fiscal year 2010, RCFLs nationwide performed 6,564 forensic examinations and processed a whopping 3,086 terabytes of data. To put that in context, the 2010 Annual Report explains it this way; "One single terabyte is equivalent to 1,024 gigabytes or approximately 1,000 copies of the Encyclopedia Britannica." Doing the math, that's about 3,086,000 encyclopedias. The RCFLs process a wide variety of digital devices and media including smartphones, hard drives, GPS (Global Positioning System) units, and flash drives. In 2010, RCFL examiners helped convict rapists, terrorists, and crooked politicians (Federal Bureau of Investigation, 2010).

Virtual Labs

Digital labs don't have to be confined to a single location. Today's technology makes it possible to run a "virtual" lab with the examiners and the central evidence repository located in geographically separate locations. This arrangement has several advantages including cost savings, greater access to more resources (tools and storage for example), access to diverse and greater expertise, and reduction of unnecessary duplication of resources (Craiger).

This virtual arrangement allows for distinct role-based access. For example, full access could be granted to examiners and laboratory management. Prosecutors, investigators, and defense attorneys would have restricted access. This restricted access would limit what those folks could see and what they could do (read only, etc.) (Whitcomb).

There are some considerable concerns with this approach:

1. **Security**—The security of the system must be robust enough to maintain the level of evidence integrity required by the courts. Otherwise there could be catastrophic consequences, such as rendering evidence from multiple cases inadmissible.
2. **Performance**—For this scheme to work, connectivity must be both speedy and reliable. No connection or a slow connection will quickly impact the organization's ability to function.
3. **Cost**—Startup costs in particular are substantial and potentially beyond what many agencies can afford (Whitcomb).

Lab Security

Lab security is always a major concern. Access to the evidence and facilities must be strictly managed. Strict security plays a key role in maintaining the integrity of the digital evidence that passes through the laboratory. Only authorized, vetted personnel should have access to critical areas such as examination stations and evidence storage. Unauthorized individuals are usually kept out using doors and other physical barriers along with access controls such as keys, swipe cards, and access codes. Digital solutions such as swipe cards and access codes offer an advantage over older methods such as keys. Electronic means provide a ready-made audit trail that can be used in support of the chain of custody. Security is further enhanced with alarm systems and the like.

Unauthorized access isn't the only threat to the evidence. The risk of fire, flooding, and other natural disasters also must be addressed.

The chain of custody continues at the lab, as does the paperwork. In the lab, the evidence must be signed in and out of the evidence storage area for examinations and court. This log must be completed each and every time the evidence is removed or returned to the evidence room or vault. This checkout and check-in process can be done the old-fashioned way with pen and paper or electronically with scanners and bar codes.

Just like in the field, network access to evidence in the lab is also a concern. This is true for both the Internet and the lab's own computers. Best practice tells us that the machine used to perform the examination should not be connected to the Internet. Removing this connection removes that argument that the evidence was somehow compromised by someone or something (malware for example) via the Internet. Virtual labs will need to be able to articulate how the integrity of their evidence is maintained, given the nature of their operation.

Malware (viruses, worms, and the like) could be hiding on any evidence drive brought in for examination. Connecting it in some manner to the internal network poses a major risk to not only the lab's computers but evidence from other cases as well. To mitigate the risk, these drives should be scanned for viruses by at least one antivirus tool prior to examination.

Evidence Storage

When the evidence is not actively being examined, it must be stored in a secure location with limited access. One of the best solutions is a data safe. These safes come in multiple sizes and are specifically designed to protect digital evidence from theft and fire. Some types of digital media are very vulnerable to heat (tape, for example). A data safe is able to keep the media at an acceptable temperature long enough (hopefully) for the fire to be extinguished.

Evidence storage locations must be kept locked at all times when not actively being used. A log or audit trail should also be maintained detailing who entered, when they entered, and what they removed or returned.

Access to evidence storage and other sensitive areas can be controlled by a variety of means including pass codes and key cards. Electronic controls have some distinct advantages over keys. One significant advantage is the ability to log each and every time an individual accesses a restricted area. This audit trail can be very helpful in monitoring and verifying the chain of custody.

POLICIES AND PROCEDURES

How the lab handles evidence, conducts examinations, keeps records, and secures its facility should not be left to chance or the whims of any one individual. These tasks should be governed by policies and **Standard Operating Procedures (SOPs)**. SOPs are documents that detail, among other things, how common forensic examinations should be performed. The art in writing SOPs lies in finding the right balance between being too narrow or overly broad. If too specific, the SOP will lack the flexibility needed to address any unusual conditions that may arise. In digital forensics, these situations occur far more often than we'd like. If too broad, they can be ineffective in keeping things consistent and ensuring the integrity of the evidence.

There are inherent dangers in not following your organization's policies and SOPs. Odds are that questions on your organization's policies and SOPs will come up during cross-examination should the case go to court.

QUALITY ASSURANCE

In the early 1980s, the Ford Motor Company told us told us that "Quality is Job 1." You may not believe that today in regard to Ford, but it's most assuredly true in regard to forensic science.

Quality assurance (QA) is a bedrock principle that underpins every discipline in forensic science. As such, every lab should have a QA program. Quality assurance is defined as "a well-documented system of protocols used to assure the accuracy and reliability of analytical results" (James & Nordby, 2009). A good QA program will cover a wide array of subjects including peer reviews of reports, evidence handling, case documentation, training of lab personnel, and more (James & Nordby, 2009).

The review process can be divided into two discrete types: a technical review and an administrative review.

- The technical review, conducted by a separate examiner, focuses on the results and conclusions. The central question in a technical review is "Are the results reported by the original examiner supported by the evidence in the case?"
- In contrast, the focus of an administrative review is ensuring that all of the paperwork is present and has been completed correctly.

An examiner's competency must be confirmed and documented on a regular basis. In the forensic community, this is known as proficiency testing. In a proficiency test, examiners must demonstrate their competence with mock evidence. There are four types of proficiency tests:

1. Open test—the analyst(s) and technical support personnel are aware they are being tested.

2. Blind test—the analyst(s) and technical support personnel are not aware they are being tested.

3. Internal test—conducted by the agency itself.

4. External test—conducted by an agency independent of the agency being tested. (Scientific Working Groups on Digital Evidence and Imaging Technology, 2011).

These tests may be conducted in-house, with other lab personnel. These results must be documented because at some point, the analyst's skills and abilities may be called into question during a court proceeding. This documentation will be critical should that happen.

The case of Glen Woodall, although concerning DNA, is a powerful example of the need for quality assurance. On July 8, 1997, Glen Woodall was convicted of the brutal sexual assault of two women by a Cabell County, West Virginia, jury. He was summarily sentenced to two life terms with an additional sentence of 203 to 335 years in prison (The DNA Initiative). The arrest and conviction of Woodall brought some much needed closure to both of the victims and peace to the community as a whole. Unfortunately for the victims and community, the relief didn't last long.

The forensic scientist in this case was West Virginia State Police serologist Fred Zain. After an investigation into Zain's work in both West Virginia and Texas, he was charged with perjury and tampering with evidence (Chan, 1994). During the investigation it was found that Woodall was innocent, and that he, too, was a victim. After serving four years in a West Virginia prison, Woodall was released and awarded $1 million from the state for his wrongful imprisonment.

What the panel found was extremely disturbing. They discovered that Zain "fabricated or altered evidence and lied about academic qualifications under oath." That's not all. The panel also found that his supervisors may have been culpable as well, overlooking or hiding complaints about his performance (Chan, 1994).

In 2011, twenty-four years later, the real suspect was arrested and eventually convicted of the crimes of which Woodall was originally found guilty. On April 1, Donald Good was sentenced to over two hundred years in prison (WSAZ, 2011). Cases like this hammer home the need for effective quality assurance programs in all forensic sciences.

Tool Validation

Our tools, be they hardware or software, must function as they are designed. Each and every tool must be validated before it's used on an actual case. A validation process clearly demonstrates that the tool is working properly, is reliable, and yields accurate results. We can't simply accept the manufacturer's word for it; assumptions aren't permitted.

The validation process is another one of those things that has to be committed to paper. To do otherwise will put any evidence found in real jeopardy of being excluded.

Documentation

The importance of complete and accurate documentation can't be overstated. The old saying "if you didn't write it down, it didn't happen" are truly words to live by in this industry. There are different types of documentation and reports used throughout the entire forensic process. These should be spelled out in the labs' or agencies' SOP and policy manuals. Submission forms, chain of custody records, examiner's notes, and the examiner's final report form the crux of the required documentation.

Normally, all the paperwork associated with a specific case is collected into a case file. The case file will contain all of the documentation pertaining to the case, including paperwork generated by the examiner and others. Usually they include case submission forms, requests for assistance, examiners' notes, crime scene reports, case reports, copy of the search authority, chain of custody, and so on (National Institute of Justice, 2004).

FORMS

Preprinted forms are widely used in both the field and the lab. They help guide personnel through the process and ensure that a high level of quality is maintained. Forms ensure all the necessary information is captured in a uniform manner. Typically, forms are used to describe the evidence in detail (make, model, serial number, etc.), document the chain of custody, request an examination, and so on.

EXAMINER NOTES

Examiner's notes cover most, if not all, of the examiner's actions and observations along with corresponding dates. They must be detailed enough to enable another examiner to duplicate the process used during the examination. Things typically recorded here include:

- Discussions with key players including prosecutors and investigators.
- Irregularities found and associated actions taken.
- Operating systems, versions, and patch state.
- Passwords.
- Any changes made to the system by lab personnel and of law enforcement. (National Institute of Justice, 2004)

If you've ever worked in the legal system, then you know that the wheels of justice can turn very, very slowly. This applies to both criminal and civil cases. It can be months or even years before a case ever gets to trial. By the time you have to testify, you may only be able to recall few, if any, facts of the case. The case documentation, and your notes in particular, will prove a great tool to refresh your recollection.

EXAMINER'S FINAL REPORT

The **examiner's final report** is the formal document that is delivered to prosecutors, investigators, opposing counsel, and so on at or near the end of an investigation. These reports typically consist of:

- Identity of the reporting agency.
- The case identification number/submission number.
- Identity of the submitting person and case investigator.
- Dates of receipt and report
- Detailed description of the evidence items submitted including serial numbers, makes, models, and so on.
- Identity of the examiner.
- Description of the steps taken during the examination process.
- Results and conclusions. (National Institute of Justice, 2004)

When drafting the final examiner's report, it's critical to take into account the intended audience, which is primarily laypeople. The lawyers, investigators, judges, and clients will most likely have little to no technical background. All too often these reports are filled with technical jargon and details that only serve to frustrate and confuse the majority of its intended audience. These reports should be comprehensible to a nontechnical audience. Jargon and acronyms should be kept to an absolute minimum.

Two major sections of the examiner's report are the summary and the details of the findings. The summary is a brief description of the results of the examination. The end users of our reports find this feature useful, especially in light of the massive caseload and amount of information they are typically dealing with. The findings included here should be supported and explained in the detailed findings.

The detailed findings provide the substance of the report. They provide the details of the examination, steps taken, results, and so on. Typically you may find details relating to:

- Files directly pertaining to the request.
- Files that support the findings.
- Email, web cache, chat logs, and so on.
- Keyword searches.
- Evidence of ownership of the device. (National Institute of Justice, 2004)

A glossary is a helpful addition to an examiner's report. Anything we can do to help our intended audience wade through any unfamiliar jargon and acronyms is always a good thing. Conveying our findings in a way that can be understood is our responsibility as forensic professionals.

DIGITAL FORENSIC TOOLS

Digital forensic tools make our work much more efficient or even possible. There are tools for specific purposes as well as tools with broader functionality.

They can come in the form of both hardware or software. They can be commercial tools that must be purchased or they can be open source that are freely available. There are advantages and disadvantages to all. Keep in mind, no single tool does everything or does everything exceedingly well. As such, it's a good practice to have multiple tools available. Using multiple tools is also a great way to validate your findings. The same results, with two different tools, significantly increase the reliability of the evidence.

Tool Selection

The digital forensic tool market boasts a large number of products, with more rolling out all the time. How does an examiner know which tools are reliable and which ones are not? How should these tools be validated? The National Institute of Standards and Technology (NIST) and the National Institute of Justice (NIJ) have taken a big step in helping to answer these and other questions.

NIST has launched the Computer Forensic Tool Testing Project (CFTT), which establishes a "methodology for testing computer forensic software tools by development of general tool specifications, test procedures, test criteria, test sets, and test hardware" (National Institute of Standards and Technology).

Let's explore what this looks like. This is an excerpt from the NIST test of a Tableau brand hardware **write blocking device (HWB)**, summarizing some of the test criteria and results:

> "An HWB device shall not transmit a command to a protected storage device that modifies the data on the storage device."
>
> "For all test cases run, the device always blocked any commands that would have changed user or operating system data stored on a protected drive."
>
> "An HWB device shall return the data requested by a read operation."
>
> "For all test cases run, the device always allowed commands to read the protected drive." (National Institute of Justice, 2009)

Each tool, be it hardware or software, must be validated before it is used on casework as well as anytime it is modified or updated. For an example, like other software you're familiar with, our forensic software gets updated on a regular basis. After each update, the tool should be validated again. Validation also proves useful in court, supporting the validity of the tool's results.

Hardware

There are many hardware tools out there designed and built specifically for digital forensics. Some of these tools include cloning devices, cell phone acquisition devices, write blockers, portable storage devices, adapters, cables, and more.

As you might expect, digital forensics is heavily dependent on an assortment of hardware such as PCs, servers, write blockers, cell phone kits, cables, and so on. Figure 3.1 shows a well-equipped digital forensic workstation.

FIGURE 3.1
One of the workstations in the West Virginia State Police Digital Forensics Lab located at the Marshall University Forensic Science Center. (Courtesy of Cpl. Bob Boggs).

Computers are the backbone of any digital forensics lab. So as an examiner you will need the best computer workstation you can afford. Digital forensic exams require quite a bit of computing power. These jobs can tax even the best systems and crush those that don't measure up. A good exam machine has multiple, multi-core processors, as much RAM as you can get (the more the better), and large, fast hard drives. Forensic software manufacturers provide detailed lists of minimum and suggested hardware requirements. Straying below the minimums is done at your own risk. To get a better understanding, let's look at the minimum and recommended system requirements (as of press time) for AccessData's Forensic Tool Kit (FTK).

AccessData's FTK comprises four distinct components and or applications. They are:

1. Oracle Database
2. FTK Client User Interface (UI)
3. Client-side Processing Engine
4. Distributed Processing Engine

The minimums and recommended specifications will vary with each component, but suffice it to say that you can never have too much RAM or computing power. For example, on a machine running the Oracle database, the FTK user interface and the primary processing engine, AccessData recommends the requirements shown in Table 3.1.

Table 3.1	Basic Recommended Requirement (AccessData Group, LLC, 2011)	
	Minimum	**Recommended**
Processor	Intel® i7 or AMD equivalent	Intel® i9 Dual Quad Core Xeon, i7 Nehalem or AMD equivalent
RAM	12GB (DDR3) 8GB (DDR2)	12GB (DDR3) 8GB (DDR2)
Operating System	Vista, 2008, Windows 7 (64 bit)	Vista, 2008, Windows 7 (64 bit)

Some components may be installed on separate machines. The minimum and recommended requirements will change depending on which configuration is used.

Examiners frequently sift through massive amounts of data. As such, digital forensics labs need to have the capacity to store voluminous amounts of data. In browsing the PCs for sale on bestbuy.com, the majority of them have between 500 GB and 699 GB of hard drive space. Multiterabyte drives are also available. With numbers like these and caseloads ever increasing, it's easy to see that storage is a major concern.

Digital forensics is no longer a "PC centric" endeavor. Small-scale devices such as cell phones and GPS units are pouring into labs across the country. These devices require different hardware from that used on laptops and desktops. Cellebrite's UFED supports over three thousand phones (Cellebrite Mobile Synchronization LTD). Paraben Corporation, a competitor of Cellebrite, boasts support for more than four thousand phones, PDAs, and GPS units (Paraben Corporation). When dealing with cell phones, having the proper cable is critical. Unlike PCs, mobile devices lack much of the standardization with regard to connectors and cables. Labs need to have a wide selection of cables on hand to cope with the vast array of handsets that walk through the doors. Fortunately, the manufacturers of mobile phone forensic hardware provide many of the required cables.

Several companies make hardware cloning devices. If you recall, a forensic clone is a "bit stream" copy of a particular piece of media such as a hard drive. These tools can really speed up the process, cloning multiple drives at once. They can also provide write protection, hash authentication, drive wiping, an audit trail, and more.

OTHER EQUIPMENT

The hardware and software we discussed earlier are not the only equipment needed. Crime scene kits are very useful outside the lab. These kits are preloaded with all of the supplies an examiner would need in the field to collect digital evidence. Kits contain standard items such as pens, digital camera, forensically clean storage media, evidence bags, evidence tape, report forms, permanent markers, and the like.

Software

There is a wide array of digital forensic software products on the market today. Some are general tools that serve a variety of functions. Others are more focused, serving a fairly limited purpose. These applications tend to focus on a very specific type of evidence, e-mail or Internet, for example.

When selecting software, a choice needs to be made between going with open source tools or a commercially produced product. There are advantages and disadvantages to both. Factors such as cost, functionality, capabilities, and support are some of the criteria that can be used to make this decision.

ADDITIONAL RESOURCES

Open Source Tools

Cory Altheide and Harlan Carvey's book *Digital Forensics With Open Source Tools* is an excellent reference for those practitioners using these applications.

One of the more popular open source tools is SIFT, or the SANS Investigative Forensic Toolkit. SIFT Workstation is a powerful, free, open source tool. It's built on the Linux Ubuntu operating system. This tool is capable of file carving as well as analyzing file systems, web history, recycle bin, and more. It can also analyze network traffic and volatile memory. It can also generate a timeline, which can be immensely helpful during an investigation. SIFT supports the following file systems:

- Windows (MSDOS, FAT, VFAT, NTFS)
- MAC (HFS)
- Solaris (UFS)
- Linux (EXT2/3/4)

(The SANS Institute)

As for commercial tools, two of the most popular general software tools are Forensic Toolkit (FTK®) from AccessData and EnCase® from Guidance Software. Both are excellent and can make exams easier and more efficient. These applications have "Swiss Army knife"–like capabilities. They perform a multitude of tasks, including:

- Searching
- E-mail analysis
- Sorting
- Reporting
- Password cracking

The search tools in these products are particularly powerful, and give examiners the capability to drill down to precisely the information they are looking for. Here is a quick list of some of the information that can be searched for:

- E-mail addresses
- Names
- Phone numbers
- Keywords
- Web addresses
- File types
- Date ranges

As helpful as these tools can be, they do have some limitations. The reality is that no single tool does it all. For that reason, budget permitting, labs need to have a variety of tools available.

More and more specialty tools are coming on the market. These tools focus on one aspect of digital evidence such as e-mail or web-based evidence. These can bring some additional capabilities to the table that some multipurpose tools don't.

ALERT!

Dependence on the Tools

GUI-based forensic tools can become a crutch. "Push-button" tools can make exams much more efficient, but they don't relieve the examiner of his or her responsibility to understand what's going on beneath the surface. Examiners need to understand not only what the tool is doing, but also how the artifact in question is created to begin with.

Some of the forensic tools that an examiner may use are listed in Table 3.2. Many of these companies offer video tutorials or demonstrations of their products. These can be a great source of additional information. They are typically available from their web site or on YouTube. This is in no way meant as an endorsement of a specific tool. These are only a representative sampling of the many tools that are available.

ACCREDITATION

Accreditation is an endorsement of a crime lab's policies and procedures, the way it does business, if you will (James & Nordby, 2009). **The American Society of Crime Laboratory Directors/Laboratory Accreditation Board (ASCLD/LAB)** is recognized as a world leader in the accreditation of forensic laboratories. Despite the name, ASCLD/LAB grants accreditation to labs both inside and outside the United States, which it has been doing since 1982 (Barbara).

Table 3.2	Some hardware and software tools that may be found in a digital forensics laboratory	
Tool	**Use**	**URL**
Forensic Toolkit Access Data Group, LLC	Multipurpose tool (acquisition, verification, searching, reporting, wiping, etc.)	http://accessdata.com
EnCase Guidance Software, Inc.	Multipurpose tool (acquisition, verification, searching, reporting, wiping, etc.)	http://www.guidancesoftware.com
SMART & SMART for Linux ASR Data, Data Acquisition and Analysis, LLC	Multipurpose tool (acquisition, verification, searching, reporting, wiping, etc.)	http://www.asrdata.com/forensic-software/
X-Ways Forensics X-Ways Software Technology AG	Multipurpose tool (acquisition, verification, searching, reporting, wiping, etc.)	http://www.x-ways.net/forensics/
Helix3 Pro e-fense, Inc.	Multipurpose tool (acquisition, verification, searching, reporting, wiping, etc.)	http://www.e-fense.com/products.php
Softblock, Macquisition, Blacklight BlackBag Technologies, Inc.	Multiple Macintosh forensic tools	https://www.blackbagtech.com/forensics.html
Mac Marshall Architecture Technology Corporation	Multiple Macintosh forensic tools	http://www.macmarshal.com/
Raptor Forward Discovery, Inc.	Linux-based acquisition and preview tool	http://www.forwarddiscovery.com/Raptor
Dossier Logicube, Inc.	Hardware acquisition	http://www.logicube.com/
Forensic hardware tools Tableau	Write blockers, bridges, storage, acquisition	http://www.tableau.com/
Wiebetech	Storage, write blockers, etc.	http://www.wiebetech.com/home.php

Based in Garner, North Carolina, ASCLD/LAB has accredited a total of 385 crime laboratories, 17 of those being outside the United States (American Society of Crime Laboratory Directors/Laboratory Accreditation Board).

According to ASCLD/LAB, they have four objectives. They are to:

1. improve the quality of laboratory services provided to the criminal justice system.
2. develop and maintain criteria that may be used by a laboratory to assess its level of performance and to strengthen its operation.

3. provide an independent, impartial, and objective system by which laboratories can benefit from a total operational review.

4. offer to the general public and to users of laboratory services a means of identifying those laboratories that have demonstrated that they meet established standards (American Society of Crime Laboratory Directors/Laboratory Accreditation Board).

Think of ASCLD/LAB as the "Good Housekeeping Seal of Approval" for forensic science. The earning and maintaining an ASCLD/LAB accreditation is no easy chore. It requires an unbelievable amount of time, planning, documentation, and money. Nothing is taken for granted. Every standard met must be backed up with extensive, detailed documentation.

ASCLD/LAB offers two accreditation programs. The first is the legacy program and the second is the international program. The legacy program is the first program instituted by ASCLD/LAB. As you might expect, there are differences between the two programs as well as some common ground. A major difference is the number of criteria that must be met under each program. The international program has considerably more standards to meet than the legacy program. Labs seeking accreditation under the international program are required to fulfill the relevant requirements to demonstrate conformance to the applicable requirements of both the ISO/IEC 17025:1999(E) General Requirements for the Competence of Testing and Calibration Laboratories and the ASCLD/LAB-International Supplemental Requirements for the Accreditation of Forensic Science Testing and Calibration Laboratories.

While accreditation is highly desirable, it's not mandatory. Non-accredited labs can and do successfully process evidence. The reality is that obtaining and maintaining an accredited forensic lab is both a cash and labor-intensive proposition. The kind of staffing and funding commitment required is tough to secure and frankly is not an option for everyone.

THE AMERICAN SOCIETY FOR TESTING AND MATERIALS (ASTM)

In addition to ASCLD/LAB, ASTM International also provides standards for the various disciplines within the forensic sciences, including digital forensics. ASTM International was formerly known as the **American Society for Testing and Materials**. It was founded in 1898 by engineers and chemists of the Pennsylvania Railroad. The standards are developed by subject matter experts that are members of ASTM (ASTM International).

Accreditation versus Certification

These terms may seem interchangeable; however, in the context of a forensic laboratory, they are not. As described earlier, accreditation refers to the laboratory, whereas certification pertains to the individual examiners. Certification normally requires an examiner to pass a written or practical test(s).

The Scientific Working Group on Digital Evidence (SWGDE) issued a paper addressing the certification of digital forensic practitioners. SWGDE asserts that any digital forensic certification must address the following core competencies, at a minimum:

1. Pre-examination procedures and legal issues
2. Media assessment and analysis
3. Data recovery
4. Specific analysis of recovered data
5. Documentation and reporting
6. Presentation of findings (Scientific Working Group on Digital Evidence, 2010)

SUMMARY

The forensic laboratory plays a critical role in our justice system. Well presented forensic evidence can be very, very persuasive to a jury. Many, many cases turn on the forensic evidence itself or the lack thereof. The forensic laboratory therefore plays a pivotal role in the search for justice.

Quality must be a priority in every forensic laboratory and to every forensic professional. Digital forensics is no different. Quality is achieved through the strict adherence to established quality standards as part of an overall quality assurance program. Accreditation of a digital forensics laboratory is one way to ensure conformance to these standards. The recognized world leader in accreditation of forensic labs is ASCLD/LAB. Standards for digital forensics are drafted by the ASTM.

Accreditation and certification are not synonymous. The primary difference is that accreditation pertains to the physical lab where certification applies to the personnel conducting the examinations. Not only should examiners be tested to demonstrate that they are "functioning properly," so to should their tools. Only tools that have been tested and proven reliable should be used when processing a case. This testing procedure is known as validation.

Digital forensic practitioners use both software and hardware tools in their work. No one single tool does everything or does it well. Most labs will have a variety of tools at their disposal to give them the broad capability they need given the wide array of technology they see coming in the door for analysis.

References

About: American Society of Crime Laboratory Directors/Laboratory Accreditation Board. (n.d.). Retrieved June 4, 2011, from: http://www.ascld-lab.org/about_us/aboutoverview.html

AccessData Group, LLC. (2011, February). *Downloads: AccessData.* Retrieved August 24, 2011, from: http://accessdata.com/downloads/media/FTK_3x_System_Specifications_Guide.pdf

American Society of Crime Laboratory Directors/Laboratory Accreditation Board. (n.d.). *Did You Know: American Society of Crime Laboratory Directors/Laboratory Accreditation Board.* Retrieved June 4, 2011, from: http://www.ascld-lab.org/largest_accreditation.html

American Society of Crime Laboratory Directors/Laboratory Accreditation Board. (n.d.). *Objectives: American Society of Crime Laboratory Directors/Laboratory Accreditation Board.* Retrieved June 4, 2011, from: http://www.ascld-lab.org/about_us/objectives.html

Barbara, J. J. (n.d.). *Digital Evidence Accreditation.* Retrieved August 25, 2011, from: http://www.forensicmag.com/article/digital-evidence-accreditation?page=0,3

Barbara, J. J. (n.d.). *Digital Evidence Accreditation: Forensic Magazine.* Retrieved June 4, 2011, from: http://www.forensicmag.com/article/digital-evidence-accreditation

Brunty, J. (2011, March 2). *Validation of Forensic Tools and Software: A Quick Guide for the Digital Forensic Examiner.* Retrieved August 24, 2011, from: http://www.dfinews.com/article/validation-forensic-tools-and-software-quick-guide-digital-forensic-examiner?page=0,2

Carrier, B. B. (2002, October). *Papers: Digital-evidence.org.* Retrieved August 24, 2011, from: http://www.digital-evidence.org/papers/opensrc_legal.pdf

Chan, S. (1994, August 21). *Scores of Convictions Reviewed as Chemist Faces Perjury Accusations.* Retrieved from LATimes.com: http://articles.latimes.com/1994-08-21/news/mn-29449_1_lab-tests-fred-zain-double-murder (Accessed 21.08.94).

Federal Bureau of Investigation. (2010). *Regional Computer Forensics Laboratory Annual Report Fiscal Year 2010.* Washington, DC: U.S. Department of Justice.

James, S., & Nordby, J. J. (2009). *Forensic Science: An Introduction to Scientific and Investigative Techniques, Third Edition.* Boca Raton, FL: CRC Press.

National Institute of Justice. (2004). *Forensic Examination of Digital Evidence: A Guide for Law Enforcement.* Washington, DC: U.S. Department of Justice.

National Institute of Justice. (2009). *Test Results for Hardware Write Block Device: T4 Forensic SCSI Bridge (FireWire Interface).* U.S. Department of Justice, Office of Justice Programs. Washington, DC: National Institute of Justice.

National Institute of Standards and Technology. (n.d.). *Computer Forensics Tool Testing Project Web Site: National Institute of Standards and Technology.* Retrieved June 6, 2011, from: http://www.cftt.nist.gov/index.html

Saferstein, R. (2006). *Criminalistics: An Introduction to Forensic Science (College Edition) (9th ed.).* Upper Saddle River, NJ: Prentice Hall.

Scientific Working Group on Digital Evidence. (2010, May 15). *Minimum Requirements for Quality Assurance in the Processing of Digital and Multimedia Evidence.* Retrieved August 24, 2011, from: http://www.swgde.org/documents/current-documents/

Whitcomb, C. A. (n.d.). *Virtual Digital Forensics Lab.* Largo, FL: National Center for Forensic Science.

WSAZ. (2011, April 1). *UPDATE: Donald Good Receives Two Life Sentences in Mall Rape Case.* Retrieved from WSAZ.com: http://www.wsaz.com/news/headlines/UPDATE_Judge_OHanlon_Will_Preside_Over_Huntington_Mall_Rape-Case.html (Accessed 17.11.11).

CHAPTER 4
Collecting Evidence

Information in This Chapter:

- Introduction to Crime Scenes
- Documenting the Scene and the Evidence
- Establishing and Maintaining the Chain of Custody
- Forensic Cloning of Evidence
- Dealing with Live Systems and Dead Systems
- Using Hashing to Verify the Integrity of Evidence
- Drafting the Examiner's Final Report

INTRODUCTION

That "smoking gun" you discovered will never get to a jury unless it's been properly collected and accounted for starting at the scene. As important as it is, you'll never see it done right on TV cop shows. Nothing kills the excitement faster than three solid hours of paperwork. In the real world, it's those three solid hours of paperwork that get your evidence into court. It all starts at the crime scene. Just locating the evidence can be tough. Especially with stamp-sized (or smaller) memory cards and the like. They could be hidden in an almost limitless number of places.

At the scene, examiners could be confronted with a variety of devices and storage media. They could find one or more running computers and wireless devices like cell phones. Together, they present some unique challenges for the investigator.

Actions during the collection process must be well documented. Notes, photos, video, and sketches record our actions and refresh our recollections. As digital evidence is extremely volatile, preservation is paramount. If at all possible, a forensic image or clone is made of the suspect media. The exam is conducted on the clone (which is an exact bit for bit copy) rather than the original.

CRIME SCENES AND COLLECTING EVIDENCE

From a practical standpoint, not all scenes involving digital evidence are created or treated equally. Digital evidence has been the focus of criminal, civil, and administrative proceedings. There are distinct differences in how the scene and the evidence may be handled and documented for these proceedings. Some cases, like a homicide, will require painstaking documentation. Others, like a civil dispute, will necessitate a somewhat less intense response. While acknowledging these subtle differences, there are certain core principles and protocols that will remain consistent.

After it's deemed safe, job one at a digital crime scene, or any other, is securing the evidence. The scene and its evidence must be protected from accidental or intentional compromise. Securing a traditional crime scene entails limiting physical access by those folks that don't have a legitimate reason to be there. Nosy neighbors, the news media, and police supervisors are typical crime scene trespassers. Securing a traditional scene is accomplished by stringing crime scene tape, posting guards, or simply asking people to leave.

In contrast, a scene with digital evidence presents an entirely new dimension of access. Most computers and digital devices are connected to the Internet, cellular, or other kinds of networks. It's this connection that permits remote access and puts the evidence at risk. Computers and wireless devices must be made inaccessible as soon as you're sure that no volatile data would be lost (Association of Chief Police Officers, 2011). For computers, it may be a matter of removing the Ethernet cable or unplugging a wireless modem or router. With wireless devices such as cell phones, we must take steps to isolate the phone from network signals.

Removable Media

If legally permissible (such as with a warrant), we want to search anywhere that could contain a piece of storage media. Considering today's "stamp-sized" memory cards, this piece of evidence could be hidden almost anywhere such as in books, wallets, hat bands, etc.

Despite their small size, memory cards can hold a ton of potential evidence such as child pornography or stolen credit card numbers. Let's break it down. A quick check of Amazon.com shows that you can buy a 64 gigabyte memory card for around $120. Gigabytes (GB) are pretty abstract for most of us. Instead of using a standard unit of data storage, we'll use an example that is less conventional yet more relatable.

We're going to convert the 64 GB memory card into our own unit of measure, which we will call "Potters"—Harry "Potters," to be exact. Picture a set of all seven books in the Harry Potter series. In rough numbers, each GB contains about 109 complete sets. With some simple math, we find that our 64 GB memory card can hold approximately seven thousand complete sets of books on something about the size of a postage stamp! Think about the amount of evidence that could be pulled from just one memory card.

REMOVABLE STORAGE MEDIA

Removable storage media include things like DVDs, external hard drives, thumb drives, and memory cards.

We're not just interested in the devices and storage media at the scene; the surrounding area and items are also worth a look. For example, books and manuals can give investigators clues as to the skill level of the target and what kind of technology they may be up against. Perhaps the biggest payoff is an alert to the possible use of encryption. Discarded packaging in the trash could also be helpful. Any forensic examiner would tell you that avoiding encryption is definitely worth the trouble.

Cell Phones

Almost everyone has a cell phone these days. As such, they often contain some very valuable evidence. Text messages, e-mail, call logs, and contacts are examples of what you can recover. These items can be used to show intent, determine the last person to come in contact with a murder victim, establish alibis, determine approximate locations, and more.

As with other electronic devices, our first mandate is to make no changes to the device or its storage media. Therefore, interacting with the phone should be avoided unless absolutely necessary. Cell phones are particularly vulnerable because they can be wiped by the cell provider or even by the owner themselves. This functionality is intended to protect your data should you lose your phone or have it stolen. Apple's "Find My Phone" app is one notable example. We must address this concern by isolating or shielding the phone as soon as possible.

You have a few options to get this done:

- Turn the phone off. The concern with this approach is the same as a PC. The phone may be password-protected. Once powered down, the code may be necessary to access the phone. If possible, it may be best to isolate the phone in a Faraday bag or arson can and leave it powered on. It can then be transported to the lab to be examined in a shielded room, and so on.
- Place the phone in special containers that shield the phone from wireless signals. Empty paint cans and Faraday bags are two of the more typical choices. Both of these items are effective at safeguarding the phone from cell signals. (See Figure 4.1.)

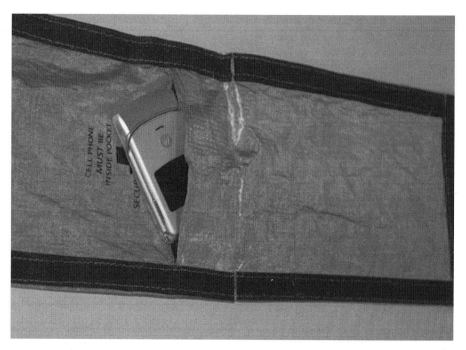

FIGURE 4.1
A Faraday bag and cell phone.

ALERT!

Protecting Cell Phones from Network Signals

It's essential to isolate a live cell phone from the network. If not, it can receive calls, text messages, or even commands to delete all the data. A **Faraday bag** is one way to prevent a network signal from reaching the phone. A Faraday bag is made of "some type of conducting material or mesh" that repels these signals. The function of the bag is based on the work of Michael Faraday, an English scientist who specialized in electromagnetism (Microsoft Corporation).

ALERT!

Power

Power is a concern whenever you seize a cell phone. If the phone is on, it will continuously try to connect to a tower, draining the battery. If the phone is off, you should also seize the power cables. Lab personnel may very well need to recharge the device in order to complete their exam.

Failing to remove connectivity to these devices not only risks destruction of the evidence; it can raise serious concerns about its integrity as well. A competent attorney could successfully argue that this evidence is untrustworthy and should be excluded.

After securing the evidence, a survey of the scene will give investigators an accurate sense of what's ahead. Several questions need to be answered:

- What kinds of devices are present?
- How many devices are we dealing with?
- Are any of the devices running?
- What tools will be needed?
- Do we have the necessary expertise on hand?

Once these questions are answered, the real work begins.

Order of Volatility

It's a good idea to prioritize the evidence to be collected. Generally, we want to start with the most volatile evidence first. In computer parlance, this is known as the **order of volatility**. This descending list works from the most volatile (RAM) to the least volatile (archived data). The order of volatility is:

1. CPU, cache, and register content
2. Routing table, ARP cache, process table, kernel statistics
3. Memory
4. Temporary file system/swap space
5. Data on hard disk
6. Remotely logged data
7. Data contained on archival media (Henry, 2009)

DOCUMENTING THE SCENE

There is an old tried and true saying in law enforcement: *"If you don't write it down, it didn't happen."* These are words of wisdom indeed. Regardless of the situation, any time evidence is collected, documentation is a vitally important part of the process. There are several different types of documentation. The most common in terms of digital forensics are photographs and written notes; video is also an option for documenting evidence.

This documentation process begins the moment investigators arrive at the scene. Typically, we start by noting the date and time of our arrival along with all the people at the scene. The remainder of our notes consists of detailed descriptions of the evidence we collect, its location, the names of who discovered and collected it, and how it was collected. It's also a good idea to note the item's condition, especially if there is visible damage.

Accurately and precisely describing the evidence is of critical importance. A piece of digital evidence is described by type, make, model, serial number, or other similar descriptors. It's also important to note whether a device is on or off or if it's connected to other devices (such as printers) or a network (like the Internet). Virtually everything we see, find, and do should be documented.

While we're talking about peripheral connections, it is good practice to label each so that the entire system can be reconstructed in the lab should that become necessary.

After the scene and evidence are secure, our attention can turn to the documentation as well as identifying and collecting potential sources of evidence. Before anything is done, it's prudent to do a walk-through to survey the scene, pinpointing the type and number of devices as well as resources that will be needed.

Photography

Next, the entire scene should be photographed. Photos should be taken of the scene before anything is disturbed, including the evidence. It's helpful to think of the photos as telling a story. Remember, at some point, you may have to walk a judge or jury through this scene weeks, months, or even years later.

Start with a broad perspective, perhaps the outside of the house or office being investigated. After the overall scene has been photographed, we can then focus on each individual piece of evidence. Long-, medium-, and close-range photos show the item in the context of its surroundings. The photos of each item should clearly show the condition of the item as it was found. We need to pay particular attention to and capture things like identifying information such as serial numbers, damage, and connections. Connection examples could include networks and peripherals such as printers and scanners. It's very important to keep in mind that this is likely the only chance we'll get to capture the scene. So, when in doubt shoot more, not less.

You've probably seen photos with both the evidence item and a ruler of some sort. This is done to give some perspective to the item. It gives us an idea as to the size of that particular piece of evidence. Remember, we want to record the scene before it's disturbed or altered in any way so inserting anything into the scene with that item (like a ruler) can qualify as alteration. If it is necessary to show the size of the piece of evidence, it's a good idea to take a picture without the ruler first, then one with the ruler.

Photographs are used to depict the scene and the evidence exactly as we find them to help supplement our notes. They don't replace them. Notes capture our personal observations that won't be recorded in a photo. They are used to refresh our recollections when we go to court. Photos are a great aid to help us tell our story to the judge and jury. They really are worth a thousand words.

FIGURE 4.2
Marked cables from the back of a PC. Labels are placed on both ends of a cable to help document how what was connected to the PC at the time it was collected.

Notes

As we photograph the evidence, we'll also be taking detailed notes of our actions along with any potential evidence we find. There is no set standard for note-taking. It's really up to the individual on how they want to document things. Chronological order is a common method. You would want to note things such as the time you arrived, who was present at the scene, who took what action, who found and collected which piece of evidence, and so on.

Never lose sight of the fact that you will be relying on these photos, notes, and reports months or years later when you prepare for court. With that in mind, you will want more detail rather than less. Memories fade, cases run together, and details get blurry. They should also be legible for the same reason. If cost is a concern, keep in mind that digital photos are cheap. You can fit a lot photos on today's memory cards.

What you write in those notes matters to other people involved in the case, especially if they end up being turned over to the opposition. Under certain legal requirements, your notes could become discoverable and made available to the opposing side. This can happen if you take your notes with you to the witness stand. With that in mind, it's important not to draw conclusions or speculate based on your initial observations. You could very well end up eating those words and losing the case. It's best to keep those notes focused on what you do and observe at the scene. Saving the interpretations and conclusions until after the analysis is a much better approach.

CHAIN OF CUSTODY

Before a piece of evidence gets in front of a jury, it must first meet a series of strict legal requirements. One of those is a well-documented chain of custody. A computer taken in as evidence makes many stops on its road to trial. It's collected, logged in at the lab, stored, checked out for analysis, checked back in for storage, and so on. Each of these stops must be noted, tracking each and every time the evidence item changes hands or locations. Without this detailed accounting, the evidence will be deemed untrustworthy and inadmissible. It's this detailed trail that makes up the chain of custody.

Marking Evidence

The first "link" in the chain of custody in any case is the person collecting the evidence. Civil cases may differ a bit in that IT staff or others may hold the distinction of being the first link. The evidence is marked as it is collected. Typically, evidence items are marked with initials, dates, and possibly case numbers. Permanent markers are best to ensure the markings aren't smudged or removed altogether. Apart from documenting the chain of custody, these marks help authenticate the item should it be introduced in court. The person who collected the item may be asked to identify it from the witness stand. What needs to be proved is that the item presented is the same one that was collected. These marks make this identification a near sure thing. (See Figure 4.3.)

Items small enough are normally sealed in a bag with tamper-proof evidence tape. The seal is then initialed and dated. The bags are usually made of paper, plastic, or special anti-static material. The anti-static material bags are used for electronics because this material helps protect the sensitive electronics found on hard drives from being damaged by static electricity.

CLONING

A forensic clone is an exact, bit for bit copy of a hard drive. It's also known as a bit stream image. In other words, every bit (1 or 0) is duplicated on a separate, forensically clean piece of media, such as a hard drive. Why go to all that trouble? Why not just copy and paste the files? The reasons are significant. First, copying and pasting only gets the active data. That is, data that are accessible to the user. These are the files and folders that users interact with, such as a Microsoft Word document. Second, it does NOT get the data in the unallocated space, including deleted and partially overwritten files. Third, it doesn't capture the file system data. All of this would result in an ineffective and incomplete forensic exam.

FIGURE 4.3
A marked piece of evidence, sealed in an evidence bag. (Photo courtesy of Marshall University.)

We will want to make a forensic clone of the suspect's hard drive(s) as soon as we reasonably can. Cloning a drive can be a pretty time-consuming process, and for that reason it usually makes more sense to do the cloning in the lab as opposed to at the scene. Cloning in the lab eliminates the need to be on scene for what could be hours. It also provides a much more stable environment, affording us better control of the process.

Before we take a computer off premises, we must have the legal authority to do so. In a criminal case, this request and the rationale behind it should be part of the search warrant application. In civil cases, this provision can be negotiated by the parties or ordered by a judge.

Although taking the hardware back to the lab is routine in criminal cases, the cloning may have to be done at the scene in a civil case. Most civil cases with digital evidence focus on business computers. A business computer sitting in a lab isn't generating any revenue, which tends to get business folks understandably cranky. If the hard drive in a business computer can't be replaced, then the machine is often cloned and put right back into service.

Purpose of Cloning

We know from earlier chapters that digital evidence is extremely volatile. As such, you never want to conduct your examination on the original evidence unless there are exigent circumstances or there is no other option available. Exigent circumstances could include situations in which a child is missing. Sometimes there are no tools or techniques available to solve the problem at hand.

Examining the clone affords us the chance at a "mulligan" should something go wrong. If possible, the original drive should be preserved in a safe place and only brought out to reimage if needed.

Hard drives are susceptible to failure. Having two clones gives you one to examine and one to fall back on. Ideally, all examinations are done on a clone as opposed to the original.

Sometimes that isn't an option, especially in a business setting when the machine and drive must be returned to service. In the eyes of the court, a properly authenticated forensic clone is as good as the original.

The Cloning Process

Cloning a hard drive should be a pretty straightforward process, at least in theory. Typically, you will clone one hard drive to another. The suspect's drive is known as the source drive and the drive you are cloning to is called the destination drive. The destination drive must be at least as large (if not slightly larger) than our source drive. Although it is not always possible, knowing the size of the source in advance is pretty handy. Bringing the right size drive will save a lot of time and aggravation.

The drive we want to clone (the source) is normally removed from the computer. It's then connected via cable to a cloning device of some kind or to another computer. It's **critical** to have some type of write blocking in place before starting the process. A write block is a crucial piece of hardware or software that is used to safeguard the original evidence during the cloning process. The hardware write block is placed between the cloning device (PC, laptop, or standalone hardware) and the source. The write block prevents any data from being written to the original evidence drive. Using this kind of device eliminates the possibility of inadvertently compromising the evidence. Remember, the hardware write blocking device goes in between the source drive and the cloning platform.

There is a little prep work involved in making a clone. The destination drive must be forensically cleaned prior to cloning a suspect's drive to it. Most if not all forensic imaging tools will generate some type of paper trail, proving that this cleaning has taken place. This paperwork becomes part of the case file.

Once the connections are made, the process is started with the press of a couple of buttons or clicks of a mouse. When complete, a short report should be generated by the tool indicating whether or not the cloning was successful. Cloning is successful when the hash values (think "digital fingerprint") for the source and clone match. We'll dig deeper into hash values in just a bit.

Forensically Clean Media

A forensically clean drive is one that can be proven to be devoid of any data at the time the clone is made. Being sterile is another way of looking at it. It is important to prove the drive is clean because comingled data is inadmissible data. Drives can be cleaned with the same devices used to make the clones. The cleaning process overwrites the entire hard drive with a particular pattern of data such as 111111111111 (Casey, 2011).

Forensic Image Formats

The end result of the cloning process is a forensic image of the source hard drive. Our finished clone can come in a few different formats. The file extension is the most visible indicator of the file format. Some of the most common forensic image formats include:

- EnCase (Extension .E01)
- Raw dd (Extension .001)
- AccessData Custom Content Image (Extension .AD1)

There are differences in the formats, but they are all forensically sound. Some, like DD, are open source, while others, like AD1, are proprietary. Choosing one format over the other can simply be a matter of preference. Most forensic examination tools will read and write multiple image formats.

In addition to being forensically sound, the other major consideration is that the tools to be used can read the image. The documentation with the tool should provide this information. Compatibility is a concern. This is especially true when exchanging image files between examiners.

Risks and Challenges

The biggest risk during the cloning process is in writing to the source or evidence drive. Any writes to the evidence will compromise its integrity and jeopardize its admissibility. Getting a functioning write-blocking device or software in place will keep this from happening. Proper cloning should be pretty boring. Any time it gets exciting, you've got problems. What can ratchet up the adrenaline? Bad sectors and damaged or malfunctioning drives come to mind. A corrupt boot sector or a failing motor can also create complications.

Value in eDiscovery

The Sedona Conference, the leading think tank on electronic discovery, defines eDiscovery as: "The process of identifying, preserving, collecting, preparing, reviewing, and producing electronically stored information ("ESI") in the context of the legal process" (Sedona Conference, 2010).

Forensic cloning provides some additional value in the eDiscovery process. Preservation of potentially relevant data is paramount in electronic discovery. Parties that fail to preserve evidence can face some very stiff punishment. Forensic cloning is one option available to preserve some kinds of media such as hard drives and removable media such as flash drives. It serves as the "gold standard" of data preservation in that it preserves all of the data on a piece of media, not just the active data. The down side of cloning is that it can be expensive and just not practical in all situations.

ALERT!

Sanctions in Electronic Discovery

Take the case of *E.I. du Pont de Nemours v. Kolon Industries (2011)*. In this case, the jury awarded $919 million to DuPont in an eye-popping verdict. Earlier in the case, the court determined that Kolon had destroyed e-mails and other potentially relevant data connecting it to the theft of trade secrets. As a result of that determination, the judge instructed the jury that Kolon (both executives and employees) deleted important evidence even though they had a duty to preserve it. Kolon's suffering may not end there. DuPont plans on requesting $50 million in punitive damages plus $30 million more for attorney fees (Favro, 2011).

LIVE SYSTEM VERSUS DEAD SYSTEM

Up to now, we've been talking about "dead" or powered off machines. What happens when we come across a running computer? At the moment there is no consensus on the answer. A growing debate exists in the digital forensics community about how to handle a "live" or running machine. The "old school" solution is simply to pull the plug, instantly removing power to the computer. Today, that approach is garnering second thoughts. There are compelling reasons not to pull the power on a running computer. Next, we'll look at the reasons both for and against this somewhat controversial method.

Live Acquisition Concerns

On the plus side, pulling the plug eliminates the need to interact with the running machine. Interacting with a running computer, in any way, causes changes to the system. Any change to a piece of evidence is bad and can cause major problems from a legal standpoint. These alterations can call the integrity of the evidence into question. Even when a machine is just sitting powered on, things are changing. When a person interacts with a running machine, even more things are changing. Knowing that change is a forensic faux pas; it's easy to see why pulling the plug is an attractive option. On a side note, these changes may have no impact on the artifacts relevant to the case. But the system is changing nonetheless.

We are now starting to second-guess this approach, recognizing that pulling the plug has some significant downsides.

For starters, yanking the plug means that any evidence in RAM will be under real threat of destruction. Data in RAM start to dissipate or fade when power is removed. There is a technique that can be used to preserve data in memory after the power is off, but it's not yet been widely adopted. (See the sidebar.)

MORE ADVANCED

Preserving Evidence in RAM

It's widely thought that data in RAM vanish when the power is turned off. That's really not true. Research by Princeton University has shown that data in RAM fade rather than disappear. This dissipation can be further slowed if the RAM is cooled to –58 deg Fahrenheit (–50 Celsius). This cooling will give examiners more time to collect this volatile data. To see this technique in action, see the video here: http://www.youtube.com/watch?v=JDaicPlgn9U.

Second, is encryption. The system or files may be unencrypted while the machine is powered on. Abruptly pulling the plug could return it to an encrypted state, potentially putting that evidence out of reach for good. Avoiding encryption is a good idea any time.

Third, a sudden loss of power could damage the data, rendering them unreadable. Fourth, some evidence may not get recorded on the drive unless and until the computer is properly shut down.

The old school solution of pulling the plug is not the only option on the table these days. There are now tools and techniques that will capture volatile memory from a live machine in a forensically sound manner. With these advances, it's time to start recognizing the advantages of live collection.

Advantage of Live Collection

Until fairly recently, pulling the plug was the only real option. Capturing data in a running computer's main memory (RAM) wasn't a realistic option. The potential solutions that existed just weren't practical to be used in the field. In contrast, present-day examiners do have some forensically sound alternatives. There are several commercial and open source tools that can be used to collect these volatile data. Unlike the older lab-bound approaches, these tools are very simple to use—so simple, in fact, that they are being marketed to nontechnical folks like most first responders. First responders could include patrol officers and IT staff among others. While these tools do simplify the process, they still require training for proper use.

Principles of Live Collection

Doing a live collection is not a rudimentary task. The following is an example of one approach.

After coming across a running computer at the scene, a couple of questions will need to be answered right from the start. Is the potential evidence to be recovered truly worth the time and effort? In some instances, the answer may be "no." In cases involving malware, RAM is vitally important. In others, such as a clear-cut possession of child pornography, RAM will likely have little value. Second, are the necessary resources available? To successfully capture the evidence in memory will require some specialized tools and training. Without these key ingredients, it could be best to punt and simply pull the plug. The risk of compromising the evidence may simply be too great. It's important to be able to recognize when you are in over your head and when you should call for help.

When interacting with a live machine, it's best to always choose the least invasive approach possible. This will require thinking before you click. Haste is not your friend in this situation. As mentioned earlier, we want to collect the most volatile information first.

ALERT!

Evidence in RAM

A computer's **volatile memory** (RAM) can contain some very valuable evidence, including running processes, executed console commands, passwords in clear text, unencrypted data, instant messages, Internet Protocol addresses, and Trojan horse(s) (Shipley & Reeve, 2006).

Conducting and Documenting a Live Collection

Now comes the tricky part. It's time to get focused. Once you start, you should work uninterrupted until the process is complete. To do otherwise only invites mistakes. Before getting underway, gather everything you will need: report forms, pens, memory capture tools, and so on. Every interaction with the computer will need to be noted. You could use an action/response approach ("I did this ... The computer did that.").

If the desktop isn't visible, you can move the mouse slightly to wake it up. If that fails to bring up the desktop, pressing a single key should solve the problem. You should of course document which key was depressed in your notes. Now that you can see the desktop, the first thing to note is the date and time as it appears on the computer. Next, record the icons and running applications. You don't want to stop there. Documenting the running processes could help identify any malware that is in residence on the computer. The running processes can be documented by accessing the task manager. Why would that matter? One of the more popular defenses, especially in child pornography cases, is to claim that the contraband images were deposited by an unknown third party by way of a Trojan.

Now it's time to use a validated memory capture tool to collect that volatile evidence in the RAM. After this step is complete, the process ends with proper shutdown. The proper shutdown allows any running application a chance to write any artifacts to the disk, allowing us to recover them later.

HASHING

How do we know our clone is an exact duplicate of the evidence drive? The answer comes in the form of a hash value. A hash is a unique value generated by a cryptographic hashing algorithm. **Hash values (functions)** are used in a variety of ways including cryptography and evidence integrity. Hash values are commonly referred to as a "digital fingerprint" or "digital DNA." Any change to the hard drive, even by a single bit, will result in a radically different hash value. Therefore, any tampering or manipulation of the evidence is readily detectable.

Types of Hashing Algorithms

There are multiple types of hashing algorithms. The term algorithm may strike fear in the hearts of the mathematically challenged. Never fear. We won't be getting into any higher-level math here, but we will get comfortable with some of the basic concepts and terms. The most common hash functions used in digital forensics are Message Digest 5 (MD5), and Secure Hashing Algorithm (SHA) 1 and 2.

Hashing Example

Let's hash a short phrase to demonstrate what happens with only a minor change. Apologies up front to any Baltimore or Cleveland fans. For this exercise, we'll use SHA1.

> Phrase - Go Steelers!
> SHA1 - c924 4cac 47b3 4335 5aed 06f3 cc85 ea82 885f 9f3e

Now let's make one small alteration, changing the "S" from upper case to lower case. When we rehash, we get this:

> Phrase - Go steelers!
> SHA 1 - 1a10 ffd1 db12 c88f 88e6 b070 561f 6124 f632 26ec

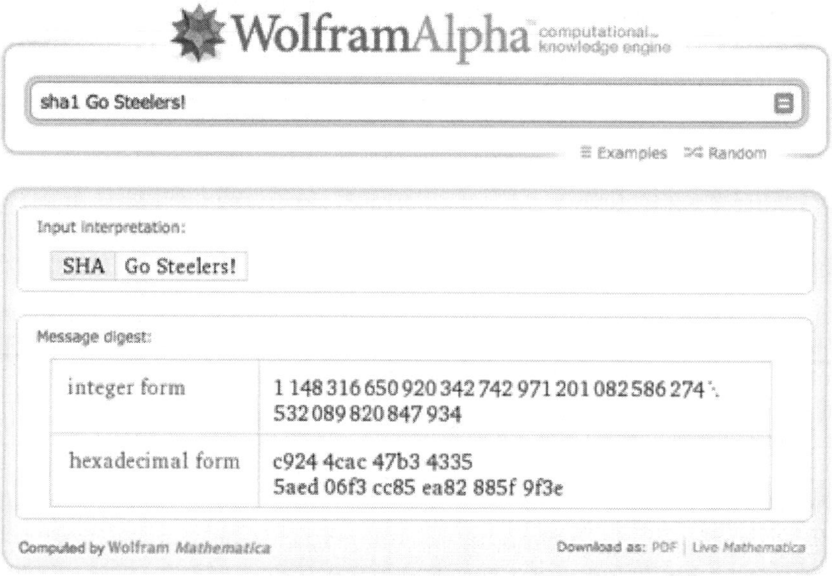

FIGURE 4.4
WolframAlpha results.

Note the drastic change in the resulting hash values. Here they are stacked for an easier comparison:

    c924 4cac 47b3 4335 5aed 06f3 cc85 ea82 885f 9f3e
    1a10 ffd1 db12 c88f 88e6 b070 561f 6124 f632 26ec

As you can see, small changes make a big difference. If you'd like to try this yourself, it's easy to do. Go to http://www.wolframalpha.com and enter the hash function you would like to use (MD5, SHA1, etc.), followed by a space and then the phrase Go Steelers! (See Figure 4.4.)

Uses of Hashing

Hash values can be used throughout the digital forensic process. They can be used after the cloning process to verify that the clone is indeed an exact duplicate. They can also be used as an integrity check at any point it is needed. Examiners often have to exchange forensic images with the examiner on the opposing side. A hash value is sent along with the image so that it can be compared with the original. This comparison verifies that the image is a bit for bit copy of the original.

The relevant hash values that were generated and recorded throughout the case should be kept and included with the final report. These digital fingerprints are crucial to demonstrating the integrity of the evidence and ultimately getting them before the jury.

FINAL REPORT

At the conclusion of the analysis, the examiner will generate a final report detailing what was done, what was found, and their findings. Ideally, final reports need to be crafted with the intended audience in mind. In reality, far too many final reports read like the owner's manual for the space shuttle. Not only can these reports be difficult to read, they can be downright intimidating.

Because they are often filled with jargon and code, these reports aren't very useful to non-technical reader's such as judges, attorneys and juries. It is important to remember that these people must be able to comprehend information contained in your report. Even the best, most compelling evidence can be ignored if the jury can't understand it.

The major forensic tools, such as EnCase and FTK, have very robust reporting features, generating quite a bit of customizable information. However, as helpful as these reports are, they are just not adequate to stand on their own. They are difficult for most non-technical readers to understand. This information should be included in the final report, but they should not serve as the lone piece of documentation for the entire examination.

The best reports will consist of much more than the standard report generated with the tool alone. The final report should include a detailed narrative of all the actions taken by the examiner, starting at the scene if they were present. The examination should be documented with sufficient detail so that the procedure can be duplicated by another examiner.

A digital forensic report written in plain English is both much appreciated and much more effective (can I get an "Amen" from the lawyers out there?).

SUMMARY

As we discussed in this chapter, the first step in the collection process is to secure both the scene and the evidence. If the device containing the evidence is a cell phone, you will need to isolate the phone from the network signal to prevent evidence from being destroyed.

Photographs are an excellent way to document the evidence and the scene. You will photograph the entire scene (e.g., the entire room, not just the computer on the desk). You must ensure that the chain of custody is fully documented and that the evidence is properly marked.

Preservation of the evidence is critical. Capturing a forensic image or clone eliminates the need to examine the original evidence. Examining the original could lead to the evidence being excluded.

Cloning the device will produce an exact, bit-for-bit copy of the original evidence. Hash values are used to verify that the cloned evidence is identical to the original. These hash values, such as MD5 or SHA1, are often likened to "Digital DNA" or a "Digital Fingerprint." We discussed the differences between live and dead acquisitions and the benefits and challenges of each. The final report should include detail about the scene, the collection process, the analysis, and the what conclusions, if any, were reached. It's critical that the final report be understandable to a nontechnical audience.

References

About: American Society of Crime Laboratory Directors/Laboratory Accreditation Board. (n.d.). Retrieved June 4, 2011, from: http://www.ascld-lab.org/about_us/aboutoverview.html

AccessData Group, LLC. (2011, February). *Downloads: AccessData.* Retrieved August 24, 2011, from: http://accessdata.com/downloads/media/FTK_3x_System_Specifications_Guide.pdf

American Society of Crime Laboratory Directors Laboratory Accreditation Board. (n.d.). *ASCLD/LAB Guiding Principles of Professional Responsibility for Crome Laboratories and Forensic Scientists.* Retrieved September 3, 2011, from: http://www.ascld-lab.org/about_us/guidingprinciples.html

American Society of Crime Laboratory Directors/Laboratory Accreditation Board. (n.d.). *Did You Know: American Society of Crime Laboratory Directors/Laboratory Accreditation Board.* Retrieved June 4, 2011, from: http://www.ascld-lab.org/largest_accreditation.html

American Society of Crime Laboratory Directors/Laboratory Accreditation Board. (n.d.). *Objectives: American Society of Crime Laboratory Directors/Laboratory Accreditation Board.* Retrieved June 4, 2011, from: http://www.ascld-lab.org/about_us/objectives.html

Association of Chief Police Officers. (2011). *Good Practice Guide for Computer-Based Electronic Evidence.* Cambridge, MA: 7Safe.

ASTM International. (n.d.). *ASTM Overview.* Retrieved October 1, 2011, from: http://www.astm.org/ABOUT/overview.html

Barbara, J. J. (n.d.). *Digital Evidence Accreditation.* Retrieved August 25, 2011, from: http://www.forensicmag.com/article/digital-evidence-accreditation?page=0,3

Barbara, J. J. (n.d.). *Digital Evidence Accreditation: Forensic Magazine.* Retrieved June 4, 2011, from: http://www.forensicmag.com/article/digital-evidence-accreditation

Barbara, J. J. (n.d.). *Triage a Computer.* Retrieved June 14, 2011, from: http://www.forensicmag.com/article/triage-computer

Brunty, J. (2011, March 2). *Validation of Forensic Tools and Software: A Quick Guide for the Digital Forensic Examiner.* Retrieved August 24, 2011, from: http://www.dfinews.com/article/validation-forensic-tools-and-software-quick-guide-digital-forensic-examiner?page=0,2

Carrier, B. B. (2002, October). *Papers: Digital-evidence.org.* Retrieved August 24, 2011, from: http://www.digital-evidence.org/papers/opensrc_legal.pdf

Carvey, H. (2009). *Windows Forensic Analysis DVD Toolkit* (2nd ed.). Burlington, MA: Syngress.

Casey, E. (2009). *Handbook of Digital Forensics and Investigation.* Burlington, MA: Academic Press.

Casey, E. (2011). *Digital Evidence and Computer Crime, 3rd ed.: Forensic Science, Computers, and the Internet.* Waltham, MA: Academic Press.

Cellebrite Mobile Synchronization LTD. (n.d.). *UFED Physical Pro.* Retrieved October 2, 2011, from: http://www.cellebrite.com/forensic-products/forensic-products/ufed-physical-pro.html

Chan, S. (1994, August 21). *Scores of Convictions Reviewed as Chemist Faces Perjury Accusations: Forensics.* Retrieved September 27, 2011, from: http://articles.latimes.com/1994-08-21/news/mn-29449_1_lab-tests-fred-zain-double-murder

Craiger, P. J. (n.d.). *Virtual Digital Evidence Laboratory.* Retrieved September 16, 2011, from: http://www.ncfs.org/VDEL.Craiger.Report.NIJ.final.pdf

DNA Initiative, The. (n.d.). *Glen Woodall (Huntington, West Virginia)*. Retrieved September 27, 2011, from: http://www.dna.gov/postconviction/convicted_exonerated/woodall

EC-Council. (2009). *Computer Forensics: Investigation Procedures and Response*. Clifton Park, NY: Cengage Learning.

Favro, P. (2011, September 15) *Breaking News: $919 Million Verdict for DuPont in Trade Secret Theft and eDiscovery Sanctions Case*. E-Discovery blog: http://www.clearwellsystems.com/e-discovery-blog/

Federal Bureau of Investigation. (2010). *Regional Computer Forensics Laboratory Annual Report Fiscal Year 2010*. Washington, DC: U.S. Department of Justice.

Henry, P. (2009, September 12). *Best Practices in Digital Evidence Collection*. Retrieved October 15, 2011, from: http://computer-forensics.sans.org/blog/2009/09/12/best-practices-in-digital-evidence-collection/

James, S., & Nordby, J. J. (2009). *Forensic Science: An Introduction to Scientific and Investigative Techniques* (3rd ed.). Boca Raton, FL: CRC Press.

Microsoft Corporation. (n.d.). *Encarta: Michael Faraday*. Retrieved June 13, 2011, from: http://www.webcitation.org/5kwc3quLs

National Institute of Justice. (n.d.). *Collecting Digital Evidence Flowchart: National Institute of Justice*. Retrieved June 14, 2011, from: http://www.nij.gov/publications/ecrime-guide-219941/ch5-evidence-collection/collecting-digital-evidence-flowchart.htm

National Institute of Justice. (n.d.). *Digital Evidence and Forensics: National Institute of Justice*. Retrieved June 14, 2011, from: http://www.nij.gov/nij/topics/forensics/evidence/digital/welcome.htm

National Institute of Justice. (2004). *Forensic Examination of Digital Evidence: A Guide for Law Enforcement*. Washington, DC: U.S. Department of Justice Office of Justice Programs.

National Institute of Justice. (2008). *Electronic Crime Scene Investigation: A Guide for First Responders* (2nd ed.). Washington, DC: U.S. Department of Justice.

National Institute of Justice. (2009a). *Electronic Crime Scene Investigation: An On-the-Scene Reference for First Responders*. Washington, DC: U.S. Department of Justice.

National Institute of Justice. (2009b). *Test Results for Hardware Write Block Device: T4 Forensic SCSI Bridge (FireWire Interface)*. U.S. Department of Justice, Office of Justice Programs. Washington, DC: National Institute of Justice.

National Institute of Standards & Technology. (n.d.). *CFTT Project Overview*. Retrieved September 30, 2011, from.gov: http://www.cftt.nist.gov/project_overview.htm

National Institute of Standards and Technology. (n.d.). *Computer Forensics Tool Testing Project Web Site: National Institute of Standards and Technology*. Retrieved June 6, 2011, from: http://www.cftt.nist.gov/index.html

Paraben Corporation. (n.d.). *Device Seizure v4.5*. Retrieved October 2, 2011, from: http://www.paraben.com/device-seizure.html

Phillip, A., Cowen, D., & Davis, C. (2009). *Hacking Exposed Computer Forensics: Computer Forensics Secrets & Solutions*. New York: McGraw-Hill.

Princeton University Center for Information Technology Policy. (2008, February 21). *Lest We Remember: Cold Boot Attacks on Encryption Keys*. Retrieved October 19, 2011, from: http://www.youtube.com/watch?v=JDaicPIgn9U

Saferstein, R. (2006). *Criminalistics: An Introduction to Forensic Science (College Edition)* (9th ed.). Upper Saddle River, NJ: Prentice Hall.

Scientific Working Group on Digital Evidence. (2009, January 15). *SWGDE Recommended Guidelines for Validation Testing v1.1*. Retrieved September 19, 2011, from: http://www.swgde.org/documents/current-documents/

Scientific Working Group on Digital Evidence. (2010a, May 15). *Minimum Requirements for Quality Assurance in the Processing of Digital and Multimedia Evidence.* Retrieved August 24, 2011, from: http://www.swgde.org/documents/current-documents/

Sedona Conference. (2010, September). *The Sedona Conference Glossary: E-Discovery & Digital Information Management* (3rd ed.). Retrieved October 21, 2011, from: http://www.thesedonaconference.org/publications_html

Shipley, T. G. (n.d.). *Collection of Evidence from the Internet: Part 1.* Retrieved June 14, 2011, from: http://www.dfinews.com/article/collection-evidence-internet-part-1?page=0,1

Shipley, T. G. (n.d.). *Collection of Evidence from the Internet: Part 2.* Retrieved June 14, 2011, from: http://www.dfinews.com/article/collection-evidence-internet-part-2

Shipley, T. G., & Reeve, H. R. (2006). *Collecting Evidence from a Running Computer: A Technical and Legal Primer for the Justice Community.* Search Group, Incorporated. Sacramento, CA: Search Group, Incorporated.

Warrington, D. (n.d.). *Crime Scene 101: Locating and Documenting Evidence.* Retrieved June 14, 2011, from: http://www.forensicmag.com/article/crime-scene-101-locating-and-documenting-evidence

Whitcomb, C. (n.d.). *A Virtual Digital Forensics Lab.* Retrieved September 28, 2011, from: http://www.ascld.org/files/digital%20VDEL%20Craiger%20ASCLD%20cmw.pdf

WSAZ. (2011, April 1). *UPDATE: Donald Good Receives Two Life Sentences in Mall Rape Case.* Retrieved September 27, 2011, from: http://www.wsaz.com/news/headlines/105522183.html

CHAPTER 5

Windows System Artifacts

INTRODUCTION

Many say that the eyes are the window to the soul, but for the forensic examiner, Windows can be the "soul" of the computer. The odds are high that examiners will encounter the Windows operating system more times than not when conducting an investigation. The good news for us is that we can use Windows itself as a tool to recover data and track the footprints left behind by the user. Because of this, it is imperative that examiners have an extensive understanding of the Windows operating system and all of its functions.

Love it or hate it, it's a Windows world. With about 90% (Brodkin, 2011) of the desktop market share, a forensic examiner will face a Windows machine the majority of the time. Getting cozy with Windows is an absolute necessity in this line of work. In the course of using Windows and its multitude of compatible applications, users will leave artifacts or footprints scattered throughout the machine. As you can imagine, this is pretty handy from an investigative perspective. These artifacts are often located in unfamiliar or "hard to reach" places. Even a savvy individual, bent on covering their tracks, can miss some of these buried forensic treasures.

The forensic challenge is to identify, preserve, collect, and interpret this evidence correctly. In this chapter, we'll take a closer look at many of these artifacts, their purpose, and their forensic significance.

DELETED DATA

For the average user, hitting the delete key provides a satisfying sense of security. With the click of a mouse, we think our data are forever obliterated, never again to see the light of day. Think again. We know from Chapter 2 that, contrary to what many folks believe, hitting the delete key doesn't do anything to the data itself. The file hasn't gone anywhere. "Deleting" a file only tells the computer that the space occupied by that file is available if the computer needs it. The **deleted data** will remain until another file is written over it. This can take quite some time, if it's done at all.

MORE ADVANCED

File Carving

The unallocated space on a hard drive can contain valuable evidence. Extracting this data is no simple task. The process is known as file carving and can be done manually or with the help of a tool. As you might imagine, tools can greatly speed up the process. Files are identified in the unallocated space by certain unique characteristics. File headers and footers are common examples of these characteristics or signatures. Headers and footers can be used to identify the file as well as marking its beginning and end.

Allocated space refers to the data that the computer is using and keeping tabs on. These are all the files that we can see and open in Windows. The computer's file system monitors these files and records a variety of information about them. For example, the file system tracks and records the date and time a particular file was last modified, accessed, and created. We'll revisit this kind of information when we talk about metadata later in this chapter.

HIBERNATION FILE (HIBERFILE.SYS)

Computers sometimes need their rest and can nap just like we do. Through this "cybernap" process, more potential evidence can be generated, depending on how "deep" the PC goes to sleep. "Deep sleep" modes like hibernation and hybrid sleep save data to the hard drive as opposed to just holding it in RAM (like "sleep"). As we know, data written to the drive itself are more persistent and can be recovered. It's possible that files deleted by a suspect could still be found here. How? Let's say that the suspect is working on an incriminating document on Monday. She has to step away for awhile to make a phone call. She puts the laptop into **hibernation** mode, which causes the computer to save everything she is doing to the hard drive. When she returns forty-five minutes later and brings the laptop back up, everything is just like she left it, including the incriminating document. Generally, a computer can go into three different modes or states when it sleeps. Those modes are: sleep, hibernation, and hybrid sleep. (Microsoft Corporation). The different modes are intended to conserve power and can vary from laptop to desktop.

Sleep

Sleep mode is intended to conserve energy but is also intended to get the computer back into operation as quickly as possible. Microsoft compares this state to "pausing a DVD player" (Microsoft Corporation; TechTarget). Here, a small amount of power is continuously applied to the RAM, keeping those data intact. Remember, RAM is considered volatile memory, meaning that the data disappear when power is removed. Sleep mode doesn't do much for us forensically because all the data remain in the RAM.

Hibernation

Hibernation is also a power-saving mode but is intended for laptops rather than desktops. It is here that we start to see some potential investigative benefit. In this mode, all of the data in RAM are written to the hard drive, which, as we know, is much harder to get rid of.

Hybrid Sleep

As the name implies, hybrid sleep is a blend of the previous two modes and is intended mainly for desktops. It keeps a minimal amount of power applied to your RAM (preserving your data and applications) and writes the data to disk.

Like the page file, suspects bent on destroying evidence can overlook these hibernation files. Pedophiles or corporate crooks will often attempt to avoid detection by deleting or destroying evidence on their hard drive as the investigation closes in around them. These hibernation files, unknown to most users, are often missed during these last minute "delete-a-thons."

REGISTRY

The **Windows Registry** plays a crucial role in the operation of a PC. Microsoft's TechNet defines the registry as "simply a database for configuration files." You could also describe it as the computer's central nervous system. In that context, you can see just how critical the registry is to the Windows computer.

The registry keeps track of user and system configuration and preferences, which is no simple task. From a forensic standpoint, it can provide an abundance of potential evidence. Many of the artifacts we look for are kept in the registry. Some of the potential evidence could include search terms, programs that were run or installed, web addresses, files that have been recently opened, and so on.

Registry Structure

The registry is set up in a tree structure similar to the directories, folders, and files you're used to working with in Windows. The registry is broken into four tiers or levels.

Inspecting the registry is something that is done in nearly every forensic examination. Looking at the registry requires a tool that can translate this information into something we can understand. Two of the major multipurpose forensic tools, EnCase and FTK, do just that.

As a key repository of critical system information, the registry could contain quite a bit of evidence. As an added bonus, the Registry can also hold the information we need to break any encrypted files we find.

FROM THE CASE FILES: THE WINDOWS REGISTRY

The Windows Registry helped law enforcement officials in Houston, Texas crack a credit card case. In this case, the suspect's stolen credit card numbers were used to purchase items from the Internet. The two suspects in this case, a married couple, were arrested after a controlled drop of merchandise ordered from the Internet. Examination of the computer's NTUSER.DAT, Registry, and Protected Storage System Provider information, found a listing of multiple other names, addresses, and credit card numbers that where being used online to purchase items. After further investigation, investigators discovered that these too were being used illegally without the owners consent.

The information recovered from the registry was enough to obtain additional search warrants. These extra searches netted the arrest of 22 individuals and lead to the recovery of over $100,000 of illegally purchased merchandise. Ultimately, all of the suspects plead guilty to organized crime charges and were sentenced to jail time.

FROM THE CASE FILES: THE WINDOWS REGISTRY AND USBSTOR

In a small town outside of Austin, Texas, guests at a local hotel called police after observing an individual at the hotel who was roaming mostly naked and appearing somewhat intoxicated. When the police arrived, they found the individual and determined he was staying at the hotel. They accompanied him back to his room and were surprised by what they found. When the door opened, they discovered another individual in the room and a picture of child pornography being projected on the wall. The projector was attached to a laptop. Two external hard drives were found lying next to the laptop. The unexpected occupant said that the laptop was his but that the two external drives belonged to the other gentlemen and had never been connected to his laptop. All of the equipment was seized and sent for examination. Forensic clones were made of the laptop and both external drives. The initial examination of the external drives found both still images and movies of child pornography.

Next, examiners wanted to determine if either of those drives had ever been connected to the laptop. The system registry file of the laptop was searched for entries in the USBStor key. Listings for external hard drives were discovered along with the hardware serial numbers from both external hard drives.

Next, examiners sought to validate their results. Using a lab computer system with a clean installation of Windows, they connected the defendants external drives to the lab system. A write blocker was connected between the drives and the system to prevent any changes or modifications to the clones of the external drives.

The lab computer's system registry file was then examined and the USBStor keys showed the same external hard drive listings as the suspect's with matching hardware serial numbers. These results proved that the suspect's external hard drives had in fact been hooked to the laptop at one time. The suspect was eventually convicted of possession of child pornography.

Attribution

Digital forensics can be used to answer many questions, such as, *what terms were searched using Google?* We can find that. *Did Bob type those terms?* Houston, we've got a problem. Unfortunately, we can rarely put someone's sticky fingers on the keyboard when a particular artifact is created. We may need to uncover other evidence in order to connect those dots.

Tracking something back to a specific user account or identifying the registered owner of the system is a much easier task. A single PC can have multiple user accounts set up on the machine. In a technical sense, user accounts establish what that specific user can and can't do on the computer (Microsoft Corporation). A PC will set up two accounts by default, the administrator and a guest account. Other accounts may be created, but they are not required. The administrator has all rights and privileges on the machine. They can do anything. A guest account (which doesn't require any login) generally has less authority.

For example, a family PC could have separate accounts for mom, dad, and each of the kids. Each of these accounts could be password-protected.

Each account on the machine is assigned a unique number called a security identifier or SID. Many actions on the computer are associated with, and tracked by, a specific SID. It's through the SID that we can tie an account to some particular action or event.

External Drives

Information has value, sometimes substantial value. They don't keep the formula for Coke under lock and key for grins. Theft of intellectual property is a huge concern. One way that would-be thieves could easily smuggle data out of an organization is by way of one of these external storage devices, such as a thumb drive. As a result, examiners are often asked to determine whether any such device has been attached to a computer.

These devices can take a variety forms such as thumb drives or external hard drives. In addition to stealing information, these devices can also be used to inject a virus or store child pornography. Whether or not such a device was attached can be determined by data contained in the registry. The registry records this kind of information with a significant amount of detail. It tells us both the vendor and the serial number of the device.

PRINT SPOOLING

In some investigations, a suspect's printing activities may be relevant. As you might expect, printing can also leave some tracks for us to follow. You've probably noticed that there's a bit of a delay after you click Print. This delay is an indication of a process called **spooling**. Essentially, spooling temporarily stores the print job until it can be printed at a time that is more convenient for the printer (TechTarget). During this spooling procedure, Windows creates a pair of complementary files. One is the Enhanced Meta File (EMF) which is an image of document to be printed. The other is the spool file which contains information about the print job itself.

There is one of each for every print job. What kind of information can we recover from the spool file? The spool file (.spl) tells us things like the printer name, computer name as well as the user account that sent the job to the printer. Either or both of these files may have evidentiary value. The problem is they don't stick around long. In fact, they are normally deleted automatically after the print job is finished. However, there are a few exceptions.

The first exception occurs if there is some kind of problem and the document didn't print. The second is that the computer that is initiating the print job may be set up to retain a copy. Some companies may find this setup appealing if they have some reason to hang onto a copy.

Spool and EMF files can be used to directly connect targets to their crimes. Copies of extortion letters, forged contracts, stolen client lists, and maps to body dump sites are but a few pieces of evidentiary gold potentially mined from their computers.

RECYCLE BIN

The "trash can" has been a familiar presence on our computer desktops starting with the early Macintosh systems. It's a really good idea, especially from the casual user's perspective. Users may not understand sectors and bytes, but most everyone "gets" the trash can. Sometimes, though, the trash can "gets" them. This is especially true when they count on the trash can to erase their evidence. They assume that their incriminating data have disappeared into a digital "Bermuda Triangle," never again to see the light of day. Unlike Amelia Earhart, that's definitely not the case. Using forensic tools such as Forensic Toolkit and EnCase, we can quite often bring those files back in mint condition.

ALERT!

Recycle Bin Function

Here's a quick question. Where is a file moved when it's deleted? I bet some of you said the recycle bin. That would make the most sense. I mean, that's where we put the unwanted files, right? But it would also be wrong. When you delete a file, it's moved to … wait for it … nowhere. The file itself stays exactly where it was. It's a common notion that when deleted, the file is actually picked up and moved to the **recycle bin**. That's not the case.

Unwanted files can be moved to the recycle bin a few different ways. They can be moved from a menu item or by dragging and dropping the file to the recycle bin. Finally, you can right-click on an item and choose Delete. The benefit of putting files into the recycle bin is that we can dig through it and pull our files back out. I've worked in places where digging through office trash can be a pretty hazardous undertaking. Fortunately, things aren't nearly as dicey on our computers. As long as our files are still "in the can," we can get them back. However, emptying the recycle bin (i.e., "taking out the trash") makes recovery pretty much impossible for the average user.

Not everything that's deleted passes through the recycle bin. A user can actually bypass the bin altogether. Bypassing can be done a couple of ways. First, if you press Shift+Delete, the file will go straight to unallocated space without ever going through the recycle bin. You can also configure your machine to bypass the recycle bin altogether. Your deleted files won't even brush the sides of the recycle bin.

The recycle bin is obviously one of the first places that examiners look for potential evidence. The first instinct suspects have is to get rid of any and every incriminating file on their computer. Not fully understanding how their computer works, they put all their faith in the recycle bin. Now you know that's a bad move. Lucky for us, many folks still don't recognize how misplaced their faith is. As a result, the recycle bin is a great place to look for all kinds of potentially incriminating files.

MORE ADVANCED

Recycle Bin Bypass

If an examiner suspects that the system has been set to bypass the recycle bin, the first thing they would check would be the registry. The "NukeOnDelete" value would be set to "1" indicating that this function had been switched on. (See Figure 5.1.)

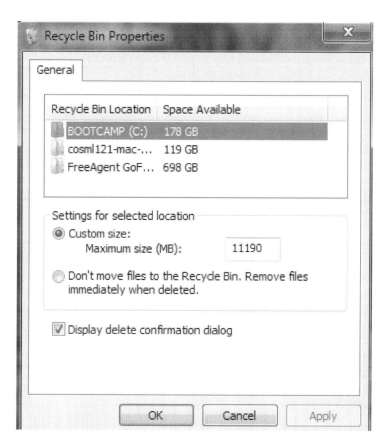

FIGURE 5.1
The recycle bin bypass option.

METADATA

Metadata is most often defined as data about data. Odds are you've come across metadata at some point. You may not have known that's what you were looking at. There are two flavors of metadata if you will: application and file system. Remember, the file system keeps track of our files and folders as well as some information about them. File system metadata include the date and time a file or folder was created, accessed, or modified. If you right-click on a file and choose "Properties," you can see these date/time stamps as shown in Figure 5.2.

Although this information can prove quite valuable to an investigation, we must keep in mind that all these date/time stamps may not be what they seem. One problem is that the system's clock can be changed by the user. Time zone differences can also cause some issues. Let's take a little closer look at the created, accessed, and modified date/time stamps.

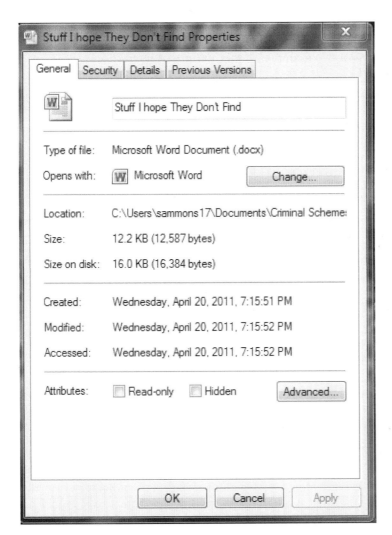

FIGURE 5.2
Metadata information as seen after right-clicking on the file and choosing "Properties." Note the created, modified, and accessed dates and times.

Created—The created date/time stamp frequently indicates when a file or folder was created on a particular piece of media, such as a hard drive (Casey, 2009). How the file got there makes a difference. By and large, a file can be saved, copied, cut and pasted, or dragged and dropped.

Modified—The modified date and time are set when a file is altered in any way and then saved (Casey, 2009).

Accessed—This date/time stamp is updated whenever a file is accessed by the file system. Accessed does not mean the same thing as opened. You may be asking how a file can be accessed without being opened, and that's a good question. You see, the computer itself can interact with the files. Antivirus scans and other preset events are just two examples of this automated interaction.

> **ALERT!**
>
> **Date and Time Stamps**
>
> System date and time stamps should NOT be taken simply at face value. These settings are readily accessible and can be easily changed. Determining an accurate timeline can be further complicated if the case involves more than one time zone. Just because the metadata say a file was created at a certain date and time doesn't necessarily make it so.

Applications themselves can create and store metadata as well. Like the file system, they can track the created, accessed, and modified dates and times. But it doesn't stop there. They can also track a variety of application-specific attributes as well. Examples could include the name of the author, the name of the company or organization, and the computer name, just to name a few (Casey, 2009).

Removing Metadata

Although metadata used to be one of our best-kept secrets, it's not any more. The criminals aren't the only ones taking notice. Corporations, law firms, and private citizens are just some of the folks concerned about metadata and the information contained therein. These legitimate concerns are being addressed by actually removing the metadata prior to sharing those files with other folks. Many tools exist for just that purpose. For example, law firms routinely scrub the metadata from all of their outbound documents, like those transmitted via e-mail. For the privacy-minded individual, the newer versions of Microsoft Word have the ability to detect and remove metadata. (See Figures 5.3 and 5.4.)

Recovered metadata can be used to refute claims by a suspect that they had no knowledge of a file's existence. It's tough to claim you didn't know it was there

Check for
Issues ▾

Prepare for Sharing

Before sharing this file, be aware that it contains:

- ▪ Document properties, author's name and related dates
- ▪ Footers
- ▪ Custom XML data
- ▪ Content that people with disabilities are unable to read

FIGURE 5.3
Menu item to choose scrubbing inside of Microsoft Word 2010.

☑ **Document Properties and Personal Information**
  Inspects for hidden metadata or personal information saved with the document.

FIGURE 5.4
The option to scan for metadata in Microsoft Word 2010.

when you not only opened the file but you changed or deleted the file as well. These dates and times can also be used to construct timelines in a case.

FROM THE CASE FILES: METADATA

Metadata can help investigators identify all the suspects in a case and recover more evidence. Take this case from Houston, Texas regarding the production of counterfeit credit cards. The suspects in this case used "skimmed" card information in their card production process. Credit card "skimming" is when thieves grab the data from the magnetic strip on the back of credit and debit cards. This often occurs during a legitimate transaction, such as when you use your card to pay for dinner.

After identifying their prime suspect, police arrested him and searched his computer. In the end, the search of the computer was disappointing. The search only found one Microsoft Word document that contained "skimmed" information. Furthermore, the search of the residence found no skimmer hardware and there was no skimming software located on the computer. Not exactly the treasure trove they had hoped to find.

The exam didn't stop there. Further examination of the Word document hit pay dirt. A review of the metadata revealed the author of the document, a female. Further investigation found that she was the suspect's girlfriend and that she worked as a waitress in a neighboring town. This information gave investigators the probable cause needed to obtain a second search warrant for her apartment. During the second search, the skimmer (the piece of hardware used to extract the data from the magnetic strip) was recovered. The examination of the computer found not only the skimming software, but additional lists of debit cards and related information. Fortunately, this information was seized before it could be used. Both suspects were eventually found guilty.

THUMBNAIL CACHE

To make it easier to browse the pictures on your computer, Windows creates smaller versions of your photos called **thumbnails**. Thumbnails are just miniaturized versions of their larger counterparts. These miniatures are created automatically by Windows when the user chooses "Thumbnail" view when using Windows Explorer. Windows creates a couple of different kinds of thumbnail files, depending on the version being used. Windows XP creates a file called thumbs.db. Microsoft Vista and Windows 7 create a similar file called thumbcache. db.

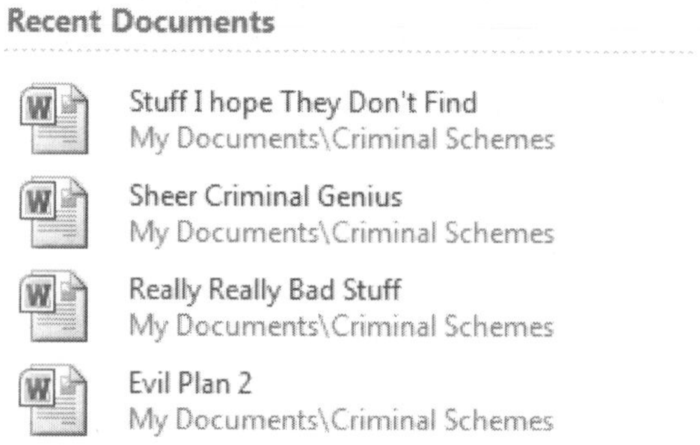

Recent Documents

 Stuff I hope They Don't Find
My Documents\Criminal Schemes

 Sheer Criminal Genius
My Documents\Criminal Schemes

 Really Really Bad Stuff
My Documents\Criminal Schemes

 Evil Plan 2
My Documents\Criminal Schemes

FIGURE 5.5
An Example of an MRU in Microsoft Word 2010.

Most users are completely unaware that these files even exist. The cool thing about these files is that they remain even after the original images have been deleted. Even if we don't recover the original image, thumbnails can serve as the next best evidence. Their mere existence tells us that those pictures existed at one point on the system.

MOST RECENTLY USED (MRU)

Windows tries to make our lives, at least on our computers, as pleasant as possible. They may not always succeed, but their hearts are in the right place. The **Most Recently Used (MRU)** list is one such example of Microsoft thinking of us. The MRU are links that serve as shortcuts to applications or files that have recently been used. You can see these in action by clicking on the Windows Start button through the file menu on many applications. (See Figure 5.5.)

RESTORE POINTS AND SHADOW COPY

Do you ever wish you could go back in time? We're not there yet, but lucky for us, Windows is. There may come a time when it's just easier (or necessary) for our computers to revert back to an earlier point in time when everything was working just fine. In Windows, these are called **restore points (RP)**, and they serve as time travel machines for our computers.

Restore Points

Restore points are snapshots of key system settings and configuration at a specific moment in time (Microsoft Corporation). These snapshots can be used to return the system to working order. Restore points are created in different ways. They can be created by the system automatically before major system events, like installing software. They can be scheduled at regular intervals, such as weekly.

Finally, they can be created manually by a user. The restore point feature is on by default, and one snapshot is automatically produced every day.

Before you start looking around for your restore points, you should know that Microsoft has taken steps to keep them from your prying eyes. They are normally hidden from the user.

These RPs have metadata (data about the data) associated with them. This information could be valuable in determining the point in time when this snapshot was taken. If the RP contains evidence, this can tell us exactly when that data existed on the system in question.

Digging through the restore points may reveal evidentiary gems that don't exist anywhere else. For the average person trying to conceal information from investigators, restore points are likely not the first place they would start destroying evidence. Obviously, that works in our favor.

FROM THE CASE FILES: INTERNET HISTORY & RESTORE POINTS

A defendant accused of possessing child pornography claimed that he had visited the site in question on only one accession, and that was only by accident. To refute this claim, examiners turned to the restore points for the previous two months. Examination of each of the registry files found in the various restore points told a significantly different story. The evidence showed that not only had multiple child pornography sites been visited, but the URLs had been typed directly into the address bar of the browser, destroying his claim that the site was visited by accident. Confronted with this new evidence, the defendant quickly accepted a plea deal.

Shadow Copies

Shadow copies provide the source data for restore points. Like the restore point, shadow files are another artifact that could very well be worth a look. We can use them to demonstrate how a particular file has been changed over time. They can likewise hold copies of files that have been deleted (Larson, 2010).

FROM THE CASE FILES: RESTORE POINTS, SHADOW COPIES, AND ANTI-FORENSICS

Officers from the Texas OAG (Office or the Attorney General) Cyber Unit, responding to a tip, served a search warrant at the suspect's residence. The OAG Cyber Unit obtained the search warrant after they were alerted that the suspect was uploading child pornography to the Internet. When the officers served the search warrant, they found the house unoccupied. Officers called the suspect letting him know they were in his home and that he should come home immediately and meet with them. When the suspect arrived, officers interviewed the suspect and searched his vehicle. Inside the car was a laptop computer.

All items seized were taken to the OAG offices for forensic examination. During the exam of the suspect's laptop, an alarming discovery was made. It appeared the suspect, on the drive home to meet the officers, used a wiping tool to get rid of not only incriminating images but the Internet history from his laptop. While the initial exam found no child pornography on the laptop, other compelling evidence was recovered.

For example, the examiner was able to recover logs from the wiping program itself showing that it had indeed been run. That wasn't all. Since the operating system was Windows Vista, the examiner decided to check the shadow copies found on the machine. Remember, these Shadow Copies (or System Restore Points) are essentially snap shots of data at a given point in time.

Next, the forensic image (clone) of the suspect's laptop was loaded into a virtual environment. This enabled the examiner to see the computer system as the suspect saw it. The examiner exported out the restore points from the suspects laptop, then imported those same files into his forensic tool. This process allowed the examiner to use his tools to extract images and other information from the suspect's system restore points. This procedure hit pay dirt. More than 3000 images of child pornography were recovered. In addition, log files were found showing searches and downloads of those same files. When it was all said and done, the suspect plead guilty and is currently serving 10 years in a Texas state prison.

PREFETCH

Speed kills. Or in the case of computers, it's that *lack* of speed that kills. Developers at Microsoft know this and work hard to squeeze every millisecond out of the system. Prefetching is one of the ways they try to speed up the system.

Prefetch files can show that an application was indeed installed and run on the system at one time. Take, for example, a wiping application such as "Evidence Eliminator." Programs like this are designed to completely destroy selected data on a hard drive. Although we may not be able to recover the original evidence, the mere presence of "Evidence Eliminator" can prove to be almost as damning as the original files themselves. Stay tuned for more discussion on "Evidence Eliminator."

LINK FILES

We all love shortcuts. They help us avoid road construction and steer clear of traffic jams. They save us time and make our travels easier, at least in theory. Microsoft Windows also like shortcuts. It likes them a lot.

Link files are simply shortcuts. They point to other files. Link files can be created by us, or more often by the computer. You may have created a shortcut on your desktop to your favorite program or folder. The computer itself creates them in several different places. You've likely seen and used these link files before. Take Microsoft Word, for example. If you look under the File menu, you'll see an option called "recent." The items in that list are link files, or shortcuts, created by the computer.

Link files have their own date and time stamps showing when they were created and last used. The existence of a link file can be important. It can be used to show that someone actually opened the file in question. It can also be used to refute the assertion that a file or folder never existed. Link files can also contain the full file path, even if the storage device is no longer connected, like a thumb drive.

Installed Programs

Software that is or has been installed on the questioned computer could also be of interest. This is especially true if the same application has now been removed after some relevant point in time (i.e., when the suspect became aware of a potential investigation). There are multiple locations on the drive to look for these artifacts. The program folder is a great place to start. Link and prefetch files are two other locations that could also bear fruit.

SUMMARY

The computer records a tremendous amount of information unbeknownst to the vast majority of users. These artifacts come in a variety of forms and can be found throughout the system. For example, it's possible to identify external storage devices, like thumb drives, that have been attached to the system. Items moved to the Windows Recycle Bin can tell us when they were deleted and by which account.

Even if a file has been deleted or overwritten, copies of the file could still exist on the drive in multiple forms. These often-overlooked copies are generated by print jobs and hibernation functions as well as restore points. These files can also be found in the swap space, a specific portion of a hard drive that is used when the system is out of RAM.

One major takeaway from this chapter is that valuable evidence of specific files, actions, or events can be recorded in multiple locations. As such, truly getting rid of it can be a highly technical process beyond the reach of most crooks.

Even deleting data and defragging your hard drive don't get rid of it. The computer stores data in a way that permits fragments of older files to be carved out for further analysis. The partial files removed from the slack space could contain just enough information to become a useful piece of evidence. Attribution is a major challenge in digital forensics. Saying with absolute certainty that a specific individual was responsible for a given artifact is often impossible. Identifying the account is often the best that can be done.

The system and the applications we use generate data about data. This information, known as metadata, can tell us when the file was created, accessed, modified, and deleted. Knowing what software has been installed and run could be relevant to an investigation. Drive wiping software, for example, could be of particular interest. The Windows Registry and the prefetching function are two sources of this potentially relevant information.

References

Bard, J. (n.d.). *The Windows Registry*. Retrieved May 2, 2011, from: http://technet.microsoft.com/en-us/library/cc751049.aspx

Brodkin, J. (n.d.). *Windows on Verge of Dropping Below 90% Market Share*. Retrieved May 2, 2011, from: http://www.networkworld.com/news/2011/011311-windows-on-verge-of-dropping.html

Casey, E. (2009). *Handbook of Digital Forensics and Investigation*. Burlington, MA: Academic Press.

Gupta, M. R., Hoeschele, M. D., & Rogers, M. K. (2006). Hidden Disk Areas: HPA and DCO. *International Journal of Digital Evidence*, 1–8.

Larson, T. (2010, July 8). *Windows 7: Current Events in the World of Windows Forensics*. Retrieved May 3, 2011, from: http://computer-forensics.sans.org/summit-archives/2010/files/12-larson-windows7-foreniscs.pdf

Microsoft Corporation. (n.d.). *How the Recycle Bin Stores Files*. Retrieved May 2, 2011, from: http://support.microsoft.com/kb/136517

Microsoft Corporation. (n.d.). *Sleep and Hibernation: Frequently Asked Questions*. Retrieved May 2, 2011, from: http://windows.microsoft.com/en-US/windows7/Sleep-and-hibernation-frequently-asked-questions

Microsoft Corporation. (n.d.). *System Restore: Frequently Asked Questions*. Retrieved May 2, 2011, from: http://windows.microsoft.com/en-US/windows-vista/System-Restore-frequently-asked-questions

Microsoft Corporation. (n.d.). *User Accounts Overview: Microsoft Corporation*. Retrieved May 2, 2011, from: http://www.microsoft.com/resources/documentation/windows/xp/all/proddocs/en-us/usercpl_overview.mspx?mfr=true

Phillip, A., Cowen, D., & Davis, C. (2009). *Hacking Exposed Computer Forensics: Computer Forensics Secrets & Solutions*. New York: McGraw-Hill.

TechTarget. (n.d.). *Spool: Whatis.com*. Retrieved May 2, 2011, from: http://whatis.techtarget.com/definition/0,,sid9_gci214229,00.html

CHAPTER 6

Antiforensics

Information in This Chapter:

- Introduction of Encryption Technology and the Threat It Poses
- Attacks Used to Break Encryption
- Techniques Used to Hide and Destroy Data

INTRODUCTION

Computer examinations and the resulting evidence make regular appearances in police blotters all across the country. To counter these relatively new forensic advances, antiforensic tools and techniques are cropping up in significant numbers. They are being used by criminals, terrorists, and corporate executives alike. In February 2011, Valerie Caproni, the General Counsel for the FBI, addressed the House Subcommittee on Crime, Terrorism, and Homeland Security. Regarding encryption and the threat it represents, she told the subcommittee, "As the gap between authority and capability widens, the government is increasingly unable to collect valuable evidence in cases ranging from child exploitation and pornography to organized crime and drug trafficking to terrorism and espionage—evidence that a court has authorized the government to collect. This gap poses a growing threat to public safety" (Caproni, 2011).

There are many definitions for the term *antiforensics*. John Barbara defines it this way "an approach to manipulate, erase, or obfuscate digital data or to make its examination difficult, time consuming, or virtually impossible" (Barbara, 2008).

There's even a web site devoted to the subject, and they're not the least bit subtle about their objectives. Anti-Forensics.com is a "community dedicated to the research and sharing of methods, tools, and information that can be used to frustrate computer forensic investigations and forensic examiners." It goes on to describe the web site's purpose, saying, "A major goal of some anti-forensics software, and the focus of Anti-Forensics.com, is to make the analysis and examination of digital evidence as difficult, confusing, and time consuming as possible" (What Is Anti-Forensics.com?).

The use of antiforensics techniques is not limited to terrorists and pedophiles. Corporate executives have put them to use as well, using these tools and techniques to hide or destroy incriminating e-mails, financial records, and so on. Even everyday applications such as web browsers have features that could be used to obstruct a forensic examination—clearing the Internet history, for example. Most newer browsers come with a "private browsing" mode that doesn't record things such as web sites visited and searches. In the latest version of Firefox, running in private mode will no longer save visited pages, form and search bar entries, passwords, download list entries, cookies, and web cache files (Mozilla Foundation, 2011). See Figure 6.1.

In this chapter we're going to take a look at several techniques used to hide or destroy digital evidence. As you'll see, some of these techniques are highly effective when used properly. Other techniques have little or no impact on a forensic examination. Even using one of the commercially available drive wiping tools is no guarantee that the data will truly disappear.

From an investigative perspective, it's important to know that there are legitimate uses of these antiforensic tools and techniques. Proving the intent, therefore, is critical. Suspects could assert that the wiping application was used only to protect their privacy or they used the defragmentation utility to improve performance. That's possible. However, that defense gets a little tougher to swallow if the tool was only used once and that was three hours after the target became aware of the investigation.

Tools	Window	Help	
Web Search			⌘K
Downloads			⌘J
Add-ons			
Error Console			⇧⌘J
Page Info			⌘I
Start Private Browsing			⇧⌘P
Clear Recent History...			
Exif Viewer			

FIGURE 6.1
The "Start Private Browsing" menu option in Firefox 6.0. Also note the option to "Clear Recent History."

HIDING DATA

Hiding techniques range from the simple to the very complex. Changing file names and extensions, burying files deep within seemingly unrelated directories, hiding files within files, and **encryption** are some of the most common hiding techniques. It's the last two techniques that can cause digital forensics practitioners to lose sleep at night.

Encryption

We all have secrets. Companies, governments, and individuals share this universal truth. The Colonel's recipe for fried chicken, our bank account numbers, and the Army's plans for war are just a few examples of information that needs to be kept from under wraps. Before our world became such a wired one, keeping this material safe was, in many respects, a lot less complicated.

The legitimate use of encryption has enabled us to enjoy many of the Internet services that we now take for granted. For example, encryption used in ecommerce permits us to buy our favorite books and book our summer vacation. It keeps our businesses running and our country safe. These modern conveniences, however, are not without a cost. Encryption is a double-edged sword with serious consequences when used by criminals, terrorists, unfriendly nations, and crooked CEOs alike.

Today, we have less direct control over these secrets as they travel over the Internet or fly through the air on a wireless network. It is encryption that provides us with both the mechanism and confidence to store and transmit our most sensitive digital information. In this book, however, the focus is on the darker side of this technology and the threat that it poses. Its value is certainly not lost on many people with bad intentions. Take terrorists, for example; despite their seemingly low-tech lifestyle, they are embracing technology including encryption.

"To a greater and greater degree, terrorist groups, including Hezbollah, Hamas, and bin Laden's al Qaida group, are using computerized files, e-mail, and encryption to support their operations," wrote then–CIA Director George Tenet last March to the Senate Foreign Relations Committee. Ramzi Yousef, the architect of the 1993 World Trade Center bombing, is one of those terrorists putting encryption to use. Yousef saved detailed plans to destroy U.S. airliners encrypted on his laptop (Dick, 2001). If done properly, encryption can keep examiners at bay until hell freezes over, literally.

What Is Encryption?

Encryption is the conversion of data into a form, called **cipher text**, which cannot be easily understood by unauthorized people (Bauchie, Hazen, Lund, Oakley, & Rundatz, 2000). Encryption starts with plain text. **Plain text** is the original, unencrypted message. The plain text message is in the clear and can be read by anyone. A cryptographic algorithm is then applied to the plain text, producing cipher text. Cipher text is basically a scrambled version of plain text that is unintelligible. The algorithm is the method used to encrypt the message. The key is data used to encrypt and decrypt the information. A password or passphrase is commonly used as the key.

Early Encryption

Encryption itself isn't a by-product of computer technology alone. It's been around for thousands of years in one form or another. One of the earliest and best-known encryption schemes is the Caesar Cipher. The Caesar Cipher is a shift cipher and encrypts the data by replacing the original letters with those "x" number of characters ahead in the alphabet. For example, using the Caesar Cipher and a key of five, an "A" would become an "F." Table 6.1 shows the entire alphabet both as plain text and as cipher text after the same cipher has been applied. Note that each letter has been shifted five spaces below its original position.

Now let's encrypt "forensics" using the Caesar Cipher with a key of eight. Table 6.2 shows us the conversion of plain text to cipher text.

This simple process is still employed today. It's frequently used to obfuscate computer code. At first glance, it appears that the terms encryption and obfuscate are interchangeable. They are similar enough to sometimes be confused, but the differences are significant enough to merit clarification. **Obfuscation** and encryption are both intended to make things harder to understand. Obfuscation, however, is used to protect computer code, rather than the data itself (Tyma, 2003). Obfuscation also protects code from reverse engineering. Encryption can't be used in this way because it would render the code totally unreadable to the computer.

ROT13 is a modern version of the Caesar Cipher in use today for obfuscation. In ROT13, letters are shifted 13 positions. In this scheme, an "A" becomes an

Table 6.1	The Alphabet with Simple Encryption (Caesar Cipher). The Key in This Example is Five	
Plain text	A B C D E F G H I J K L M N O P Q R S T U V W X Y Z
Cipher text	F G H I J K L M N O P Q R S T U V W X Y Z A B C D E

Table 6.2	Shows a Letter by Letter Conversion Using the Caesar Cipher and a Key of Eight								
Plain text	F	O	R	E	N	S	I	C	S
Cipher text	N	W	Z	M	V	A	Q	K	A

Table 6.3	The Opening of Lincoln's Gettysburg Address Encrypted Using ROT13										
Fourscore	**and**	**seven**	**years**	**ago**	**our**	**fathers**	**brought**	**forth**	**on**	**this**	
Sbhefpber	naq	frira	lrnef	ntb	bhe	snguref	oebhtug	sbegu	ba	guvf	

continent	**a**	**new**	**nation**	**conceived**	**in**	**liberty**	**and**	**dedicated**			
pbagvarag	n	arj	angvba	pbaprvirq	va	yvoregl	naq	qrqvpngrq			

to	**the**	**proposition**	**that**	**all**	**men**	**are**	**created**	**equal**			
gb	gur	cebcbfvgvba	gung	nyy	zra	ner	perngrq	rdhny			

"N," and so on. Table 6.3 shows an excerpt from Lincoln's Gettysburg Address after ROT13 has been applied.

Algorithms

For the mathematically challenged, like myself, just the word *algorithm* can cause some anxiety. The algorithms we use to send our credit card numbers across the Internet are exponentially more complex than the cipher Julius used in Rome. Although algorithms are complicated and well beyond the scope of this book, we can still get a handle on their basic use and functionality. Put simply, an algorithm is just a set of instructions used to accomplish a certain task. As an example, we can create an algorithm for sending an e-mail about an upcoming meeting.

1. Go to office.
2. Turn on computer
3. Open Microsoft Outlook
4. Click "New Email"
5. Fill in the "To" information
6. Type "Meeting" in the subject line
7. Type the body of the message
8. Press send

Fundamentally, there are two types of encryption algorithms: symmetrical and asymmetrical. **Symmetrical encryption** uses the same key to encrypt and decrypt the data. In contrast, **asymmetrical encryption** uses two separate and distinct keys.

There are many encryption algorithms in use today serving a variety of purposes. You may have already heard of some of them. AES, TripleDES, Blowfish, and RSA are just a few.

ALGORITHMS: IT'S NO SECRET

It may come as a surprise, but the algorithms themselves are open and well published. Why in the world would they put this information out there? It sure seems counterintuitive. Believe it or not, the answer is security. Best practice in cryptography states that the security of algorithms should be "independent of their secrecy" (Schneier, 2002).

This fundamental cryptographic principle has been around for quite some time. In 1883 Auguste Kerckhoffs, a Dutch linguist and cryptographer, said that in any truly effective crypto system, the key should be the only secret. Any system that relies on the secrecy of the algorithm is less secure (Schneier, 2002).

"The #1 lesson I've learned from my work at AccessData is 'you cannot trust closed-source crypto.' You have no idea if it is secure or not," said Nephi Allred, a cryptanalyst with AccessData. "I've reverse-engineered a lot of applications in my time: some good, some bad. While there are some good closed-source apps and some bad open-source apps (actually very few), the best apps are invariably open-source and the worst are invariably closed-source. Personally, I would never trust my own data to a closed source application" said Allred.

Key Space

Key space is a metric that is often discussed when talking about the strength of a particular encryption scheme. The key space or key length has a direct impact on our ability to break the encryption, particularly with a brute force attack. A brute force attack tries to break the password by attempting every possible key combination until the right one is found.

This is where this gets particularly troubling when you consider all the possible key permutations and how long it would take to "guess" the password. An encryption scheme with a 128-bit key would have roughly 340,282,366,920, 938,000,000,000,000,000,000,000,000 possible key combinations. How long would that take a computer to guess the password? Crunching some rough numbers will give us an idea. Using one computer, guessing 500,000 passwords per second would break that key in about 21,580,566,141,612,000,000, 000,000,000 years. Let's crank up the number of computers guessing passwords to 1000. That gets us to a much more "manageable" wait time of only 21,580, 566,141612,000,000,000,000 years. Remember these numbers represent rough estimates; the truth is that they can be much higher depending on the algorithm used. Complex encryption schemes such as Pretty Good Privacy (PGP) can radically drop the number of attempts per second to only a few hundred (Schneier, 2007).

Some Common Types of Encryption

With privacy being such a major concern, encryption tools are now included with some versions of the newer operating systems including Windows 7 and Apple OS X. These tools are **BitLocker** and **FileVault**, respectively. These encryption schemes can be applied selectively, only encrypting certain files or folders. They can also be used to encrypt an entire drive. This is known as full or whole disk encryption.

Full disk encryption (FDE) has some noteworthy advantages. We know from previous chapters that operating systems in their course of normal operation will leave artifacts scattered across the drive. Take swap space, for example. Even though we encrypt an entire folder containing our sensitive files, remnants (or the entire file) could be located in the swap space. Full disk encryption takes care of these data "leaks." The term *full disk encryption* is a little misleading. It doesn't really encrypt the entire disk. In order to run BitLocker, there must be two partitions (sections) on the hard drive: one, known as the "operating system volume," and the other, which contains the files to boot the machine, system tools, and so on. The operating system volume contains everything else including the vast majority of the items of most interest to us (Microsoft Corporation, 2009).

As they say, there is no free lunch. FDE has some drawbacks as well. Performance will likely suffer as the data are being encrypted and decrypted. This encryption/decryption is done "on the fly," meaning that it occurs just before the data are saved or loaded into RAM. Passwords and keys are another concern. Recovering your data is dependent on having the proper authentication. If you lose or forget your password, you will very likely never get your data back. Encryption cuts both ways.

ENCRYPTING FILE SYSTEM (EFS)

Encrypting File System (EFS) is used to encrypt files and folders. EFS is simple to use, using nothing more than a check box in a file's properties. It is "not fully supported on Windows 7 Starter, Windows 7 Home Basic, and Windows 7 Home Premium" (Microsoft Corporation). EFS uses the Windows username and password as part of the encryption algorithm. EFS is a feature of the New Technology File System (NTFS), not the Windows operating system (Microsoft Corporation).

BITLOCKER

Unlike EFS, BitLocker can be used to encrypt an entire hard drive, whereas BitLocker To Go is used to encrypt removable media such as a USB drive (Microsoft Corporation). BitLocker isn't available in all versions of Windows. Currently it's only available on the Windows 7 Ultimate systems (Microsoft Corporation). BitLocker doesn't usually function alone. It normally works in conjunction with a piece of hardware called a **Trusted Platform Module (TPM)**. The TPM is a microchip on the motherboard of a laptop or PC that is intended to deliver cryptographic functions (Microsoft Corporation). The TPM generates and encrypts keys that can only be decrypted by the TPM. If configured to work without the TPM, then the required keys are stored on a USB thumb drive.

BitLocker encryption is pretty stout, making decryption doubtful without the key.

Encountering a running BitLockered machine affords an examiner an excellent opportunity to recover data without having to defeat the BitLocker encryption. Files stored in a BitLocker protected area of the hard drive are decrypted when they are requested by the system (Microsoft Corporation, 2009). Any time you can avoid going toe to toe with encryption is a good thing.

When dealing with a running computer, recognizing the presence of BitLocker could make all the difference in a case. That running BitLockered machine may very well represent the only chance you would have to recover any evidence from that computer.

APPLE FILEVAULT

Apple's latest version of OS X, Lion, comes with FileVault 2. FileVault2 uses 128 bit, AES encryption. With FileVault 2 you can encrypt the content of your entire drive. Apple gives customers the chance to store their recovery key with them. Passwords stored with Apple could be retrievable with the proper legal search authority (Apple, Inc., 2011).

TRUECRYPT

TrueCrypt is a free, open source software that provides on-the-fly-encryption functionality. In on-the-fly encryption, the data are automatically encrypted and decrypted as they are saved and opened. All of this is done behind the scenes without any user involvement. TrueCrypt also is capable of providing full disk encryption. This includes file names, folder names, as well as the contents of every file. It also includes those files that can contain sensitive data that the system creates on its own. These files include things like log files, swap files, and registry entries. Decryption requires the correct password and or key file(s). TrueCrypt supports Windows, Mac, and Linux operating systems (TrueCrypt Developers Association, 2011). TrueCrypt can use multiple encryption algorithms including AES, Serpent, Twofish, or some combination of these three. The key space is 256 bits.

Breaking Passwords

Breaking passwords, or cryptanalysis, can be daunting or practically impossible. In order to give us the best chance for success, we'll need to use any advantage we can get. There are multiple ways to break passwords; some are technical, some are not. Sometimes it's as simple as asking. Options include **brute force attacks**, **dictionary attacks**, and **resetting passwords**. They can all yield positive results. We'll dig into these attacks more in an upcoming section.

The good news is that it's not all gloom and doom. In most cases, we are still dealing with people, and they represent the weakest point in this entire process. Humans can be both lazy and careless, giving us the chance we need to crack the encryption. Far too many people use simple passwords that are easy to break. Some of the best include "password," "letmein," or the ever-popular "123." Birthdays, pet names, or the name of our favorite sports team are also used routinely. Memorizing long random passwords is not easy or convenient for the majority of us. Even if a strong password is used, oftentimes it is written down on a Post-It note and stuck to the monitor. Furthermore, encryption keys can be left unsecured and subject to compromise.

People, being creatures of habit, quite often reuse at least a portion of their passwords. We can exploit this behavior to our advantage. If we can get one password, many times we can get them all. "Sometimes if we can go in and find one of those passwords, or two or three, I can start to figure out that in every password, you use the No. 3," said Stuart Van Buren, a U.S. Secret Service agent (Homeland Security Newswire, 2011).

What exactly qualifies as a strong password? According to Microsoft, a strong password uses a variety of letters, numbers, punctuation, and symbols, and has a minimum length of fourteen characters (Microsoft Corporation).

Examiners may get lucky and find the password in the swap space on the hard drive. Capturing the RAM of a running machine can also help in breaking passwords. You've probably entered a password on a web site at one time or another. As you entered your password, dots appeared, concealing the text as you type. What you may not realize is that the actual password is recorded in RAM. Failing to grab the RAM from a running machine could truly be a missed opportunity.

When the need arises, we have special tools available to us that can break passwords through a variety of attacks. These tools can break some simple passwords in less than a second. One of the leading tools of this type is the Password Recovery Toolkit (PRTK) from AccessData, the Utah-based computer forensic software company. Other tools include John the Ripper and Cain and Abel.

PASSWORD ATTACKS

Passwords can be attacked and broken in multiple ways, but avoiding encryption is always preferable to having to attack passwords. There are tools and techniques we can use to increase our chances of success. One thing working in our favor is the vulnerability that humans bring to the table. Long random strings of letters, numbers, and characters make for excellent passwords. Unfortunately, they are also tough for people to remember. As such, most passwords are based on actual words, recognizable patterns, or both.

Brute Force Attacks

A brute force attack is just what it sounds like. We are using as much computing power as we can muster to guess the correct password. The more computers (or, more precisely, central processing units) we can throw at it, the faster we can break it. As you'll see, "faster" is a relative term when it comes to breaking passwords. Products are available now that harness otherwise idle computers and use them against the encrypted file, folder, or drive. This is known as a distributed attack since the computational burden is spread among multiple computers. Some agencies are getting quite creative in breaking encryption.

The digital forensic folks with the U.S. Immigration and Customs Enforcement Cybercrime Center are using networked Sony PS3 gaming consoles to attack passwords. This approach leverages the power of these devices as well as their cost-effectiveness. "Bad guys are encrypting their stuff now, so we need a methodology of hacking on that to try to break passwords," said Claude E. Davenport, an agent in the U.S. Immigration and Customs Enforcement Cyber Crimes Center. "The Playstation 3—its processing component—is perfect for large-scale library attacks" (Wawro, 2009).

Password Reset

Sometimes we will go after the software rather than the password. Some applications have vulnerabilities that can be exploited to simply reset the password, giving us the access we need. Unfortunately, the password reset isn't widely effective, working only on a relatively small number of applications. In instances where it becomes necessary to bypass Windows system passwords, bootable CDs can get the job done. They do this by overwriting data in the Security Account Manager, or SAM for short. Elcomsoft's System Recovery tool is one of many products that fill this need (Elcomsoft Co. Ltd.).

Dictionary Attack

A dictionary attack is more precise, using words and phrases that can be collected from multiple sources. For example, a forensic application can create an index of all the words found on a suspect's hard drive. These words would come from both the allocated and unallocated space. Other dictionary sources could be terms commonly used in certain criminal circles such as child pornography or narcotics trafficking. Dictionaries can also contain words from specific sources such as web sites.

Intelligence, the background information on our suspect or target, can really increase our chances of success. This information can be used to build a dictionary of potential passwords. Gathering this information starts at the scene. We are not solely interested in the digital devices alone, but photos, books, etc. We want to know the name of our subject's children and pets. We want to know their hobbies and interests. The terms and words associated with these interests could provide clues to the suspect's password. For example, if the suspect is a huge Lord of the Rings (LOTR) fan, we can employ a tool that will index (record the content) of a web site devoted to LOTR. The tool will grab names and places such as Aragorn and Rivendell. These terms can then be used to create custom dictionaries that can help unlock the password.

Let's look at creating a custom dictionary based on biographical information on our suspect, Bill Thehacker. We'll be using AccessData's Password Recovery Toolkit. We enter a total of seven bits of information including names, birth date, and some keywords related to Bill. (See Figure 6.2.)

From the seven words in Figure 6.2, the tool then generates over twenty-six hundred permutations, a sampling of which is shown in Table 6.4. Note the combinations of terms with a multitude of prefixes and suffixes.

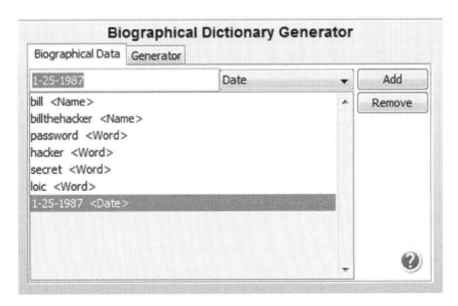

FIGURE 6.2
Biographical Dictionary Generator in PRTK.

Table 6.4	A Sampling of the Over Twenty-six Hundred Keywords Generated from Our Original List of Seven	
1	b25billthehacker	251987secret
25	billthehacker251b	251987 secret
1987	billthehacker125b	secret1987h
1251987	b251billthehacker	h1987secret
billbill	b125billthehacker	secret198725h
bill bill	25billthehacker1b	secret251987h
bill-bill	25b1billthehacker	h198725secret
bill_bill	1billthehacker25b	h251987secret
billb	1b25billthehacker	1987secret25h
bill b	billthehacker1b25	1987h25secret
bill-b	b1billthehacker25	25secret1987h
bill_b	billthehacker25b1	25h1987secret
billbillthehacker	b25billthehacker1	secret25h1987
bill billthehacker	billthehacker25bill	h25secret1987
bill-billthehacker	bill25billthehacker	secret1987h25
bill_billthehacker	billthehacker251bill	h1987secret25
billb	billthehacker125bill	secret1987
bill b	bill251billthehacker	secret 1987
bill-b	bill125billthehacker	1987secret
bill_b	25billthehacker1bill	1987 secret
	25bill1billthehacker	

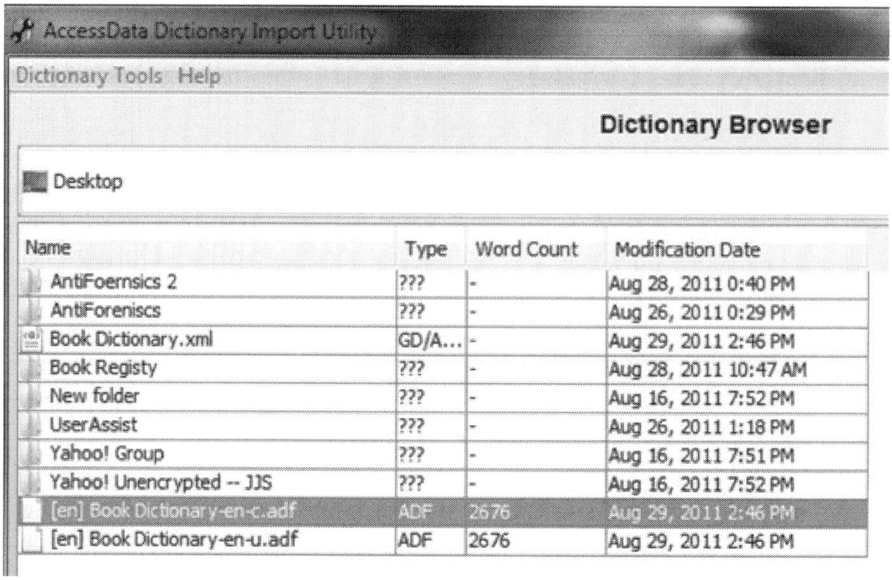

FIGURE 6.3
The final word count generated by our seven original entries.

ADDITIONAL RESOURCES

Encryption

Bruce Schneier is a well-respected author and cryptographer who regularly publishes on encryption and security-related issues. He is the author of several books as well as the Blowfish Encryption Algorithm. His book *Secrets & Lies: Digital Security in a Networked World* is both fascinating and highly readable. He also publishes a blog and the Crypto-Gram Newsletter. A visit to his web site, http://www.schneier.com/, is highly recommended.

STEGANOGRAPHY

Steganography, or stego for short, is another and very effective way to conceal data. The word steganography comes from the Greek words "Stegos" meaning covered and "Graphie" meaning writing. Its exact roots equate to covered writing. SearchSecurity.com defines steganography as "the hiding of a secret message within an ordinary message and the extraction of it at its destination" (TechTarget, 2000).

There are two files composing the finished stego file. The file that contains the secret message is called the **carrier file**. Carrier files can be image files, video files, audio files, and word processing documents, just to name a few. The embedded secret document is called the **payload**. The underlying concept behind steganography is fairly straightforward. Let's start with the carrier files.

These file types are used because they have a significant amount of redundant data, also known as "noise." The redundant data are replaced with the data composing the hidden message. Payload files don't necessarily have to be text based. An image file can be inserted into another image file. There are multiple variants or combinations that are possible.

Steganography applications are widely available on the Internet, and many are free. Backbone Security, a company that makes one of the more popular steg detection tools, has cataloged more than 960 separate steganography applications available for download on the internet (Backbone Security. com, 2011).

What makes stego such a concern? First, it's very difficult to detect. Second, once discovered it's very tough, if not impossible, to extract the payload without knowing the steg application and password used to create it.

Before his demise at the hands of Seal Team Six, Osama Bin Laden and his colleagues made extensive use of steganography to communicate. Stego files were posted in sports chat rooms and pornographic bulletin boards (Kelley, 2005).

Detecting the use of steganography is pretty tough. One of the most popular tools is Stego Suite™ from the Steganography Analysis and Research Center (SARC). The current version identifies over five hundred known steganography applications and has the ability to crack and extract payloads from carrier files (Wetstone Technologies, Inc.).

In June 2010, The FBI arrested ten Russian spies who had been in the United States for roughly a decade. These spies made extensive use of steganography as they passed secret messages to the SVR, the Russian intelligence service (CBS News, 2010). A criminal complaint in the case, filed in the Southern District of New York, provided some insight into the use of steganography by the Russians. In the complaint, Special Agent Maria Ricci said in part:

> "In addition, and among other things, a number of the Boston Conspirators' Electronic Messages appear directly to concern communication by means of steganography. For example, one message, dated December 15, 2004, discussed the process of 'decrypt[ing]' messages embedded in images; another message, dated February 22, 2005, discussed 'decypher [ing] [sic]' data embedded in images. Similarly, on or about October 3, 2004, law- enforcement agents, acting pursuant to a judicial order, intercepted aural communications taking place inside the Boston townhouse. Tracey Lee Ann Foley, the defendant, was heard saying to Donald Howard Heathfield, the defendant: 'Can we attach two files containing messages or not? Let's say four pictures ....' Based on my training, experience, and participation in this investigation, I believe that this was a reference to conveying messages by means of steganography—placing 'files containing messages' in 'pictures.' On or about March 7, 2010, law-enforcement agents, acting pursuant to a judicial order, intercepted aural communications taking place inside the Boston townhouse. As a

final example, in or about March 2010, Foley and Heathfield were heard discussing Foley's use of steganography and the schedule of her communications with Moscow Center"

(*United States of America v. Christopher R. Metsos*, 2010)

DATA DESTRUCTION

Sometimes hiding data isn't enough, and perpetrators try to destroy the data instead. Actually destroying the data is a little more complicated than many people think. The uninitiated may simply hit the delete key, assuming that the data no longer exist. As we've seen, this approach is not effective because the "deleted" data remain on the media and are easily recovered. In contrast, many drive wiping tools can be very effective. Using utilities such as these can leave telltale signs of their use, providing substantial evidence even without the original data in question.

Data destruction can be accomplished or attempted in several ways. Some of them are better than others. **Drive wiping** software is commercially available and can be effective in destroying potential evidence. Much of its effectiveness rests with the quality of the software, how it is used, and the number of "wipes" that are made. Defragmenting or reformatting a drive is frequently attempted, but often delivers limited results.

Drive Wiping

Drive wiping utilities are used to overwrite data on a hard drive in such a way as to make them unrecoverable. Most of these applications are promoted and/or intended to keep personal or corporate information private. Both are noble causes indeed. Unfortunately, these same utilities can be used for other, less honorable purposes. Examples of these tools include "Darik's Boot and Nuke," "DiskWipe," "CBL Data Shredder," "Webroot Window Washer," and "Evidence Eliminator."

Using these tools is not an "all or none" proposition. They can be somewhat surgical in their application, wiping only specified files while leaving others untouched. Operating system files, for example, could be left intact. They can target specific files and folders as well as potentially incriminating system values like those found in the Windows Registry.

These tools do have a legitimate use and are available at many technology stores such as Best Buy. Privacy is a major concern for everyone, and wiping utilities can help. If we want to donate our old computers we certainly don't want our e-mails and other personal information going with it to Goodwill.

Using these tools is no guarantee that the data can't be recovered. Success depends largely on the quality of the tool and the skills of the user.

From an evidentiary or investigative perspective, the presence or use of these applications can serve as the next best thing to the original evidence. Suspects may find it hard to explain why "Evidence Eliminator" software was installed

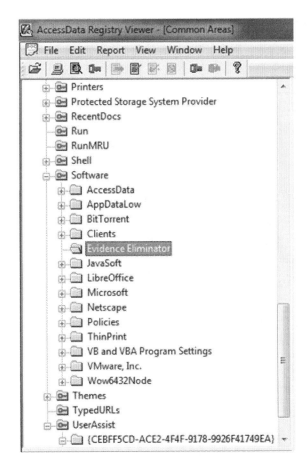

FIGURE 6.4
Note the presence of "Evidence Eliminator" in the Windows Registry software key.

and run on their computer the day before their computer was searched. Figure 6.4 shows the entry for "Evidence Eliminator" in the software key in the Windows Registry. This is an indicator that this software was installed on the machine.

Wiping utilities can leave telltale signs of their use. When looking at the drive at the bit level, a distinct repeating pattern of data may be seen. This is completely different from what would normally be found on a hard drive in everyday use. (See Figure 6.5.)

Evidence of their use can be found elsewhere on the drive. Figure 6.6 shows signs of Evidence Eliminator being opened on that machine.

Some operating systems, Apple OSX Lion for example, ship with a drive wiping utility installed. Called Secure Erase, this utility offers multiple options for data destruction. (See Figure 6.7.)

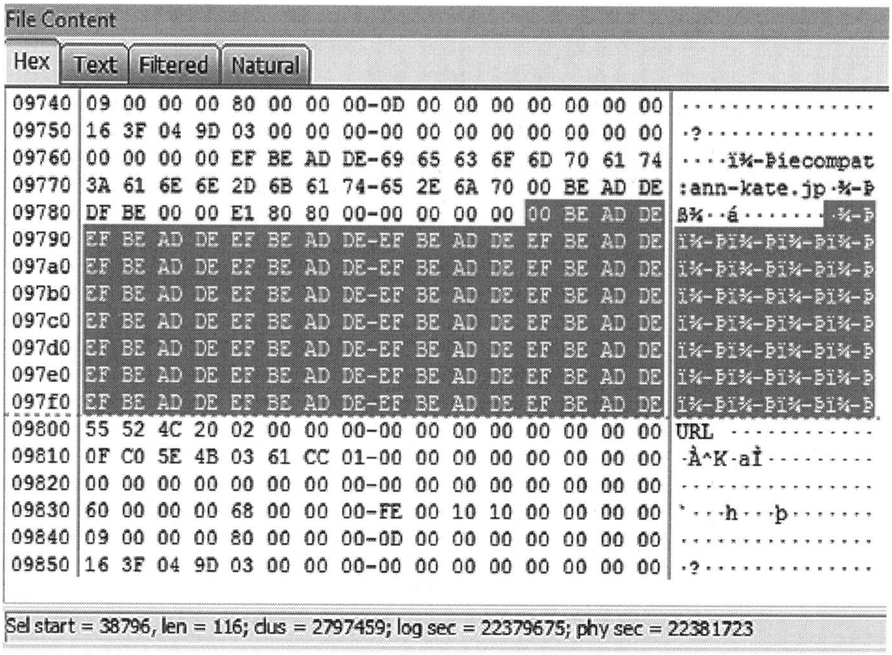

```
File Content

Hex  Text  Filtered  Natural

09740  09 00 00 00 80 00 00 00-0D 00 00 00 00 00 00 00  ................
09750  16 3F 04 9D 03 00 00 00-00 00 00 00 00 00 00 00  .?..............
09760  00 00 00 00 EF BE AD DE-69 65 63 6F 6D 70 61 74  ....ï¾Þiecompat
09770  3A 61 6E 6E 2D 6B 61 74-65 2E 6A 70 00 BE AD DE  :ann-kate.jp.¾Þ
09780  DF BE 00 00 E1 80 80 00-00 00 00 00 00 BE AD DE  ß¾..á........¾Þ
09790  EF BE AD DE EF BE AD DE-EF BE AD DE EF BE AD DE  ï¾Þï¾Þï¾Þï¾Þ
097a0  EF BE AD DE EF BE AD DE-EF BE AD DE EF BE AD DE  ï¾Þï¾Þï¾Þï¾Þ
097b0  EF BE AD DE EF BE AD DE-EF BE AD DE EF BE AD DE  ï¾Þï¾Þï¾Þï¾Þ
097c0  EF BE AD DE EF BE AD DE-EF BE AD DE EF BE AD DE  ï¾Þï¾Þï¾Þï¾Þ
097d0  EF BE AD DE EF BE AD DE-EF BE AD DE EF BE AD DE  ï¾Þï¾Þï¾Þï¾Þ
097e0  EF BE AD DE EF BE AD DE-EF BE AD DE EF BE AD DE  ï¾Þï¾Þï¾Þï¾Þ
097f0  EF BE AD DE EF BE AD DE-EF BE AD DE EF BE AD DE  ï¾Þï¾Þï¾Þï¾Þ
09800  55 52 4C 20 02 00 00 00-00 00 00 00 00 00 00 00  URL ............
09810  0F C0 5E 4B 03 61 CC 01-00 00 00 00 00 00 00 00  .À^K.aÌ.........
09820  00 00 00 00 00 00 00 00-00 00 00 00 00 00 00 00  ................
09830  60 00 00 00 68 00 00 00-FE 00 10 10 00 00 00 00  `...h...þ.......
09840  09 00 00 00 80 00 00 00-0D 00 00 00 00 00 00 00  ................
09850  16 3F 04 9D 03 00 00 00-00 00 00 00 00 00 00 00  .?..............

Sel start = 38796, len = 116; clus = 2797459; log sec = 22379675; phy sec = 22381723
```

FIGURE 6.5
Note the distinct repeating pattern of hexadecimal numbers. This pattern is unusual and may be an indication that a wiping utility was used.

```
000  5B 00 5D 00 44 00 65 00-6D 00 6F 00 6E 00 6F 00  [.].D.e.m.o.n.o.
010  69 00 64 00 2E 00 6D 00-65 00 5B 00 5D 00 2D 00  i.d...m.e.[.].-.
020  45 00 76 00 69 00 64 00-65 00 6E 00 63 00 65 00  E.v.i.d.e.n.c.e.
030  5F 00 45 00 6C 00 69 00-6D 00 69 00 6E 00 61 00  _.E.l.i.m.i.n.a.
040  74 00 6F 00 72 00 5F 00-39 00 35 00 30 00 32 00  t.o.r._.9.5.0.2.
050  37 00 35 00 38 00 2E 00-30 00 32 00 31 00 36 00  7.5.8...0.2.1.6.
060  2E 00 74 00 6F 00 72 00-72 00 65 00 6E 00 74 00  ..t.o.r.r.e.n.t.
070  00 00 DA 00 32 00 00 00-00 00 00 00 00 00 00 00  ..Ú.2...........
080  5B 5D 44 65 6D 6F 6E 6F-69 64 2E 6D 65 5B 5D 2D  []Demonoid.me[]-
090  45 76 69 64 65 6E 63 65-5F 45 6C 69 6D 69 6E 61  Evidence_Elimina
0a0  74 6F 72 5F 39 35 30 32-37 35 38 2E 30 32 31 36  tor_9502758.0216
0b0  2E 6C 6E 6B 00 00 96 00-08 00 04 00 EF BE 00 00  .lnk....ï¾..
0c0  00 00 00 00 00 00 2A 00-00 00 00 00 00 00 00 00  ......*.........
```

FIGURE 6.6
Shows signs in the MRU that the program Evidence Eliminator has been opened on this machine.

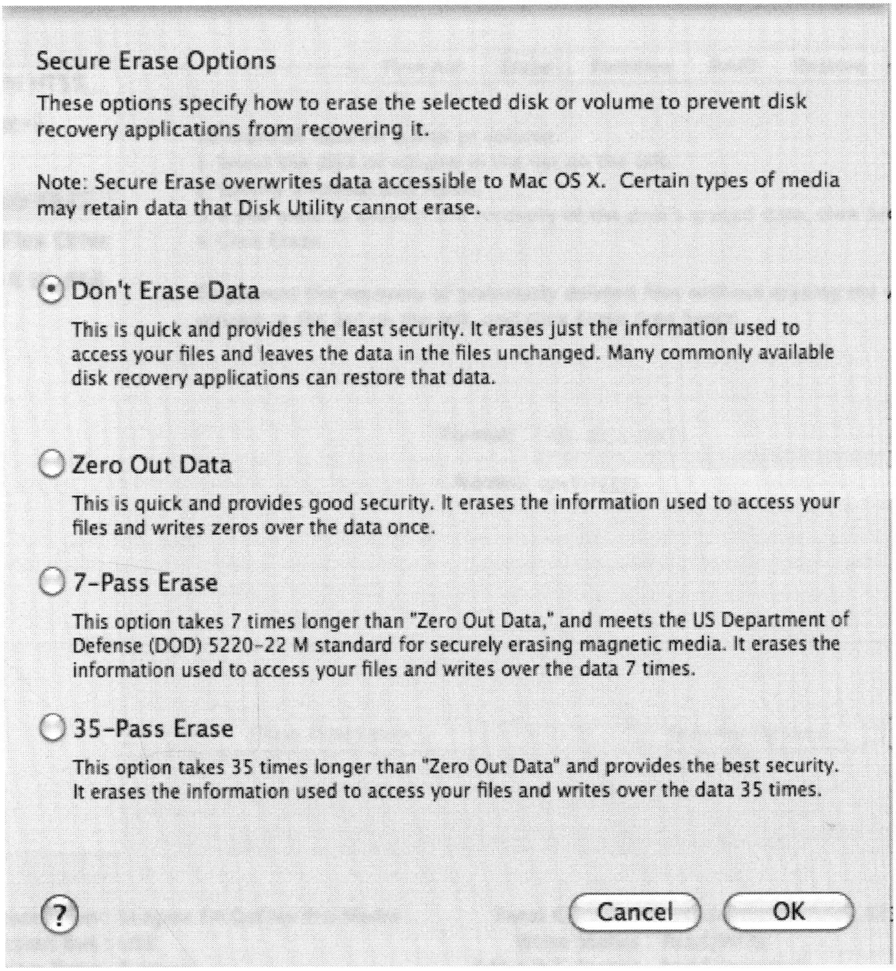

Secure Erase Options

These options specify how to erase the selected disk or volume to prevent disk recovery applications from recovering it.

Note: Secure Erase overwrites data accessible to Mac OS X. Certain types of media may retain data that Disk Utility cannot erase.

⦿ Don't Erase Data

This is quick and provides the least security. It erases just the information used to access your files and leaves the data in the files unchanged. Many commonly available disk recovery applications can restore that data.

◯ Zero Out Data

This is quick and provides good security. It erases the information used to access your files and writes zeros over the data once.

◯ 7-Pass Erase

This option takes 7 times longer than "Zero Out Data," and meets the US Department of Defense (DOD) 5220-22 M standard for securely erasing magnetic media. It erases the information used to access your files and writes over the data 7 times.

◯ 35-Pass Erase

This option takes 35 times longer than "Zero Out Data" and provides the best security. It erases the information used to access your files and writes over the data 35 times.

(?) (Cancel) (OK)

FIGURE 6.7
Secure Erase options from Apple OS X. Note the array of options, particularly the number of passes over the data.

MORE ADVANCED

Defragmentation as Antiforensic Technique

Defragmentation or "Defragging" as it's commonly called is often done to improve computer performance. Defragging is the process of moving clusters as close together as possible in order to speed the system up. This procedure involves moving data from one location on the drive to another. As such, data can be overwritten in the process. These overwritten (destroyed) data may have had some evidentiary value.

(Continued)

(Continued)

The defragmentation process can occur in three ways; it can be user scheduled, manually initiated by the user, or done automatically by the operating system (Casey, 2009).

There are a few different ways you can attempt to determine whether a drive has been recently defragmented. One way is to boot the drive image in Windows and look at the amount of file fragmentation. Drives in regular use normally show a significant amount of file fragmentation. Drives that show otherwise, without a plausible explanation, would be suspect.

Q & A With Nephi Allred, Cryptanalyst with AccessData, the Maker of Password Recovery Toolkit (PRTK).

By now it should be clear that encryption is a major concern to the digital forensics community. As such, we must be prepared to deal with encrypted data. Decryption tools are one weapon we can bring to the fight. One of the premier decryption tools on the market is Password Recovery Toolkit (PRTK) from AccessData. In the Q&A below, we get a closer look inside PRTK and the encryption it aims to break. PRTK is widely used worldwide by law enforcement, intelligence agencies, and private corporations such as large financial institutions. U.S. users include the FBI, CIA, and Secret Service, just to name a few.

[Q] About how many passwords per second does PRTK guess on a "standard" machine?

[A] Allred: We get this question a lot. It's impossible to answer as it stands because the question itself has an implicit assumption, which is wrong. Namely: all password schemes are not the same. It's a bit like asking how fast animals can go. Which animal? Every program or application or other system that uses passwords does it differently. The way they do it makes all the difference in the world in how much computation is required to test a password.

For example, a "typical" machine might guess two million passwords per second trying to crack an Office 97 file, while the same machine might only guess five hundred passwords per second cracking an Office 2010 file.

And of course the answer also depends on what you mean by a "typical" machine (and that changes as time goes on, too).

[Q] PRTK guesses passwords in a certain order to improve the speed and efficiency. Can you talk a little about how that works and why it's important?

[A] Allred: Not all passwords are created equal. In the space of all possible passwords, some are more likely to be used by humans than others. (For example, "Br1tn3y" is much more likely to be used than "H*i3}-aV.K=TyG7"). So if you are trying to guess passwords, you will be faster and more successful on average if you guess the more probable passwords first.

Of course which passwords are more probable is not always easy to determine, and certainly varies from person to person. PRTK defines a default ordering of passwords that we have tried to make as effective as possible, given what is known about how people tend to choose passwords. But an investigator often has specific knowledge about a suspect and can use that to make a password ordering more tailored to that individual. This is why PRTK gives its users a great deal of password space customization. For example, rather than going with the default, you can specify that a job first try all the passwords in a (possibly customized) dictionary, then all of those words in reverse order, then all of those words with "123," "4eva," or "asdf" appended. And lots more.

[Q] I know that PRTK also relies on identified patterns of passwords (roots and appendages). What are those based on and how does that work?

[A] Allred: Based on various password lists that we've obtained over the years (some from clients of ours, others freely available), we've tried to make password "rules" that generate passwords that people actually use in real life. At this point, this is still more an art than a science. That is, there is no deep statistical analysis going on (yet)—mostly we eyeball the lists and look for patterns. For example, a lot of passwords seem to end with "1". So one of our password rules is "Dictionary followed by common suffixes" (and "1" is one of those common suffixes).

[Q] Do you know just how effective PRTK is in breaking passwords?

[A] Allred: Again, this varies widely over the kinds of files and suspects. I don't have any numbers for you, unfortunately. You should probably talk to people who use PRTK (or DNA) on real cases.

It's worth noting that not all attacks PRTK does are password guessing attacks. Some crypto systems have flaws that allow their passwords to be recovered instantly, with no "guessing" involved. For example, PRTK can instantly recover the master password on the "Whisper32" password manager. This was not uncommon in applications a decade ago, but these days it's becoming much more rare as software developers become more crypto savvy.

[Q] Is there anything that slows down the decryption process? Can you talk about that and why that is?

[A] Allred: Yes, there is. These days, most developers of password using applications are aware of tools like PRTK, and they will use measures to slow down password guessing attacks. As I explained in #1, the speed at which we can guess passwords all depends on how the application uses the password.

An application could deliberately choose a very slow password-to-key methodology. It might hash the password ten thousand times, for example, instead of just one, while transforming the password into a key. (This is a simplification, but you get the idea). This forces the password-guessing tool to also hash the password ten thousand times per password guessed, which leads to many fewer passwords per second.

[Q] How is encryption changing? What do you see is the next "big thing" in cryptography? What challenges do you see ahead?

[A] Allred: Cryptography is a big subject, and I'm hardly an expert in any of the cutting edges of new research. But in the arena of password based encryption, things are changing.

It's not exactly a new insight, but people are becoming more and more aware that passwords as a security device are often inadequate. What we'll use instead of them (or, more likely, in addition to them) is not yet entirely clear, but encryption providers are trying new things.

For example, several applications, like TrueCrypt, allow users to enhance their password with "key files." A key file can be any file, and it is used to scramble a password before use. This means that to run a successful password-guessing attack, PRTK needs to have any and all key files used. It may not be easy for the investigator to figure out what key files were used, if any.

SUMMARY

Antiforensic tools and techniques can have a significant impact on a forensic examination of a computer. To frustrate examiners, subjects generally attempt to either hide the incriminating data in some fashion, or try to destroy it altogether. Encryption is one of the most common and potentially potent forms of data hiding. Powerful encryption is available free on the Internet and included with some versions of both Microsoft and Apple operating systems. These tools can make it practically impossible to recover the encrypted data.

Should encryption be encountered, it can be attacked in different ways. In a brute force attack, every possible password is tried until the right one is found. This is the slowest and least desirable of all the attacks. Increasing the processing power used in an attack can reduce the time needed to break the password. Some password-protected applications have vulnerabilities that can be exploited. These vulnerabilities can allow us to reset the password to one of our choosing.

Dictionaries can be created and used to break passwords. These can range from standard dictionaries to custom ones based on information specific to the target. Pet names, hobbies, interests, and birth dates are just some of the details that can compose a custom dictionary.

Messages or data can be hidden within other files. In a process known as steganography, files (called payloads) are inserted into other files such as pictures or movies (called carrier files). Steganography can be very difficult to detect. If it is detected, it can also prove tough to extract the message from the carrier file.

A subject may choose to destroy the data with a commercially available drive wiping tool. The effectiveness of these tools is far from foolproof. Incriminating data can still be recovered even after the tool has been used. Even if data have been successfully deleted, the software can leave behind telltale signs of their use. Proof of their use can be potent evidence as well.

References

AntiForensics Community. (n.d.). *About AntiForensics: AntiForenics*. Retrieved May 13, 2011, from: http://www.antiforensics.com/

Apple, Inc. (2011, July 26). *OS X Lion: About FileVault 2*. Retrieved August 14, 2011, from: http://support.apple.com/kb/HT4790

Backbone Security.com. (2011, April 26). *Backbone's Digital Steganography Database Exceeds 925 Applications*. Retrieved August 14, 2011, from: http://www.sarc-wv.com/news/press_releases/2011/safdb_v39.aspx

Barbara, J. (2008, December 01). *Anti-Digital Forensics, The Next Challenge: Part 1*. Retrieved August 15, 2011, from: http://www.forensicmag.com/article/anti-digital-forensics-next-challenge-part-1

Bauchie, R., Hazen, F., Lund, J., Oakley, G., & Rundatz, F. (2000, July). *Encryption*. Retrieved August 17, 2011, from: http://searchsecurity.techtarget.com/definition/encryption

Berghel, H. (2011, February 17). Hiding Data, Forensics, and Anti-forensics. *Communications of the ACM*, 15–20.

Caproni, V. (2011, February 17). *Going Dark: Lawful Electronic Surveillance in the Face of New Technologies*. Retrieved August 15, 2011, from: http://www.fbi.gov/news/testimony/going-dark-lawful-electronic-surveillance-in-the-face-of-new-technologies

Casey, E. (2009). *Handbook of Digital Forensics and Investigation*. Burlington, MA: Academic Press.

Casey, E. (2011). *Digital Evidence and Computer Crime, 3rd ed.: Forensic Science, Computers, and the Internet*. Waltham, MA: Academic Press.

CBS News. (2010, June 29). *FBI: 10 Russian Spies Arrested in U.S.* Retrieved September 11, 2011, from: http://www.cbsnews.com/stories/2010/06/28/world/main6627393.shtml

Dick, Ronald, L., (2001, April 5). *Issue of Intrusions into Government Computer Networks*, Retrieved August 14, 2011, from: http://www.fbi.gov/news/testimony/issue-of-intrusions-into-government-computer-networks

Elcomsoft Co. Ltd. (n.d.). *System & Security Software*. Retrieved August 27, 2011, from: http://www.elcomsoft.com/esr.html#forgot%20administrator%20password

Geiger, M. (2005). Evaluating Commercial Counter-Forensic Software. *DFRWS*. New Orleans.

Gupta, M. R., Hoeschele, M. D., & Rogers, M. K. (2006). Hidden Disk Areas: HPA, and DCO. *International Journal of Digital Evidence*, 1–8.

Homeland Security Newswire. (2011, March 18). *Feds Forced to Get Creative to Bypass Encryption*. Retrieved August 14, 2011, from: http://www.homelandsecuritynewswire.com/feds-forced-get-creative-bypass-encryption

HowStuffWorks, Inc. (n.d.). *What Is a Computer Algorithm?* Retrieved August 17, 2011, from: http://computer.howstuffworks.com/question717.htm

Kelley, J. (2005, February 5). *Terrorist Instructions Hidden Online*. Retrieved August 14, 2011, from: http://www.usatoday.com/life/cyber/tech/2001-02-05-binladen-side.htm

Microsoft Corporation. (n.d.). *BitLocker Drive Encryption Overview*. Retrieved June 20, 2011, from: http://windows.microsoft.com/en-US/windows-vista/BitLocker-Drive-Encryption-Overview

Microsoft Corporation. (n.d.). *Compare Windows*. Retrieved June 20, 2011, from: http://windows.microsoft.com/en-US/windows7/products/compare

Microsoft Corporation. (n.d.). *Create Strong Passwords*. Retrieved August 13, 2011, from: http://www.microsoft.com/security/online-privacy/passwords-create.aspx

Microsoft Corporation. (n.d.). *The Encrypting File System*. Retrieved September 11, 2011, from: http://technet.microsoft.com/en-us/library/cc700811.aspx

Microsoft Corporation. (n.d.). *Unique Technology for Enterprise Customers*. Retrieved August 27, 2011, from: http://www.microsoft.com/windows/enterprise/products/windows-7/features.aspx#bitlocker

Microsoft Corporation. (n.d.). *What Is Encrypting File System (EFS)?* Retrieved June 20, 2011, from: http://windows.microsoft.com/en-US/windows7/What-is-Encrypting-File-System-EFS

Microsoft Corporation. (n.d.). *Windows BitLocker Drive Encryption Step-by-Step Guide: Microsoft Corporation*. Retrieved May 13, 2011, from: http://technet.microsoft.com/en-us/library/cc766295%28WS.10%29.aspx

Microsoft Corporation. (2009, July 10). *Windows BitLocker Drive Encryption Frequently Asked Questions*. Retrieved August 18, 2011, from: http://technet.microsoft.com/enus/library/cc766200%28WS.10%29.aspx#BKMK_EntireDisk Microsoft.

Mozilla Foundation. (n.d.). *Private Browsing*. Retrieved August 27, 2011, from: http://support.mozilla.com/enUS/kb/Private%20Browsing#w_what-does-private-browsing-not-save

Phillip, A., Cowen, D., & Davis, C. (2009). *Hacking Exposed Computer Forensics: Computer Forensics Secrets & Solutions*. New York: McGraw-Hill.

Rogers, M. (2005). *Anti-Forensics. Lockheed Martin*. San Diego.

Schneier, B. (2002, May 15). *Crypto-Gram Newsletter*. Retrieved June 20, 2011, from: http://www.schneier.com/crypto-gram-0205.html#1

Schneier, B. (2007, January 15). *Secure Passwords Keep You Safer*. Retrieved August 25, 2011, from: http://www.schneier.com/essay-148.html

Strickland, J. (n.d.). *How Stuff Works: How Computer Forensics Works*. Retrieved May 13, 2011, from: http://computer.howstuffworks.com/computer-forensic3.htm

Symantec Corporation. (n.d.). *PGP Encryption Products*. Retrieved May 13, 2011, from: http://www.symantec.com/business/theme.jsp?themeid=pgp

Symantec Corporation. (n.d.). *Whole Disk Encryption: Symantec Corporation*. Retrieved May 13, 2011, from: http://www.symantec.com/business/whole-disk-encryption

TechTarget. (2000, December). *Steganography*. Retrieved August 15, 2011, from: http://searchsecurity.techtarget.com/definition/steganography

TrueCrypt Developers Association. (2011, July 11). *System Encryption*. Retrieved August 14, 2011, from: http://www.truecrypt.org/docs/?s=version-history

TrueCrypt Developers Association. (n.d.). *Documentation: TrueCrypt Developers Association*. Retrieved May 13, 2011, from: http://www.truecrypt.org/docs/

Tyma, P. (2003, April 8). *Encryption, Hashing, and Obfuscation*. Retrieved June 20, 2011, from: http://www.zdnet.com/news/encryption-hashing-and-obfuscation/128604

United States of America v. Christopher R. Metsos, et al. (2010, June 1). Southern District, New York.

Vijayan, J. (2008, February 4). *Updated Encryption Tool for al-Qaeda Backers Improves on First Version, Researcher Says: Computerworld*. Retrieved May 13, 2011, from: http://www.computerworld.com/s/article/9060939/Updated_encryption_tool_for_al_Qaeda_backers_improves_on_first_version_researcher_says.

Wawro, A. (2009, November 19). *US Government Using PS3s to Crack Encryption, Catch Paedophiles*. Retrieved August 17, 2011, from: http://www.computerworlduk.com/news/security/17680/us-government-using-ps3s-to-crack-encryption-catch-paedophiles/

Wetstone Technologies, Inc. (n.d.). *Stego Suite™—Discover the Hidden*. Retrieved August 18, 2011, from: http://www.wetstonetech.com/product/stego-suite/

What Is Anti-Forensics.com? (n.d.). Retrieved August 14, 2011, from: http://www.anti-forensics.com/about-anti-forensics

CHAPTER 7
Legal

Information in This Chapter:

- The Legal Aspects of Digital Forensics
- The Fourth Amendment and Its Impact on Digital Forensics
- Electronic Discovery
- Duty to Preserve Potential Digital Evidence in Civil Cases
- Private Searches and Establishing the Need for Off-Site Analysis
- Overview of The Electronic Communications Privacy Act
- Searching Digital Evidence With & Without a Search Warrant

INTRODUCTION

No discussion on digital forensic fundamentals can be complete without including the legal aspects of the discipline. The legal community has been playing a perpetual game of catch-up with technology since the very beginning. With computer and other technologies becoming so intertwined in our work and private lives, it was inevitable that electronic data would find its way into the courts. It's not just the child pornographers and identity thieves; digital evidence plays a huge role in civil litigation as well.

With these newfangled technologies came new criminal behaviors that necessitated new statutes outlawing them. Some of these are simply old crimes with a new twist. In this instance, the technology just facilitated the crime in an up-to-date, more efficient way.

Search authority is the very first step in the digital forensic process. The authority itself can take many forms, depending on which venue you're working in at the time.

Whether it be a civil or criminal case, having valid search authority is a requirement. In fact, it's the first step in the digital forensic process. In this chapter, we'll examine the fundamental legal issues in both criminal and civil litigation.

THE FOURTH AMENDMENT

The **Fourth Amendment** serves as the "litmus test" for all governmental searches and seizures. Any evidence deemed to be seized in violation of the Fourth Amendment is inadmissible in a court of law. Americans have had a long distaste for governmental intrusion into their private lives. Before the American Revolution, British soldiers, operating under Writs of Assistance, routinely invaded the homes of citizens without cause. The Fourth Amendment to the Constitution was crafted with this travesty in mind. The Fourth Amendment says: "The right of the people to be secure in their persons, houses, papers, and effects, against unreasonable searches and seizures, shall not be violated, and no Warrants shall issue, but upon **probable cause**, supported by Oath or affirmation, and particularly describing the place to be searched, and the persons or things to be seized" (FindLaw).

CRIMINAL LAW—SEARCHES WITHOUT A WARRANT

There are two key questions that must be answered from the beginning. First, did the government act? Second, did that action violate the individual's reasonable expectation of privacy? If the answer to the first question is "no," then the Fourth Amendment doesn't apply. It only covers searches by the government (or its agents), not private citizens.

For Fourth Amendment purposes, a person becomes an agent of the government if they are acting at the request of law enforcement. Under that scenario, it would be no different than if the police officer conducted the search.

Reasonable Expectation of Privacy

What exactly is a "reasonable expectation of privacy"? That's a great question with no easy answer. There is no clear cut rule or test that would help us define it. Much of the interpretation centers on what society as a whole would consider as being reasonable. For example, a person would reasonably have a greater expectation of privacy on their personal computer than they would at a public library. As a rule of thumb, you can consider the computer as a closed container. If the officer lacks the authority to open a desk drawer or box, then the same would be true with a computer (Executive Office for United States Attorneys, 2009).

If the person has a reasonable expectation of privacy, then the government must first obtain a search warrant, or the search would have to meet one of the documented exceptions to the warrant requirement.

What about individual files? Should they be seen as separate, closed containers? It seems that courts aren't sure either. Rulings have been handed down supporting both positions. In (United States v. Slanina, 2002), the Fifth Circuit ruled that when a proper search is conducted on a portion of a disk, defendants no longer have a reasonable expectation of privacy in regards to other files.

In contrast, the Tenth Circuit took the opposite stance saying "[b]ecause computers can hold so much information touching on many different areas of a person's life, there is greater potential for the 'intermingling' of documents and a consequent invasion of privacy when police execute a search for evidence on a computer" (United States v. Walser, 2001).

Information that an individual knowingly exposes to others is not protected by the Fourth Amendment. Examples here could include public computers such as those in a classroom or "shared drives" on a network (Executive Office for United States Attorneys, 2009).

Private Searches

Private searches are not afforded Fourth Amendment protection unless the search is done at the request of the government or with their knowledge or involvement. Take the Geek Squad at Best Buy, for example. Let's say that someone gives them permission to work on their home computer and in the process they find child pornography images on their machine. The images found by the repair technician would be admissible as long as they were not searching at the request of the government, thereby acting as their agent.

E-mail

By and large, an individual maintains their Fourth Amendment protections when an e-mail is being transmitted, but would lose those protections when it reaches its final destination. E-mail is viewed in a similar fashion as regular "snail mail." The legal interception of an individual's e-mail or other electronic communication is something that is tightly controlled. Known as the Wiretap Act, Title III of the Omnibus Crime Control and Safe Streets Act of 1968 prohibits unauthorized monitoring and lists the procedures needed to obtain a warrant for wiretapping (U.S. Department of Justice, Office of Justice Programs, 2010).

The Electronic Communications Privacy Act (ECPA)

The purpose of the ECPA was to ban a third party from intercepting and/or disclosing electronic communication without prior authorization. This federal statute was passed originally in 1968 as an amendment to the Wiretap Act of 1968. The ECPA underwent its first change in 1994 when it was amended by the Communications Assistance to Law Enforcement Act, also known as CALEA. It was modified once again after the 9/11 attacks by the USA Patriot Act. The Patriot Act was authorized again in 2006 (TechTarget, 2005).

Exceptions to the Search Warrant Requirement

There are several well-known exceptions to the search warrant requirement. A warrantless search is valid with **consent** as long as the person giving the consent is authorized and the consent is truly voluntary. The voluntariness of the consent is judged on the totality of the circumstances. The Supreme Court recognized age, education, intelligence, and the physical and mental condition of the person giving consent as important factors to consider. Other considerations would be whether the person was under arrest at the time of consent and whether the person had been advised of his right to refuse consent. If the validity of the search relies on consent, the burden is on the government to prove it was indeed given voluntarily.

Consent may be revoked at anytime. The search must cease immediately when the consent is withdrawn. So what happens if the suspect has second thoughts after his computer has been collected and taken to the lab for processing? The same standard applies (almost). The search must stop when they revoke their consent. That said, courts have said that this does NOT apply to forensic clones. In other words, although the original must be returned, any clones that have been made do not. Defendants do not have a reasonable expectation of privacy with a forensic clone (United States v. Megahed, 2009). For this very reason, cloning a drive sooner rather than later is a very wise move.

The scope of a consent search is sometimes at issue in a criminal case. If they give you consent to search the house, does that include closed containers and computers? Well, that depends on the particular details of the situation. Courts will again apply the "reasonableness" standard in making a determination. What would a reasonable person have understood the scope to be under those conditions?

The party granting consent may set forth restrictions on the search. Should that be the case, officers must abide with this request. To do otherwise could very well result in the suppression of any evidence recovered.

MORE ADVANCED

Consent Forms

In searches that hinge on consent, it often comes down to one side's word over the other. What exactly was said, how it was said, and what the suspect understood at the time could all be scrutinized. A well-crafted consent-to-search form will go a long way in countering any attack on the search. The form should include details specifically relating to digital evidence. The form should seek permission to search not just computers but any storage media including cell phones, manuals, printers, and more. The form should ask for permission to take these items from the location for offsite examination (Executive Office for United States Attorneys, 2009).

In the end, it's important to remember that consent searches can be highly nuanced and heavily dependent on the facts or circumstances that arise during that specific incident. While searching without a warrant is sometimes a necessity, the best practice is to get a search warrant whenever possible. Your case will rest on much more solid ground with a warrant than without.

Third parties can sometimes consent to the search of private property. Room-mates, spouses, and parents are just a few of the examples. Normally, if a device is shared, all parties have the authority to provide consent to search its common areas. In this situation, none of them would have a reasonable expectation of privacy in the common areas since it's shared with other people. The notion of common areas is significant. Areas such as those that are password protected would not qualify as a common area. The third party would likely not have the authority to consent to its search. However, if the suspect has shared the password with the third party, then this constraint no longer applies. The suspect's reasonable expectation of privacy has been greatly diminished.

It's foreseeable that in the end, the third party in question really didn't have the authority to consent. This is not necessarily a deal breaker as far as the admissibility is concerned. Officers in the field can only do what a reasonable person would do when determining a third party's legal ability to provide consent. If the suspect is present at the scene, a third party is not permitted to grant consent.

Spouses, under normal circumstances, can consent to the search of common areas. Parents may or may not be able to provide consent to search a child's property. If the child in question is less than eighteen years of age, parents are generally permitted to give consent. If the child is over eighteen, then it gets a bit more complicated. Factors that will impact this determination include the child's age, whether or not they pay rent, and what steps (if any) they have taken to restrict access.

Technicians are often in the position of uncovering evidence during the course of their work. The courts have been split when deciding if the technician has the authority to consent. Officers may recreate the technician's search or observe them retrace their steps. They may not, however, expand the technician's search or direct them to look deeper. Should a technician locate evidence, their findings are normally used as the basis for a search warrant.

Exigent circumstances arise from time to time requiring the immediate seizure and possible search of a digital device. This is generally permitted under one of these three conditions: the evidence is under immanent threat of destruction, a threat puts law enforcement or the public in general in danger, and when the suspect is expected to escape before a search warrant can be acquired. This exception may apply to the seizure of an item or device, but not automatically the search of it. Once the item has been seized (secured), the exigency may no longer exist, thus requiring a search warrant to continue.

Officers have the right to charge suspects with evidence they see if they are legally permitted to be where they are, and if the item is immediately apparent to be incriminating. This is known as the **plain view** doctrine. This situation typically arises in a digital forensic context when an examiner is analyzing a drive for evidence of one crime and finds evidence of a completely different one. For instance, an examiner searching a hard drive for photos of stolen artwork comes across images of child pornography. At this juncture, the search should cease until a separate warrant pertaining to the possession of child pornography can be obtained.

Border searches and searches by probation and parole officers are afforded much more latitude than those conducted by police officers. From the court's perspective, individuals entering the country can be searched with probable cause or even reasonable suspicion. The court recognizes the government's need to secure the border from contraband and like material. Those individuals on probation or parole have less of an expectation of privacy than other citizens. For example, sex offenders may be prohibited from using the Internet during their supervised release. This stipulation would permit the parole or probation officer the authority to search the offender's computer at any time to ensure compliance. There is even some case law permitting this type of search without these specific conditions in place.

Employees in the workplace may or may not possess a reasonable expectation of privacy on their work computers. This expectation will vary depending on the facts including whether or not the employee is a government employee. Normally, officers can search an employee's computer without a warrant if the employer or another coworker (with shared authority) gives permission. Government employees are looked at a bit differently. That's not to say that employers can't search the employee's system; it just means that the search must be "work-related, justified at their inception, and permissible in scope" (Executive Office for United States Attorneys, 2009).

SEARCHING WITH A WARRANT

Absent one of the well-defined exceptions described here, police officers must have a search warrant before searching someone's private property, including their computer.

A search warrant is an order that is obtained by a law enforcement officer from a judge, granting them permission to search a specific place and seize specific persons or things.

A judge will issue the warrant when he or she believes that there is probable cause that a crime was committed and that the people or things specified in the warrant will be found at that location. The Supreme Court said that probable cause is established when there is "a fair probability that contraband or evidence of a crime will be found in a particular place" (Illinois v. Gates, 1983). Another way to look at it is more likely than not the items or persons to be seized will be found at that specific location. Mathematically, this would equate to a probability of 51 percent.

When applying for a warrant, it's helpful to determine the role of the computer in the crime. The computer can be considered contraband if it contains child pornography or is stolen property. The computer can also be used to store evidence, such as incriminating documents. Finally, the computer can serve as a tool or instrumentality of the crime. This is the case when the computer is used to hack into a company's network, for example.

Seize the Hardware or Just the Information?

We know from the Fourth Amendment that a search warrant must "particularly describe the place to be searched and the person or things to be seized." To effectively meet that requirement, we first need to understand what precisely we need to seize. In short, is it the hardware or the information held by the hardware? If the computer is contraband, evidence, or fruits or instrumentalities of a crime, then we need to establish probable cause to seize the hardware. Otherwise, our focus is on the information alone.

Particularity

Courts frown heavily on overly broad affidavits that lack the particularity mandated by the Fourth Amendment. Affidavits should make it clear what items can be seized and what can't. "Particularly" describing things that you likely have never seen may seem like an impossible task. It's really not. Serial numbers and the like are not required.

Here is some sample language that could be used:

> "Any and all personal computer(s)/computing system(s) located at the residence of (INSERT ADDRESS HERE), to include input and output devices, electronic storage media, computer tapes, scanners, disks, diskettes, optical storage devices, printers, monitors, central processing units, and all associated storage media for electronic data, together with all other computer-related operating equipment and materials."

Describing the information can be done in a somewhat similar fashion. Although we probably don't know the file names, for example, it's quite possible that we would know the suspect's name, the time period, and the specific crime that's being investigated. The courts are looking for some type of limiting language. Asking for "any and all files" on a suspect's hard drive stands a very good chance of being deemed overly broad, resulting in the suppression of any evidence found.

Establishing Need for Off-Site Analysis

The forensic analysis of a hard drive can be a very time-consuming process. For a variety of reasons, this is best done at the lab or police station. For all intents and purposes, doing this at the scene contemporaneously with the search should not be the first option. As such, the search warrant affidavit should spell out in clear terms the logic and need for this practice. Reasons can include the amount of time and data involved and potential use of antiforensic techniques as well as the need to perform this task under the more controlled conditions (like those found in the lab). This is one way to make this point in an affidavit:

> "Computer storage devices (like hard disks or CD-ROMs) can store the equivalent of millions of pages of information. Additionally, a suspect may try to conceal criminal evidence; he or she might store it in random order with deceptive file names. This may require searching authorities to

peruse all the stored data to determine which particular files are evidence or instrumentalities of crime. This sorting process can take weeks or months, depending on the volume of data stored, and it would be impractical and invasive to attempt this kind of data search on-site.

Technical requirements. Searching computer systems for criminal evidence sometimes requires highly technical processes requiring expert skill and properly controlled environment. The vast array of computer hardware and software available requires even computer experts to specialize in some systems and applications, so it is difficult to know before a search which expert is qualified to analyze the system and its data. In any event, however, data search processes are exacting scientific procedures designed to protect the integrity of the evidence and to recover even "hidden," erased, compressed, password- protected, or encrypted files. Because computer evidence is vulnerable to inadvertent or intentional modification or destruction (both from external sources or from destructive code imbedded in the system as a "booby trap"), a controlled environment may be necessary to complete an accurate analysis." (Executive Office for United States Attorneys, 2009)

Stored Communications Act

The **Stored Communications Act** (SCA), enacted in 1986, provides statutory privacy protection for customers of network service providers. The SCA controls how the government can access stored account information from entities such as Internet Service Providers (ISPs). This account information typically includes e-mail as well as subscriber and billing information. Specifically, the SCA lays out the process state and federal law enforcement officers must adhere to in order to force disclosure of these records by the provider.

The SCA seeks to codify the type of information sought, the privacy expectations associated with it, and the legal instrument required for the government to access it. The SCA breaks down service providers into two separate and distinct groups: "electronic communication service" providers and those organizations that provide "remote computing services." Understanding these differences is essential to deciphering the SCA and its legal requirements.

According to the SCA, specifically 18 U.S.C. § 2510(15), an **electronic communication service (ECS)** provider is "any service which provides to users thereof the ability to send or receive wire or electronic communications." ECS examples would include companies that deliver telephone and e-mail services (Executive Office for United States Attorneys, 2009). America Online comes to mind, as does Hotmail. It may surprise you to know that any company, no matter what its focus, can qualify as an ECS.

Title 18 U.S.C.§ 2711(2) defines a **remote computing service (RCS)** as "the provision to the public of computer storage or processing services by means of an electronic communications system." Put another way, an RCS is provided by an "off-site computer that stores or processes data for a customer" (Executive Office for United States Attorneys, 2009).

The SCA also addresses the variety of information these providers store. This can include basic subscriber information like name, address, and credit card number. Other potential information includes logs and opened, unopened, draft, and sent e-mails.

ELECTRONIC DISCOVERY (eDiscovery)

Digital evidence is alive and well in civil cases. Parties involved in litigation need to review all of the potentially relevant data as well as any data that may have to be disclosed to the opposing party. Common means of discovery include interrogatories, depositions, and requests for document production (Sedona Conference, 2007). Electronically stored information (ESI) presents some challenges that paper records do not. For example, ESI is easily modified, volatile, and easily duplicated and dispersed. As such, the rules of evidence for both state and federal courts are changing to specifically address ESI.

The (Sedona Conference, 2007) defines eDiscovery as "The process of collecting, preparing, reviewing, and producing electronically stored information ("ESI") in the context of the legal process" (Sedona Conference, 2007)

Duty to Preserve

Evidence that was once confined to paper memos and filing cabinets is now found in Microsoft Word documents and back-up tapes. Digital evidence is significantly different from the paper-based evidence so many lawyers were accustomed to dealing with. For example, digital evidence is far more volatile and easier to alter or destroy. Volume is another key difference. There can be such a mind-boggling amount of data in a case that it can cost millions of dollars just to produce and review them.

In December 2006, the federal courts took the first substantive step in addressing and dealing with digital evidence, changing the Rules of Civil Procedure. These rule changes mandate that opposing attorneys work together to deal with the **electronically stored information (ESI)** in the case very early in the process. Addressing ESI early in a case reduces costs, time, and the chance of relevant evidence being overlooked. Not all lawyers and judges have embraced these changes. Like many folks, some lawyers and judges are very uncomfortable with technology, even going as far as to have someone else check and then print their e-mail.

Zubalake v. USB Warburg was a series of landmark electronic discovery cases. Judge Shira Scheindlin's rulings addressed many of the fundamental concerns in cases that involve ESI. Some of the concerns included the duty to preserve electronic data, a lawyer's duty to oversee their client's compliance with these guidelines, data sampling, cost shifting, and sanctions.

The **duty to preserve** potentially relevant data begins when there is a "reasonable anticipation of litigation." Failing to recognize this trigger and take action can result in **spoliation** of the evidence and potentially severe sanctions to boot. Like other legal standards addressed in this chapter, defining a reasonable anticipation of litigation can be difficult, quite difficult in fact. The duty to preserve is not just caused by the arrival of a subpoena. It's very likely that the duty kicked in well before that time. It's a very fact-specific determination that will vary from case to case. The firing of a disgruntled employee could be enough to trigger it; likewise, so could an accusation of sexual harassment by an employee against his or her supervisor.

Judge Scheindlin also addressed a lawyer's duty to oversee their client's attempts to identify, preserve, collect, and produce potentially relevant evidence. She said, in part, "[c]ounsel must take affirmative steps to monitor compliance so that all sources of discoverable information are identified and searched." Furthermore, she said that attorneys should draft and distribute a "litigation hold" that directs a company and its employees to protect the relevant data and ensure they're not destroyed or compromised in any way.

Data sampling is a way to test a large collection of ESI for the "existence or frequency of relevant information" (Sedona Conference, 2007). The volume of potentially relevant data can be staggering, especially in a large corporate environment. Data sampling is one of the best ways to save time and reduce costs during the eDiscovery process.

The costs incurred during the eDiscovery process can be massive, rising into hundreds of thousands or even millions of dollars. Typically, in traditional discovery, the producing party bears the cost of production. Under certain conditions, the costs of production may be shifted to the requesting party. In the *Zubalake* case, Judge Scheindlin addressed this concern and devised a seven-factor test to be used to determine if cost shifting is warranted.

The seven factors are "(1) the extent to which the request is specifically tailored to discover relevant information; (2) the availability of such information from other sources; (3) the total cost of production compared to the amount in controversy; (4) the total cost of production compared to the resources available to each party; (5) the relative ability of each party to control costs and its incentive to do so; (6) the importance of the issue at stake in the litigation and; (7) the relative benefits to the parties of obtaining the information" (*Zubulake v. UBS Warburg, 2003*).

Private Searches in the Workplace

It's not uncommon for work computers to be the subject of a search for criminal, civil, or administrative actions. From the private side, employers have a fair bit of latitude to search an individual's company computer. A company computer use policy that clearly spells out that work computers, e-mail, and so on are for work purposes only and that they may be searched at any time is an accepted best practice. For Fourth Amendment purposes (law enforcement or their agents), a work computer can be searched with consent of a supervisor or another employee as long as they have common authority over the area to be searched. It is also important to note that federal privacy statutes and the Stored Communications Act may come into play as well.

In the end, consult with the prosecuting attorney or corporate/in-house counsel for guidance. Getting their input can help ensure that the case is on the strongest legal footing (Executive Office for United States Attorneys, 2009)

ALERT!

International eDiscovery

With the cloud environment and data regularly flying across borders, international electronic discovery is becoming an issue. Not every country has the same views on privacy or the same legal standards and procedures for discovery. As a result, gaining access to data in a foreign country is very complex. The Sedona Conference's *Framework for Analysis of Cross-Border Discovery Conflicts: A Practical Guide to Navigating the Competing Currents of International Data Privacy and e-Discovery* is an excellent introduction to the complexities involved in international eDiscovery. You can download it for free from http://www.thesedonaconference.org/.

EXPERT TESTIMONY

As a digital forensic examiner, you must be prepared to testify in court as an expert witness as to your findings and procedures. What's the difference between a witness and an expert witness? A major difference is that a qualified expert witness can give an opinion, but a "regular" witness can't.

Determining whether or not an individual is an expert is a matter for the court to decide. An expert doesn't have to have a Ph.D or other lofty credentials. FindLaw defines an expert as someone "who by virtue of special knowledge, skill, training, or experience is qualified to provide testimony to aid the factfinder in matters that exceed the common knowledge of ordinary people" (FindLaw).

Under this definition, bakers, tailors, accountants, medical doctors, and school bus drivers could be qualified as an expert. Certainly credentials help, but they are not a requirement.

There are two cases that form the foundation for the admissibility of expert testimony. The first is a 1923 case, *United States v. Frye*. The *Frye* (1923) case centered on the admissibility of new lie-detection technology. Out of this case came what became known as the "Frye Test." The test said that "the results of scientific tests or procedures are admissible as evidence only when the tests or procedures have gained general acceptance in the particular field to which they belong" (United States v. Frye, 1923).

Eventually, the Frye Test fell by the wayside. In *Daubert v. Merrell Dow Pharmaceuticals, Inc.,* 509 U.S. 579 (1993), the U.S. Supreme Court ruled that the

Federal Rules of Evidence superseded the Frye Test. Merrell Dow Pharmaceuticals Inc. was sued by plaintiffs who claimed that their drug, Bendectin, had caused significant birth defects. The lower court granted Merrell Dow's request for summary citing that the scientific evidence presented by the plaintiff had not yet gained approval within the scientific community. The Supreme Court agreed.

In *Daubert* (1993), the Court said that the admissibility should be evaluated on "whether the testimony's underlying reasoning or methodology is scientifically valid and properly can be applied to the facts at issue. Many considerations will bear on the inquiry, including whether the theory or technique in question can be (and has been) tested, whether it has been subjected to peer review and publication, its known or potential error rate and the existence and maintenance of standards controlling its operation, and whether it has attracted widespread acceptance within a relevant scientific community" (Daubert, 1993).

Understanding this groundwork will help the examiner better comprehend the admissibility of their testimony within the context of the law.

ADDITIONAL RESOURCES

Expert Testimony

Fred Smith and Rebecca Bace's book on expert testimony, *A Guide to Forensic Testimony: The Art and Practice of Presenting Testimony as an Expert Technical Witness*, contains a tremendous amount of practical information. One of the best aspects of the book is that it is written for information technology experts. The book covers the topic well and is quite "readable."

SUMMARY

Proper search authority is a necessary first step in the forensic examination process. Evidence collected without it is very likely to be excluded. The Fourth Amendment to the U.S. Constitution protects citizens from unreasonable searches and seizures. The protections afforded by the Fourth Amendment only cover actions by the government. It does not apply to private citizens acting on their own. Law enforcement can search and seize digital evidence with and without a search warrant. Searches with a warrant are always better, from a legal standpoint, than searches without one. That said, exigent circumstances can and do arise that would permit officers to do otherwise.

On the private side, supervisors and employers will likely have broad authority to search company computers, especially if the employee read and signed a computer usage agreement clearly stating that the company computers, e-mail, and so on could be searched at any time.

Consulting with the appropriate legal counsel before searching or seizing digital evidence is never a bad idea. If you have questions or concerns, they should always be raised in advance.

References

Casey, E. (2011). *Digital evidence and computer crime, 3rd ed.: Forensic science, computers, and the Internet.* Waltham, MA: Academic Press.

Daubert v. Merrell Dow Pharmaceuticals,Inc., 509 U.S. 579 (1993).

Executive Office for United States Attorneys. (2007). *Prosecuting computer crime.* Office of Legal Education. Washington, DC: United States Department of Justice.

Executive Office for United States Attorneys. (2009). *Searching and seizing computers and obtaining electronic evidence in criminal investigations.* Office of Legal Education. Washington, DC: United States Department of Justice.

Frye v. United States, .293 F. 1013 (D.C. Cir 1923).

FindLaw. (n.d.). *Fourth Amendment—Search and Seizure.* Retrieved October 4, 2011, from: http://caselaw.lp.findlaw.com/data/constitution/amendment04/

Goldfoot, J. (2011). The physical computer and the Fourth Amendment. *Berkley Journal of Criminal Law, 16*(1), 112–167.

Illinois v. Gates, 462 U.S. 213, 238, (1983).

Kerr, O. S. (2005a). Digital evidence and the new criminal procedure. *Columbia Law Review, 105*(1), 279–318.

Kerr, O. S. (2005b). Searches and seizures in a digital world. *Harvard Law Review, 119*(2), 532–585.

Kroll OnTrack, Inc. (n.d.). *Zubulake v. UBS Warburg.* Retrieved October 10, 2011, from: http://www.krollontrack.co.uk/zubulake/

McCullagh, D. (2007, December 14). *Judge: Man Can't Be Forced to Divulge Encryption Passphrase.* Retrieved October 3, 2011, from: http://news.cnet.com/8301-13578_3-9834495-38.html

Scheindlin, S., & Capra, D. J. (2008). *Electronic discovery and digital evidence: Cases and materials.* Eagan, MN: Thomson West.

Sedona Conference. (2007). *The Sedona Conference glossary: E-Discovery & digital information management* (2nd ed.). Sedona, AZ: Sedona Conference.

TechTarget. (2005, December). *Electronic Discovery.* Retrieved November 6, 2011, from Search Financial Security. TechTarget.com: http://searchfinancialsecurity.techtarget.com/definition/electronic-discovery.

U.S. Department of Justice, Office of Justice Programs. (2010). *Privacy and Civil Liberties.* Retrieved October 10, 2011, from: http://it.ojp.gov/default.aspx?area=privacy&page=1284#contentTop

United States v. Megahed, 2009 WL 722481, at *3 (M.D. Fla. Mar. 18, 2009).

United States v. Slanina, 283 F.3d 670, 680 (5th Cir. 2002).

United States v. Walser, 275 F.3d 981, 986 (10th Cir. 2001).

Zubulake v. UBS Warburg, 217 F.R.D. 309 (S.D.N.Y. 2003).

CHAPTER 8

Internet and E-Mail

Information in This Chapter:

- Overview of the Internet and How it Works
- How Web Browsers Work and the Evidence They Can Create
- E-Mail Function & Forensics
- Chat and Social Networking Evidence

INTRODUCTION

In the beginning, the Internet was a little-known tool used by a few academics and the military. Today, it's a tool truly for the masses. We can order pizza, pay bills, look up a phone number, and take a class. For many of us, it is hard to imagine life without it. For examiners, its use can leave significant pieces of evidence. Web browsing, chat, e-mail, and social networking are just some of the technologies that we must understand how they're used, how they work, and where they leave traces.

INTERNET OVERVIEW

We'll begin with a quick introduction to the technology involved in getting your favorite web page to appear on your computer screen. Perhaps the best way is to track the process from start to finish. It all begins when someone enters a web address or **URL** (Uniform Resource Locator) into the address bar of a **browser**. A URL comprises three parts: the host, the domain name, and the file name. Let's use http://www.digitalforensics.com as an example.

In our example, "http" or **Hypertext Transfer Protocol (HTTP)** is the protocol used on the Internet to browse and interact with web sites and the like. A protocol is nothing more than an agreed-upon way for devices to communicate with one another. Next is the **domain name**, "digital forensics." Last is the **Top Level Domain (TLD)**, ".com." It's called a TLD because it is at the top of the hierarchy that makes up the Internet's domain name system. Other TLDs include .org, .edu, and .net, just to name a few.

The browser, using the HTTP protocol, sends a "get" request to the web server hosting www.digitalforensics.com. A browser is an application that is used to view and access content on the Internet. There are several browsers to choose from: the most common are Microsoft's Internet Explorer, Mozilla's Firefox, and Google's Chrome.

After hitting enter, the first order of business is to convert the domain name into an **IP (Internet Protocol)** address. The Internet functions with IP addresses. It can't do anything with the domain name itself. The domain name is for us, making it easier to remember. A **Domain Name Server (DNS)** is responsible for mapping domain names to specific IP addresses. After the DNS makes the conversion, the request is then sent on to the server hosting the web site. After receiving the request, the server returns the requested web page and associated content.

A web page comprises several components. The first is the **HTML (Hypertext Markup Language)** document. This contains quite a bit of information including directions for how the page should be rendered (displayed) by the browser, content, and more. It also contains file names for subcomponents of the web page such as images. It's important to note that HTML is not a programming language.

There are two types of web pages: static and dynamic. A static web page is one that is prebuilt. Its content, layout, etc., are predetermined. A dynamic page, however, is built "on the fly." It doesn't exist until it's called. The page is built from different pieces drawn from databases. Amazon is a great example of a dynamic web site. My page will very likely be different from your page. The books and so on that appear on my page are based on my shopping and buying habits. All this information is stored in a database(s) along with the things like the book images, descriptions, and so on. When I logon to Amazon, the server sends the items that are standard for everyone (like the Amazon logo) along with the content targeted to me.

When interacting with a web site, it's important to understand where certain things are occurring. This can be especially important to know from a forensics perspective because it can tell you where you should be looking for a given artifact. Actions can occur on either the client-side or the server-side. JavaScript (no relation to the Java the programming language) is a client-side technology. It's used for things such as roll-overs on a navigation bar. The code that makes that work is downloaded and run on the local machine. Server-side actions are just the opposite and are used when there is a need to send information to another computer (like my custom content at Amazon).

Determining the ownership and host of a particular domain name can become relevant in a criminal or civil case. A search query known as a **"whois"** can help you identify some of the individuals and/or companies associated with a given domain name. A whois search can tell you the registrant, when the domain was created, the administrative contact, and the technical contact. The contact information typically provides a name, address, and phone number. Most if not all domain name registrars now offer private registration. Any whois search for a domain name with private registration will typically get the registrar's contact information, rather than the actual owner (Network Solutions, LLC). If you'd like to give this a try, visit one of the sites offering the whois service. Network Solutions is one: http://www.networksolutions.com/whois/index.jsp.

Peer-to-Peer (P2P)

P2P is used primarily as a means to share files. A major portion of the traffic on a P2P network is pirated music and movies as well as child pornography. P2P differs from a client/server network in that computers on a P2P network can serve both roles (client and server). **Gnutella** is one of the major systems or architectures used in P2P networks.

MORE ADVANCED

Gnutella Requests

On a P2P network, what stops a file request from just propagating forever? There is actually a built-in mechanism in the information packets. In each packet, there is a Time To Live (TTL) value that is set to decrease by one every time it is delivered to another node on the network. Once that number hits 0, the packet is stopped.

To get started with a P2P network, users must first download and install a P2P client such as KaZaA, Frostwire, GigaTribe or eMule. Typically, users then create a "shared" directory containing files they want to make available to others.

To find files of interest to download, users normally enter search term(s) for the file or files he wants. If the search is successful, the software returns a list of computers that have the requested file(s). Lastly, the files are downloaded to a directory of the user's choosing or to the default location specified by the client. P2P networks use HTTP to transfer files.

Nodes on a Gnutella fall into two categories. Nodes that have the required bandwidth as well as the uptime (time on the network) are classified as Ultrapeers. Those that don't are known as leafs. Ultrapeers perform some additional duties such as searching, indexing, and facilitating connections.

The INDEX.DAT File

The **INDEX.DAT** is a binary, container-like file that is used by Microsoft's Internet Explorer (MSIE). The INDEX.DAT file holds quite a bit of value for forensic examiners. There are multiple INDEX.DAT files on a system. The INDEX.DAT tracks several pieces of information regarding the URLs visited, the number of visits, and so on. These files are hidden from the user and must be viewed using a tool of some sort. Both FTK and EnCase are able to decipher INDEX.DAT files. MSIE has three directories: History, Cookies, and Temporary Internet Files. INDEX.DAT files are used to track the information and contents of each directory (Casey, 2009).

WEB BROWSERS—INTERNET EXPLORER

Web browsers are an indispensable part of the overall computing experience and serve as our "vehicles" on the "Information Superhighway" known as the World Wide Web. Although there are multiple browsers on the market, Microsoft's Internet Explorer is far and away the most widely used. Other browsers (for the PC) also getting some traction are Mozilla's Firefox and Google's Chrome. On Macintosh computers, Safari is king, with Firefox getting some use here as well. At their foundation, these applications function in much the same way. For instance, all of them utilize some sort of caching system. They also have mechanisms to deal with cookies, Internet history, typed URLs, bookmarks, and more. They differ in the details. Space does not permit an exhaustive look at all the browsers and the details of their inner workings. Instead, we'll focus on some of the common functions as they are in MSIE, the overwhelming market leader.

Cookies

A **cookie** is a small text file that is deposited on a user's computer by a web server. Cookies can serve a variety of purposes. They can be used to track sessions as well as remember a user's preferences for a particular web site. Amazon.com is a great example. When you return to the site you are normally greeted with a "Hello, Susan" as well as customized recommendations based on your buying and browsing history. That level of individualization is made possible through cookies.

Cookies can provide valuable evidence and are tracked in a single INDEX.DAT file. They can contain Uniform Resource Locators (URLs), dates and times, user names, and more. Deciphering a cookie can be a challenge, as they aren't normally written in the clear. Fortunately for us, tools are available to get this done. It's critical to note that the existence of a web address in a cookie is not necessarily proof that the suspect actually visited the site (Casey, 2009).

Temporary Internet Files, a.k.a. web Cache

We are an impatient lot. As such, speed is vital to a user's Internet experience. Today, web browsing is expected to be nearly indistinguishable from the applications running on our own machines. web cache is one way that the browser makers shave some time off the download times. Cache speeds things along by reusing web page components like images, saving time from having to download objects more than once.

Microsoft's browser, Internet Explorer, refers to web cache as **Temporary Internet Files (TIF)**. In Microsoft Internet Explorer, TIF is organized into sub-folders bearing a random eight-character name. They are organized using a collection of INDEX.DAT files. Each file in TIF has a corresponding date and time value associated with it. This includes a "last-checked" time, which is used by the browser to determine if a newer version exists on the server. If so, then it will download the newer version.

Users can view their TIF anytime using Windows Explorer. Inside the TIF folder users will see a listing of its contents. Each item in the list will display an icon showing file type, file name, and the associated URL. It's important to understand that in this instance, what the user sees is a virtualized representation of the content. The actual items are kept in the TIF subdirectories. The only file that is actually kept here is the INDEX.DAT that keeps tabs on where the files are located inside the various subdirectories.

Webmail evidence can also be found in TIF. Hotmail, AOL, and Yahoo! can all leave messages and/or inbox information that can prove useful. These items can be recognized by the file names. Here are some examples:

- Outlook web Access Messages—Read[#].htm
- AOL Messages—Msgview[#].htm
- Hotmail messages—getmsg[#].htm
- Yahoo!—ShowLetter[#].htm
- Outlook web Access Inbox—Main[#].htm
- AOL Inbox—Msglist[#].htm
- Hotmail Inbox—HoTMail[#].htm
- Yahoo!—ShowFolder.htm

web cache can be used to determine both culpability and intent. Much of what's in web cache will be thumbnails (those small images) along with bits and pieces of web pages.

Image size can impact a case, particularly those involving child pornography. If the suspect images are comprised entirely of small, cache-like images, then some prosecutors may be reluctant to file charges. The issue then becomes intent. Those images could have been downloaded automatically, without his consent. Images of such a small size can make for a much weaker case. Larger images, those not commonly found as part of a web page, are harder to explain away.

Internet History

Microsoft's Internet Explorer, the reigning king of browsers, keeps multiple historic user records. History is used to prevent a user from having to retype URLs into the address bar of the browser. The index.dat files track other details as well. For example, it tracks the number of times the site is visited, and the name of the file. The Internet history is organized in multiple folders and index.dat files. There are three folders: Daily, Weekly, and Cumulative.

These folders use a naming convention based on a set prefix followed by a date range. For example, a folder covering the Internet history from October 1, 2011, to October 8, 2011, would look like this:

MSHist012011100120111008
MSHist01 – Folder name/prefix
2011 – Year (start)
1001 – Date (start)
2011 – Date (end)
1008 – Date (end)

People who have something to hide will often clear their history on a frequent basis. This can be done manually by the user or automatically by the system. By default, the history is set to clear every twenty days. The user can change this to clear much faster than that. Using a tool that can read the registry, you can view this information here:

NTUSERS\Software Microsoft\Windows\CurrentVersion\Internet Settings\URL History

---

MORE ADVANCED

The NTUSER.DAT File

The **NTUSER.DAT** file contains preference settings and individual information for each user profile. Browser history is part of this information. There is one NTUSER.DAT for each user profile on the system. Although technically a registry file, the NTUSER.DAT is located in the user folder. Note that we're talking about user "profiles" and not "users." Putting a specific person on the keyboard is a very difficult if not impossible determination to make. Just because a person has a profile on the machine does not mean their fingers were on the keyboard at any given moment.

If this value is set less than the default of twenty days, this can be used to show the defendant took proactive steps to remove potentially incriminating evidence.

Internet Explorer Artifacts in the Registry

As part of its everyday function, MSIE deposits artifacts in the registry. These items are stored particularly in the NTUSER.DAT hive. Here we can see if the browser stores passwords, the default search engine, the default search provider, and more.

The registry can also tell us what URLs have been typed right into the browser's address bar. These are listed from 1 to 25 with the lowest number being the most recent. Only twenty-five entries can be kept at a time. The entries are purged on a first in, first out basis. Figure 8.1 shows you what they look like through a forensic tool.

Name	Type	Data
url1	REG_SZ	http://www.google.com/
url2	REG_SZ	http://www.fileshredder.com/
url3	REG_SZ	http://www.wikileaks.org/
url4	REG_SZ	http://hackernews.com/
url5	REG_SZ	http://www.hacker.com/
url6	REG_SZ	http://www.hacer.com/

FIGURE 8.1
Typed URLs as found in the Windows Registry. Graphic courtesy of Jonathan Sisson.

Here is the file path to this registry artifact:

NTUSER\Software\Microsoft\Internet Explorer\Typed URLs

Remember, the registry is not human-readable in its native form. To examine it you will need an appropriate tool. Some of these tools include Microsoft's RegEdit, Harlan Carvey's RegRipper, and AccessData's Registry Viewer.

Chat Clients

Chat applications are both popular and numerous. They are used for instant text-based communication. Popular applications include AOL Instant Messenger (AIM), Yahoo! Messenger, Windows Live Messenger, Trillian, Digsby, and many more. These clients can be used either to commit or to facilitate a variety of crimes. Pedophiles use these tools to solicit sex from minors or to distribute child pornography. Buyers and sellers use them to negotiate the sale and transfer of narcotics. The list can go on and on. Function varies from client to client as do the artifacts they leave behind. Function and residual evidence can also vary from version to version. It's difficult to keep up with the rapid pace at which these clients change. Changes can result in artifacts moving or disappearing. Rather than get "down in the weeds" with each application and version, we'll talk in broad terms of what kind of artifacts are possible and how they can be used as evidence.

Not unlike other software, chat client will leave artifacts of its installation. Paths and directories may vary somewhat. The presence or absence of these files and folders may help in proving or disproving that a specific client was used to communicate with a victim or accomplice.

Chat programs maintain a contact or "buddy" list. This list of screen names can be used to link individuals together, particularly if the other parties' screen names appear in the logs or on the drive. Screen names are often nonsensical, like "football-fan7878," and can require some effort to connect them with a specific person. Entering screen names as part of your keyword search can also be very helpful. To complicate matters further, users can have multiple screen names. Many times these alternate identities assume a parent-child relationship with the primary identity.

Users can also choose to block people, preventing them from communicating with them. If this function is available, then this setting should be tracked somewhere, potentially leaving relevant artifacts. Often clients will also maintain a list of recent chats.

Other preferences that are under user control include embedding the date time in the chat, selecting a custom icon or image, and enabling or disabling logging. Logging can serve as a tremendous source of evidence if it's enabled.

Normally, logging is turned off by default, requiring the user to activate that function. Logs typically record the chat conversations and/or other related information like connection details, etc. Even if logging is turned off, the user can manually save that particular chat session should they need to. A major difference between having logging turned on and manually saving a session log is the location where the resulting file is saved. Auto-saved logs will normally go to a default location, whereas a destination will need to be selected for a manually saved log.

Another preference setting of interest involves the automatic acceptance of video calls, file transfers, real-time instant messages, and so on. By default, many of these features are disabled. This setting and the subsequent functionality can be used to prove that an image wasn't downloaded without consent.

A suspect will have an uphill slog trying to get a jury to believe that they "had no idea" they were downloading child pornography through their chat client when the settings prove that they had to agree to accept it.

Some chat/IM clients are now allowing users to associate a cell phone (or more than one) with their account. This allows them to have IM messages forwarded to their mobile phone. In this situation, the cell number together with the account information could be used to help connect that person to a particular screen name.

Internet Relay Chat (IRC)

Commercial chat clients like Yahoo! and AOL are quite popular and in wide use. There are two other chat clients that are well worth exploring. These tools are arguably better suited for criminal activity. **Internet Relay Chat** or IRC is one such tool. IRC is a large chat network that has little to no oversight as it is under the control of no one single entity. It affords its user near total anonymity because there is no formal registration process. IRC is also free to use. The IRC network comprises many smaller networks such as Undernet, IRCnet, and EFnet, just to name a few (Casey, 2011). IRC users create their own chat rooms or "channels." IRC attracts criminals with a wide range of interests looking to trade information or contraband. Network intrusion, identity theft, and child pornography represent some of the main criminal interests found on IRC.

IRC boasts some other features that make it attractive for criminals. Direct Client Connection (DCC) allows two users to connect directly from one machine to the other. In this mode the communication is totally private. This private traffic even avoids network servers, leaving no evidence for investigators to find.

ICQ "I Seek You"

ICQ is the second chat tool that warrants a closer look. ICQ came on the scene in 1996.

These numbers from ICQ give you an idea of just how popular this chat client is:

- Over 42 million active users
- Over 425 million downloads
- Over 1.1 billion messages sent and received every day
- The average ICQ user is connected more than five hours per day
- 47% female and 53% male
- 80% of users between the ages of thirteen and twenty-nine
- Available in sixteen languages (ICQ)

Unlike IRC, ICQ does have a registration process. Users that register are assigned a User Identification Number or UIN. Communication on ICQ maintains a high level of privacy. One must be invited to be included into a conversation. ICQ does route traffic through centralized servers so some artifacts may exist there if that server can be found.

E-MAIL

Of all the potential sources of digital evidence, e-mail is one of the best. People often draft and send e-mail that they assume will never be read by anyone other than the intended recipient. As such, these often candid exchanges can (and have) come back to haunt the parties involved. It's also persistent, residing in multiple locations, thus making it harder to get rid of.

Accessing E-mail

E-mail is accessed and managed in one of two ways. The first is web-based e-mail such as Google's Gmail or Microsoft's Hotmail. These tools function through a web browser. The second is through an e-mail application (client). E-mail clients are specialized programs designed specifically for working with e-mail. Some applications also manage calendars, tasks, contacts, and more. Outlook and Windows Live Mail by Microsoft are two of the most popular e-mail clients on Windows systems. Outlook, the more robust of the two, is used primarily in the workplace or by power users. Windows Live Mail and its predecessor Outlook Express have much more limited functionality.

Outlook stores data in either a .pst or .ost file. Windows Live Mail stores individual messages as .eml files. Microsoft Outlook Express uses .dbx. Getting at the individual messages from inside these containers is a concern, but much less so now that several current tools handle these file types natively. Individual e-mail messages (.msg files) can be exported out and given to investigators or attorneys for review.

E-mail Protocols

E-mail uses multiple protocols to send and receive e-mail. Some of them are:

- **Simple Mail Transfer Protocol (SMTP)**—Used by e-mail clients to send e-mail and by servers to both send and receive.
- **Post Office Protocol (POP)**—Used by e-mail clients to receive e-mail messages.
- **Internet Message Access Protocol (IMAP)**—Two-way communication protocol used by clients to access e-mail on a server.

E-mail as Evidence

E-mail is widely used and people tend to be uninhibited in their messages, saying things they may never say otherwise. Thus, e-mail can provide us with a wealth of potential evidence. Some of those things include:

- Communications relevant to the case
- E-mail addresses
- IP Addresses
- Dates and times

When investigating e-mail, it's important to realize that it could be found in a number of places. These include: the suspect's machine, any recipient's machine, company server or backup media, smartphone, service provider, and any server that the message may have passed through on its way to its final destination. Like most web based evidence, time is still a factor. Collecting that evidence sooner rather than later will give you a better chance of success.

The main components of an e-mail are the header, the body, and potentially attachments. Every e-mail message that's sent has a **header**. The header records information as the e-mail travels from the sender to the receiver. Think of it as a passport of sorts. At every stop (server) along the way, information is added to the header. The **body** of the e-mail is the message itself. Finally, any attachments are added. These include things such as images and user-created files such as documents, spreadsheets, and so on. Keeping the attachments connected with an associated e-mail message is very important from an evidentiary perspective.

E-mail—Covering the Trail

Especially savvy suspects may take steps to prevent someone from tracing the message back to them. For example, they could forge an e-mail (make it appear to be from someone else) or remove or modify the headers. Suspects could also create a phony e-mail account.

There is free software available on the Internet that enables users to "spoof" an e-mail. **Spoofing** is the act of making an e-mail look as though it actually came from someone else or from a different location. There are services available that will remail (forward) messages, stripping out the identifying information prior to transmission. This is known as anonymous remailing. Many of these companies don't keep logs, further ensuring the privacy of their users.

ALERT!

Shared E-mail Accounts

E-mail can be used to communicate even without being sent. This is done by creating an anonymous account, Yahoo! for example, and sharing the login information. Users then simply create messages and deposit them in the "Drafts" folder for others to read. Once the message is read it can be deleted. These accounts can be for one-time use, making it nearly impossible to trace or monitor. This is a popular practice among terrorists. "One-time anonymous accounts are extremely difficult to monitor," said Richard Clarke, former U.S. counterterrorism czar.

http://www.pbs.org/wgbh/pages/frontline/shows/front/special/techsidebar.html

---

Tracing E-mail

Tracing an e-mail message is heavily reliant on logs. As we learned earlier, each server along the e-mail's path adds information to the message's header.

One of those bits of information is the **Message ID**. The message ID is a unique number assigned to the message by the e-mail server. Correlating the message ID with the server's logs is solid evidence that the message was received and sent by that particular machine. Again, the providers may purge those logs on a regular basis if they even keep them at all. Foreign providers will likely be very tough to deal with, making collection of this evidence that much harder.

Reading E-mail Headers

The e-mail header provides a record of the path the message took from sender to receiver (assuming steps weren't taken to alter or remove it). E-mail headers should be read from the bottom to the top. Below is a sample e-mail header from a message I may have sent to legendary Steeler linebacker Jack Lambert.

```
Delivered-To: Lambert58@gmail.com

Received: by 11.48.31.1 with SMTP1 id c2ct279nzg; Fri, 25 Oct 2011
22:38:23 -0800 (PST)
Return-Path:

Received: from mail.emailprovider.com (mail.myisp.com [12.34.567.890]) by
mx.gmail.com with SMTP id f27se846431anc.2011.10.25.22.38.19; Fri, 25 Oct
2011 22:38:23 -0800 (PST)

Message-ID: <20111025233819.47097.mail@mail.myisp.com>

Received: from [12.34.567.890] by mail.myisp.com via HTTP; Fri, 25 Oct 2011
22:38:19 PST

Date: Fri, 25 Oct 2011 22:38:19 -0800 (PST)
From: John Sammons
Subject: Super Bowl
To: Jack Lambert

Delivered-To: Lambert58@gmail.com
```

The message recipient
```
Message-ID: <20111025233819.47097.mail@mail.myisp.com>

Received: from [12.34.567.890] by mail.myisp.com via HTTP; Fri, 25 Oct 2011
22:38:19 PST
```

This the record of the message being sent through Jack Lambert's email provider,
mail.myisp.com.
```
Delivered-To: Lambert58@gmail.com

Received: by 11.48.31.1 with SMTP1 id c2ct279nzg; Fri, 25 Oct 2011 22:38:23
-0800 (PST)
Return-Path:

Received: from mail.emailprovider.com (mail.myisp.com [12.34.567.890]) by
mx.gmail.com with SMTP id f27se846431anc.2011.10.25.22.38.19; Fri, 25 Oct
2011 22:38:23 -0800 (PST)
```

```
Finally,the message is transmitted from my email provider to Jack's Gmail
account, Lambert58@Gmail.com
```

Note the message ID, 20111025233819.47097.mail@mail.myisp.com. Remember, this is a unique number assigned by an e-mail server (Google, 2011).

SOCIAL NETWORKING SITES

E-mail and social media have at least one thing in common. There seems to be almost nothing that people won't send, post, or tweet. The fact that everyone seems to be on Facebook, Twitter, or some flavor of social media is not lost on law enforcement or prospective employers for that matter. Both groups routinely look to social media to learn more about suspects and prospective employees.

Social media evidence can be found in several places including the suspect's computer, smartphone, and the provider's network. Getting evidence from the provider will require relatively quick action along with a subpoena or search warrant. Remember, the provider only retains this information for a certain amount of time. At some point, the data you need will be purged without some legal intervention. All things considered, collecting the evidence from the provider might yield the best results.

Recovering evidence on the local machine can be a challenge. The page file (or swap space) is one location that could bear fruit. INDEX.DAT files also hold promise. Multiple artifacts can be found here. The confirmation e-mail (sent when the account is created) is found in the History.IE5\Index.dat file. The user's Facebook profile can be found on the local machine in a file named profile[#].htm. This is located in the Content.IE5 directories. The History.IE Index.dat file can hold Facebook friend searches.

ADDITIONAL RESOURCES

Casey Anthony Trial Testimony

The Casey Anthony trial garnered media attention across the country. Anthony was charged with murdering her young daughter Caylee. Digital forensics played a central role in the case, particularly regarding the searches for certain keywords such as "chloroform." The trial testimony in this case by computer forensic examiner Sgt. Kevin Stenger provides some insight expert testimony on browser forensics (Firefox in this instance).

http://www.myfoxorlando.com/dpp/news/060811-kevin-stenger-testifies

---

SUMMARY

The Internet functions in large part due to two protocols, specifically HTTP and TCP/IP. Another very common technology in wide use is HTML or Hyper-text Markup Language. HTML is one of the primary languages used to construct web pages. In digital forensics, evidence can be found within this code so it behooves us as examiners to be able navigate through it to locate any existing evidence.

We also looked at how web pages are found and sent to browsers using Uniform Resource Locators (URLs) and Domain Name Servers (DNS).

Peer-to-Peer (P2P) networks can be used to share not only pirated music and movies, but contraband such as child pornography as well.

Chapter 8 also looked at several artifacts generated from Internet and e-mail usage. This includes such things as INDEX.DAT records, Temporary Internet Files (TIF), the NTUSER.DAT file, cookies, and e-mail headers. Tracing an e-mail back to its origin is no easy feat as the identifying information can be forged or removed.

Chat clients and their associated logs are worth examining if found on a computer. Remember, logging may not be turned on by default.

IRC and ICQ are two modes of Internet communication that can't be ignored. These are two of the most popular ways for criminals (and others concerned with private communication) to help cover their trail.

Social networking is used worldwide today by a massive number of people. Social networking evidence can be found locally and remotely on the provider's network.

References

Casey, E. (2009). *Handbook of Digital Forensics and Investigation.* Burlington, MA: Academic Press.

Casey, E. (2011). *Digital Evidence and Computer Crime: Forensic Science, Computers and the Internet.* Waltham, MA: Academic Press.

E.I. du Pont de Nemours and Company v. Kolon Industries, Inc., 2011 U.S. Dist. LEXIS 45888 (E.D. Va. April 27, 2011).

Google. (2011, September 21). *Reading Full Email Headers.* Retrieved October 24, 2011, from: http://mail.google.com/support/bin/answer.py?hl=en&answer=29436

Network Solutions, LLC. (n.d.). *WHOIS Behind That Domain Name?* Retrieved October 13, 2011, from: http://www.networksolutions.com/whois/index.jsp

Refsnes Data. (n.d.). *HTML Introduction.* Retrieved October 13, 2011, from: http://www.w3schools.com/html/html_intro.asp

CHAPTER 9

Network Forensics

Information in This Chapter:

- Networking Fundamentals
- Types of Networks
- Network Security Tools
- Network Attacks
- Incident Response
- Network Evidence & Investigations

INTRODUCTION

It seems like hardly a day goes by that a major company or government entity isn't reporting a significant network intrusion of some kind. Take Fidelity National Information Services Inc. (FIS), for example. The Jacksonville processor of prepaid credit cards reported that an international criminal enterprise stole $13 million in a single day during 2011. They disclosed the theft in their first-quarter earnings statement released on May 3, 2011. The hackers executed a highly planned and well-coordinated operation involving ATMs from around the world along with stolen prepaid credit cards (Krebs). FIS is just one of many victims of crimes like this.

What began as a subculture motivated simply by overcoming the challenge hacking presented has now evolved into a much more sinister and significant threat, so much so that it's now a critical matter of national security. So much of the nation's critical infrastructure is reliant upon digital networks and devices. There is certainly no shortage of high-profile targets. These include governmental agencies, the power grid, and the financial and health care industries. This threat now comprises nation-states, organized criminal enterprises, terrorists, as well as individuals.

The private sector bears a significant portion of the responsibility in defending these networks. So, how does digital forensics figure into all this? Digital forensics can play a couple of roles:

Network investigations have some inherent hurdles that don't come into play in an investigation focusing on a stand-alone computer. Unlike a single machine, data (evidence) could be spread across multiple machines or devices. To further complicate things, they could also be spread across a geographically expansive area. The sheer amount of data that could be involved presents another challenge. Depending on the size of the organization and its network, the volume of data could reach truly astronomical proportions.

Hackers have many attack options at their disposal when it comes to attacking a network. The attacks can be quite sophisticated or astoundingly simple. Some attacks rely on vulnerabilities in the technology; others rely on the weaknesses found in people. Software is one example of a weakness in the technology. Flaws in the software are found in the underlying code. These flaws are identified by software developers, security professionals, or others. Hackers then develop exploits to take advantage of the vulnerability. Hopefully, the software developer will take notice and fix the issue sooner rather than later. These normally come in the form of a "patch." This is a constant struggle that never seems to end.

Human weakness also contributes to a hacker's success in a number of ways. First, people are inclined to use weak passwords. They tend to be either too short or too predictable. For example, they use the names of their pets or children or they use actual words that can be found in the dictionary. Finally, even if the password was strong, they could leave the password written down very near the computer. Second, unsuspecting users can fall prey to a **social engineering** attack.

Social Engineering

In a social engineering attack, an authorized user is persuaded by an unauthorized individual into divulging sensitive information. Common attacks include hackers posing as employees, customers, or security consultants.

These various attacks can also be conducted in combination, leveraging the vulnerabilities of both the technology and the people who control it.

NETWORK FUNDAMENTALS

Networking or linking computers together has some distinct advantages. Sharing resources and collaboration are just two such benefits.

A network has some basic necessities that are required regardless of its size or purpose. The first is some type of connection between computers or devices. This connection can be a physical one (such as via an Ethernet cable) or wireless. Next, the network must have an established way to communicate. This common language, or set of rules, is known as a protocol. **Transmission Control Protocol/Internet Protocol (TCP/IP)** is a very commonly used network protocol and is also the one used on the Internet.

To lay the foundation, we'll start by defining and identifying the various types of networks in common use today. By far, the most common type of network encountered in a commercial setting is client/server. In a **client/server network**, each computer on the network is assigned one of these two roles. Clients are utilized by end-users, such as the workstation on your desk. These machines request files, services, and information from servers. Servers, by contrast, store and provide files, services, and information to multiple clients. In essence, you can have one server sharing files with hundreds of clients. They have much more control on the network. Servers tend to function in specific role(s). File servers, e-mail servers, and print servers are but a few examples.

The other network configuration commonly in use is known as **peer-to-peer (P2P)**. As the name suggests, all machines on the network can/do function as both clients and servers. P2P networks are seldom used in a commercial setting. File sharing is the predominant use of P2P networks. Music, movies, and software are some of the more commonly shared files. Unfortunately, P2P is also a major conduit for not only pirated music, video, and software, but child pornography as well. This is a major problem not only in the United States but worldwide as well.

Now that we have a basic understanding of how networks are organized, let's take a look at how these networks can be classified.

Network Types

The **Local Area Network** or LAN is generally considered the smallest office network. It comprises computers and devices in a single office or building. The **Wide Area Network (WAN)** is larger, sometimes significantly so. A WAN consists or LANs at different locations. The WAN can be spread across great distances. Other network types include **MANs (Metropolitan Area Network)**, **PANs (Personal Area Networks)**, **CANs (Campus Area Networks)**, and **GANs (Global Area Networks)**.

In contrast to the Internet is an intranet. A company's intranet is private, and access to it is limited. Intranets are routinely used for file sharing, communication, and so on. An intranet functions like the Internet, using web browsers and typically the same protocol (TCP/IP).

On a network that uses the TCP/IP protocol, each computer or device on the network has a unique identifier or address known as an **IP address**. An IP address is used to deliver messages and data to its proper destination, functioning much like a street address. There are two versions of IP addressing we need to be concerned with: version 4 and version 6. IPv4 is being phased out because of the relatively small number of addresses when compared to the staggering numbers of devices and computers on the Internet. We're simply running out of addresses. IPv4 offers in the neighborhood of about four billion different IP addresses. It is being replaced by IPv6. IPv6, by contrast, provides for all intents and purposes a limitless number of addresses (Microsoft Corporation).

An IPv4 address is made up of four numbers that are separated by periods. Each of these four numbers, called octets, can range from 0 to 255. A typical IPv4 address would look like this: 198.122.55.16. An IPv6 address would look like this:

2008:0eb3:29a2:0000:0000:8c1d:0967:7256.

As a comparison, if you wrote an IPv6 address using IPv4 notation, it would look like this:

65535.65535.65535.65535.65535.65535.65535.65535 (Nikkel, 2007)

IP addresses can be static or dynamic. A static address is normally fixed and doesn't change. In contrast, a dynamic address changes on a regular basis. For example, certain Internet Service Providers (ISPs) use dynamic IP addressing. Here, each time you log on, the network assigns you an IP address from a pool of addresses that are currently unassigned. This enables a provider to service a large number of customers within the fixed number of IP addresses that they control. This works because not all of their subscribers will be online at any given time.

Data on a network can travel in different ways. **Packet switching** is used on the Internet and many other networks. Packet switching breaks the data into small chunks called packets. These packets then travel the network to their final destination using IP addressing.

Each packet is structured in a uniform manner. Individual packets are comprised of three parts; the header, payload, and footer. The header contains the addressing information, identifying the sender and receiver's IP address. Next, the packet identifies itself relative to the total number of packets. Something like "I'm packet 26 out 234." Then comes the payload itself. Finally, the packet is concluded with a footer or trailer. The trailer tells the receiver that this is the end of the packet. It also conducts a cyclical redundancy check (CRC). The CRC is a sum of all the ones in the packet. If the numbers don't match, the receiving computer will automatically resend the request. It's is used to verify the integrity of the packet. Figure 9.1 depicts the organization of a TCP/IP packet.

Networks routinely consist of hardware beyond just computers and servers. These devices are also important from an investigative perspective in that they can contain valuable evidence.

The TCP/IP packet: A simplified look

Addressing	Sequence number	Data	Checksum/Hash
Destination IP: Source IP:	13 of 66	1101011011011011001101011101110110110110110110111011110 1011010111011110111101001110101110110111111010111111011 1101111010101111010111111011111010101010101101111111011	821f0328884629 7c2cf43c34766a

FIGURE 9.1
A typical IP packet. Illustration courtesy of Jonathan Sisson.

A gateway is a network point that acts as an entrance to another network (Tech-Target, 2000). A bridge, by contrast, is used to connect two networks using the same protocol. Routers direct data, using the IP address, on the network to their final destination.

NETWORK SECURITY TOOLS

Regarding security, the best (and most realistic) approach is to prepare in terms of "when" there is an intrusion as opposed to "if" there is an intrusion. Working on the assumption that you will be able to keep each and every committed hacker out is just not realistic. Does that mean organizations should only take minimal measures to protect their networks, focusing more resources on response rather than prevention? Absolutely not. A robust perimeter defense should always be employed, the scope of which is normally dictated by the available budget and personnel needed to run it.

Fortunately, there are many hardware and software tools available that can help protect our networks. These tools not only serve to prevent a successful attack, they can also contain information of investigative value. Let's examine a couple of these tools.

A **firewall** is "a set of related programs, located at a network gateway server, that protects the resources of a private network from users from other networks" (TechTarget, 2000). The firewall acts as a filter for both inbound and outbound network traffic. It decides whether or not to allow the traffic to pass after carefully examining the network packets.

The purpose of an **Intrusion Detection System (IDS)** is to detect attacks from both outside and inside an organization. The IDS typically monitors a network looking for a pattern of recognized network attacks as well as unusual system and user actions and activity (TechTarget, 2000). Snort is a well-known open-source network intrusion detection system **(NIDS)**. Snort operates as a **sniffer**, watching the network in real time and firing off alerts should a potential problem be identified (TechTarget, 2002).

NETWORK ATTACKS

There are many different ways to hack and/or attack a network. These attacks change at something akin to "warp" speed, resulting in a constant strain on the security industry. Below are just some of the attacks in use today.

Distributed Denial of Service (DDoS)—This attack uses massive numbers of compromised computers to attack a lone system. The attacking computers overwhelm the target with huge numbers of messages and requests. The target simply can't deal with this large volume of inbound traffic and eventually buckles, shutting down. The "army" of attacking computers are known as a "botnet," comprising individual compromised systems called "zombies."

Identity Spoofing (IP Spoofing)—An attacker can forge or "spoof" a valid or "known" IP addresses to gain access to a targeted network.

Man-In-The-Middle-Attack—In this attack, the hacker inserts himself between you and the person or entity you are communicating with. Your communications can then be monitored, altered, or deleted. This can also enable the attacker to impersonate you.

Social Engineering—Social engineering is one of the most effective attacks at the hacker's disposal. Social engineering is often described as obtaining protected information by way of a "trick" or a "con." TechTarget defines social engineering this way: "a term that describes a non-technical kind of intrusion that relies heavily on human interaction and often involves tricking other people to break normal security procedures" (TechTarget, 2001). Legendary hacker Kevin Mitnick made wide use of this technique with tremendous success (Mitnick, 2011).

Here is just one of many such examples of Mitnick's success: Mitnick calls up the network operations center of a cell phone company during a snowstorm. After befriending one of the operators, he asks them: "I left my SecureID card on my desk. Will you fetch it for me?" Of course, the network operators are too busy to do that, so they do the next best thing: They read it to him over the phone, giving him access to their network. Once inside, Mitnick steals source code belonging to the company. In this instance, Mitnick was able to "prove" his identity by telling the network operators his office number, the department where he worked, and the name of his supervisor—all information that the attacker had gleaned from previous phone calls to the company (Garfinkel, 2002).

In 2011, Verizon Business, the United States Secret Service (USSS), and the Dutch National High Tech Crime Unit (NHTCU) issued an interesting joint report after analyzing some eight hundred security incidents. These incidents were investigated by one or more of these organizations. As part of their report, they identified the most common hacking methods used in these incidents. These include:

- Exploitation of backdoor or command/control channel.
- Exploitation of default or guessable credentials.
- Brute force and dictionary attacks.
- Footprinting and fingerprinting.
- Use of stolen login credentials.

Some, like exploiting default passwords or the use of stolen credentials, are pretty self-explanatory. Others, like the command/control channel exploit and footprinting bear a little further explanation. Exploiting a command and control channel or backdoor allows an attacker to avoid security countermeasures. This enables the attacker to avoid detection. **Footprinting** or **fingerprinting** is an automated process by an attacker to scan for open ports or services (Verizon Business Global LLC & United States Secret Sevice, 2011).

Network security must focus on threats not only outside the firewall, but behind it as well. Internal attacks, such as those launched by disgruntled employees, can be devastating. Lets take a look at two such attacks.

> **ALERT!**
>
> **Inside Threat**
> It's important to recognize the fact that threats come from not only outside of an organization, but inside as well. Preventative measures must account for both possibilities. An inside threat has a significant advantage in that it can bypass much of the security measures that are in place.

An application developer, who lost his IT sector job as a result of company downsizing, expressed his displeasure at being laid off just prior to the Christmas holidays by launching a systematic attack on his former employer's computer network. Three weeks following his termination, the insider used the username and password of one of his former coworkers to gain remote access to the network and modify several of the company's Web pages, changing text and inserting pornographic images. He also sent each of the company's customers an e-mail message advising that the web site had been hacked. Each e-mail message also contained that customer's usernames and passwords for the web site. An investigation was initiated, but it failed to identify the insider as the perpetrator. A month and a half later, he again remotely accessed the network, executed a script to reset all network passwords, and changed four thousand pricing records to reflect bogus information. This former employee ultimately was identified as the perpetrator and prosecuted. He was sentenced to serve five months in prison and two years on supervised probation, and ordered to pay $48,600 restitution to his former employer (Keeney, Cappelli, Kowalski, Moore, Shimeall, & Rogers, 2005).

A system administrator, angered by his diminished role in a thriving defense manufacturing firm whose computer network he alone had developed and managed, centralized the software that supported the company's manufacturing processes on a single server, and then intimidated a coworker into giving him the only backup tapes for that software. Following the system administrator's termination for inappropriate and abusive treatment of his coworkers, a logic bomb previously planted by the insider detonated, deleting the only remaining copy of the critical software from the company's server (Keeney, Cappelli, Kowalski, Moore, Shimeall, & Rogers, 2005). The company estimated the cost of damage in excess of $10 million, which led to the layoff of some eighty employees (Keeney, Cappelli, Kowalski, Moore, Shimeall, & Rogers, 2005).

INCIDENT RESPONSE

Organizations have to be able to respond when the breach occurs. Having a plan along with the tools and personnel to effectively respond can go a long way in mitigating the damage.

The National Institute of Standards and Technology (NIST) outlined the incident response life cycle in their *Computer Security Incident Handling Guide*. We can use this to walk us through an incident from beginning to end. The phases are: preparation, prevention, detection and analysis containment, eradication and recovery, and postincident activity (Scarphone, Grance, & Masone, 2008).

Preparation—Preparation is key for organizations to respond quickly and effectively to any network security event. There are many steps an entity can take during the preparation phase. Planning is obviously one such step. A network's defenses should also be assessed and tested at regular intervals in order to identify vulnerabilities.

Proactive measures must be taken to prevent intrusions. Some of the preventative actions that can be taken include patching systems (keeping software up-to-date), host security (hardening individual computers), network security (securing the perimeter of the network), and conducting user awareness and training. Finally, having well-thought-out policies, procedures, and guidelines adds significantly to an organization's preparedness.

Detection and Analysis—Detecting a security incident presents a significant challenge. Today's sophisticated attacks can mask themselves as "normal" network activity. Vigilance and a painstaking attention to detail are needed by network security personnel in order to improve their odds of catching an attack. It also helps them reach a proper conclusion after conducting their analysis. It's a well-known fact that Intrusion Detection Systems produce large numbers of false positives. As such, the security team must be capable of accurately sifting through data. What does an attack look like? That can be a little tough to describe. To better identify suspicious activity, it's best to get an accurate picture of what is "normal" network traffic or activity is for the organization. Some of the potential signs of an attack include antivirus software alerts, abnormally slow Internet connectivity, and abnormalities in network traffic.

Containment, Eradication, and Recovery—When a breach occurs, it must be controlled in order to minimize its impact. Left unchecked, the fallout from an attack could grow exponentially. How to contain the incident varies based on the type of incident being faced. Some containment options include shutting down the compromised system, disconnecting it from the network, or disabling some functionality. Once the attack has been identified and contained, steps could be required to remove any potentially dangerous components such as malicious code or compromised accounts.

Postincident Activity—Unfortunately, this valuable step is often overlooked. A postincident review represents a missed opportunity for the organization as a whole and its personnel to improve. A typical postincident review seeks to answer questions such as:

- What did we get right?
- What did we get wrong?
- Are our policies and procedures adequate and effective?
- Do we have the necessary resources to effectively respond?
- What, if anything, would we do differently?

Responding to a security breach effectively requires diverse skill sets. As part of an incident response plan, an organization should form a computer Incident Response Team. This multidisciplinary team should bring all of the skills necessary to manage the incident to the table. Some of the skills needed to respond include representatives from management, information security, IT support, legal, public affairs/media relations, and others (Scarphone, Grance, & Masone, 2008). Someone with digital forensics capabilities should be part of the team. Many times digital forensics resources do not exist within the company itself. In these instances this function would have to be outsourced. If this is indeed the situation, this resource should be identified well in advance of an actual incident.

NETWORK EVIDENCE AND INVESTIGATIONS

A hacker's attack typically follows a path both to and through the targeted network. As such, the potential exists to locate evidence all along the route. "Tracking" the intruder, therefore, is a critical step in the process of finding and identifying them. It is to our advantage to identify, follow, and examine as much of this trail as we can.

Our examination should include as many of the in-between or intermediary devices as possible. These intermediary devices, such as routers and servers, can hold valuable information and shouldn't be overlooked. Routers can be both an evidentiary source as well as a target for hackers. As a critical part of a network, they often serve as a valuable goal for hackers. If they can compromise a router, they can gain a significant foothold. A challenge with routers as a source of evidence is their volatility. You may recall from Chapter 2 that volatile memory requires constant electrical power to maintain its contents. Unplugging or rebooting the device will likely result in a loss of potential evidence. This will in all likelihood require a "live" examination of the device while it's running. The best advice is to handle with care and treat it as you would any other piece of volatile memory.

Digital evidence is digital evidence, regardless of its source. The fundamental principles and procedures of preservation and collection still apply.

LOG FILES

Many devices and computers in a network generate logs of events and activities. As such, log files serve as a primary source of evidence in network investigations. There are several different types of log files. Some of the logs of interest include authentication, application, operating system, and the firewall log. An **authentication log** identifies the account (and IP address) connected to a particular event.

Application logs record the date and time as well as the application identifier. The date/time stamps indicate when the application was started and how long it was used. **Operating system** logs track system reboots as well as the use of different devices. The operating system logs are useful in recognizing patterns of activity as well as anomalies (unusual occurrences) in the network.

Device logs such as those generated by routers and firewalls are also worth examining. We'll look at router logs more in just a second (Vacca & Rudolph, 2011).

There are some things to keep in mind with log files. Log files can change or disappear pretty rapidly. They can be purged at regular intervals to help keep storage space free. There's also a good chance that not all of the relevant logs will be in your possession. Attacks that originate outside of your organization will pass through devices under the control of a third party, such as an Internet Service Provider (ISP). These logs may have to be subpoenaed, which can take some time. ISPs won't likely hang onto these logs forever. They likely have document retention and destruction policies in place controlling what gets kept and for how long. Lacking a clear need or reason to keep it, those logs will be destroyed.

The router logs can contain much information of interest. Some of the things we can uncover are:

Requested Uniform Resource Locators (URLs)
Server Name
Server IP Address
Client's URL
Client IP Address
Who logged in and when

When attempting to collect evidence from a router, it's very important to minimize any interaction. Instead of accessing the router through the network itself, it's a better option to go through the router's console. Remember, our objective is to observe and record what we find, not to alter or change anything. To that end, we should avoid any command that could potentially modify any of the data. A configuration command, for example, is one that should be avoided. The "show" command is a much better option. Here are a couple of examples of "show" commands:

>(router name)#show clock detail—Displays the system time
>(router name)#show users—Displays the users that have access to the router

NETWORK INVESTIGATIVE TOOLS

The actual traffic (packets) moving on the network can hold some valuable clues. There are several tools, called "sniffers," available that can capture and analyze network traffic. Some of these tools include:

Wireshark (www.wireshark.org)
NetIntercept (http://www.niksun.com/product.php?id=16)
Netwitness Investigator (http://www.netwitness.com/products-services/investigator)
Snort (http://www.snort.org/)

Capturing network traffic can yield some great clues. For instance, we can determine what files have been stolen, what commands were executed, as well as any malicious payload that was delivered. From a legal perspective, it's important to realize that monitoring network traffic in certain instances can be considered wiretapping (Casey, 2009).

Network Investigation Challenges

Identifying the responsible hacker is by no stretch a simple task. There are many impediments along the way that can keep the attacker's identity hidden. The suspect can "spoof" his or her real IP address, potentially sending investigators on a wild goose chase. Along the same lines, the hacker can channel his or her attack through many intermediate servers scattered across the globe.

Logs can be a great source of evidence, but only if they are actually there for us to examine. Sometimes the logging function is disabled to start with, meaning that no logs were even generated. Time presents another concern. If the breach is discovered too late, then there is a significant chance that any logs maintained by an outside entity (an ISP, for example) will be destroyed pursuant to their retention and destruction policy. Hackers can also intentionally delete relevant logs during their attack, effectively covering their tracks. Lastly, jurisdiction can create a substantial obstacle. The attacker's trail can literally traverse state, national, and international boundaries. Different legal jurisdictions, especially international ones, can have wildly different requirements for obtaining this sort of information. Different countries may also have very different views of cybercrime in general, which can result in a lack of cooperation (Morris, 2005).

ADDITIONAL RESOURCES

Training and Research

Training and research are a must in the world of digital forensics. Established in 1989, the SANS Institute is one of the leading institutions meeting this critical need. They offer a wide array of courses and resources covering both information security and digital forensics. In addition, they offer many certifications that are accepted throughout the industry. They also have a strong presence on Twitter.

http://www.sans.org/
http://computer-forensics.sans.org/blog
@SANSInstitute
@sansforensics

SUMMARY

Network security should be a huge concern to all of us. Our networks and PCs are under near constant attack from lone hackers, organized criminals, and foreign countries. Cybercrime, cyberwar, and cyberterrorism are major problems threatening not only our countries and companies, but our personal computers as well. Networks represent a far greater challenge, from a forensic standpoint.

They vary wildly in size and complexity. There are several tools to help us protect our critical network infrastructure, including firewalls and intrusion detection systems. Smart organizations plan ahead for security breaches, enabling them to respond efficiently and effectively, minimizing the damage and increasing the odds that they can identify the perpetrator(s).

References

Bowden, M. (2011). *Worm: The First Digital World War*. New York: Atlantic Monthly Press.

Casey, E. (2009). *Handbook of Digital Forensics and Investigation*. Burlington, MA: Academic Press.

Casey, E. (2011). *Digital Evidence and Computer Crime: Forensic Science, Computers and the Internet*. Waltham, MA: Academic Press.

Conrad, E., Misenar, S., & Feldman, J. (2010). *CISSP Study Guide*. Burlington, MA: Elsevier.

Garfinkel, S. (2002, October 7). *Kevin Mitnick and Anti-Social Engineering*. Retrieved November 9, 2011, from CSOOnline.com: http://www.csoonline.com/article/217395/kevin-mitnick-and-anti-social-engineering-

Hadnagy, C. (2011). *Social Engineering: The Art of Human Hacking*. Indianapolis: Wiley.

Krebs, B. (n.d.). *Coordinated ATM Heist Nets Thieves $13M*. Retrieved September 19, 2011, from: http://krebsonsecurity.com/2011/08/coordinated-atm-heist-nets-thieves-13m/

Keeney, M., Kowalski, E., Cappelli, D., Moore, A., Shimeall, T., and Rogers, S. (2005, May). *Insider threat study: Computer sabotage in critical infrastructure sectors. United States Secret Service and CERT program*. Report available at http://www.secretservice.gov

Maggiora, P. D., & Doherty, J. (2003). *Cisco Networking Simplified*. Indianapolis: Cisco Press.

McClure, S., Scambray, J., & Kurtz, G. (2009). *Hacking Exposed: Network Security Secrets and Solutions*. New York: McGraw-Hill.

Microsoft Corporation. (n.d.). *IPv6*. Retrieved September 17, 2011, from: http://technet.microsoft.com/en-us/network/bb530961.aspx

Mitnick, K. (2011). *Ghost in the Wires: My Adventures as the World's Most Wanted Hacker*. New York: Little, Brown and Company.

Morris, D. A. (2005, May 3). *Tracking a Computer Hacker*. Retrieved September 19, 2011, from: http://www.justice.gov/criminal/cybercrime/usamay2001_2.htm

Nikkel, B. J. (2007). *An Introduction to Investigating IPv6 Networks*. Digital Investigation: The International Journal of Digital Forensics and Incident Response Vol. 4, No. 2. Oxford, England: Elsevier.

Poulsen, K. (2011). *Kingpin: How One Hacker Took Over the Billion-Dollar Cybercrime Underground*. New York: Crown.

Prowell, S., Kraus, R., & Borkin, M. (2010). *Seven Deadliest Network Attacks*. Burlington, MA: Syngress.

Scarphone, K., Grance, T., & Masone, K. (2008). *Computer Security Incident Handling Guide*. National Institute of Standards and Technology, Computer Security Division. Gaithersburg, TN: National Institute of Standards & Technology.

TechTarget. (2000, August). *Intrusion Detection (ID)*. Retrieved September 17, 2011, from: http://searchmidmarketsecurity.techtarget.com/definition/intrusion-detection

TechTarget. (2000, October). *Firewall*. Retrieved September 17, 2011, from: http://searchsecurity.techtarget.com/definition/firewall

TechTarget. (2001, March). *Social Engineering*. Retrieved September 18, 2011, from: http://searchsecurity.techtarget.com/definition/social-engineering

TechTarget. (2002, January). *Snort.* Retrieved September 17, 2011, from: http://searchmidmarket security.techtarget.com/definition/Snort

Vacca, J. R., & Rudolph, K. (2011). *System Forensics, Investigation, and Response.* Sudbury, MA: Jones and Bartlett Learning.

Verizon Business Global LLC, & United States Secret Sevice. (2011). *2011 Data Breach Investigations Report.* Ashburn New York: Verizon Business Global LLC.

CHAPTER 10

Mobile Device Forensics

Information in This Chapter:

- Cellular Networks and How They Work
- Overview of Cell Phone Operating Systems
- Potential Evidence Found on Cell Phones
- Collecting and Handling Cell Phones as Evidence
- Cell Phone Forensic Tools
- Global Positioning System Function and Potential Evidence

INTRODUCTION

The phones riding on our hips and sitting in our pockets are true marvels of technology. These "mini-computers" are capable of delivering much of the same functionality that was once the lone province of desktops and laptops. We can browse the Internet, send and receive e-mail, shoot pictures and videos, and plot our location on a map, just to name a few of the possibilities.

Cell phones and other mobile devices can make a case airtight. Just ask Boise, Idaho's Dan Kincaid. When the Boise police arrested Kincaid for burglary, they also seized and searched his Blackberry cell phone. It paid off. His e-mail contained several messages that would eventually help convince him to plead guilty. After being spotted, Kincaid e-mailed his girlfriend saying "Just trying to find a way out of this neighborhood without getting caught." "Dogs bark if I'm between or behind houses ..." He went on to write, "Cops know I have a blue shirt on. ... I need to get out of here before they find me" (Shachtman, 2006).

At their core, today's smart phones are fundamentally computers with radios attached to them. There is an ever-evolving world of cell phone hardware with no slowdown in sight. Like their larger cousins, these small-scale devices can create artifacts that can be recovered and used as evidence.

Cellular phones and other mobile devices present yet another challenge for examiners. Walk into any cell phone store and you'll be confronted with a vast array of cell phone makes, models, and operating systems. The various devices in turn support many different services and applications. To further complicate things, there is not an established hardware interface. You've likely run across this issue one time or another when you upgraded your phone. Odds are when you got a new phone you had to get a new charger and data cables as well. Keeping pace with the cabling, operating systems, and so on is quite a challenge. The good news is that this seems to be getting better, with many phones now including a mini-USB in their handsets.

CELLULAR NETWORKS

Evidence can be located not just in the phone or memory card, but on the network itself. As examiners we need to understand the basic operation of cellular networks and the location(s) of any potential evidence.

As the name implies, each cellular network comprises individual cells. Each cell uses a predetermined range of frequencies to provide service to a distinct geographic area. The size and shape of each cell vary. In fact, they can vary wildly. They can cover a few city blocks in an urban environment to over a couple of hundred square miles in the country. The type of terrain, particularly obstructions, is the limiting factor; see Figure 10.1.

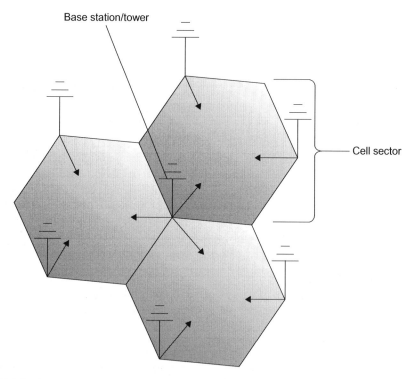

FIGURE 10.1
The layout of a typical cellular network. (Illustration by Jonathan Sisson.)

The strength of the radio signal emitted from each cell is closely controlled. This is done purposefully to limit its range. By limiting the range, providers can reuse the relatively limited number of frequencies they have to work with.

Each cell has a base station that consists of an antenna (or mast) along with the related radio equipment. Together, they are known as a **cell site**. These cell sites deliver coverage to the individual cells. You've probably seen these large towers along the interstate for example or smaller ones on rooftops in more urban locations. Normally, each cell tower will have three panels per side. The middle panel is usually the transmitter, with the other two being receivers. The receiver panels constantly listen for incoming radio signals.

It may surprise you to know that the cell sites are not located in the center of each cell. They are actually located at the junction of multiple cells, facilitating service as subscribers move from cell to cell.

Cellular Network Components

It takes quite a bit of infrastructure to get your phone call from that remote location back to your office downtown. Forensically speaking, each of these components could potentially provide information relevant to an investigation.

A **Base Station** consists of the antennas and related equipment.

A **Base Station Controller (BSC)** regulates the signals between base stations. This function is critical as phones move from place to place.

The **Mobile Switching Center (MSC)** processes calls within the network. As a key piece of the wireless network, the MSC holds a tremendous amount of possible evidence. It also coordinates calls between different wireless networks as well as land lines. The MSC handles SMS messages as well. The call detail records and logs are found here.

The **Visitor Location Register (VLR)** is a database that is linked to a MSC. All mobile devices currently being controlled by that MSC are recorded in the VLR. **Interworking Functions** serve as doorways outside data networks such as the Internet.

Information about individual subscribers is collected in the **Home Location Register (HLR)**. This information includes subscriber identification, billing, and the services they receive, along with the current location of the device. The HLR also stores encryption keys. The HLR supports the **Authentication Center (AuC)**, which is used to control access to the network. The AuC screens connections, blocking unauthorized users (Jansen & Ayers, 2007).

Text or SMS messages are the responsibility of the **Short Message Service Center (SMSC)**. Messages may be recovered from the SMSC, but there is no hard and fast rule dictating how long these messages must be kept by individual providers. It is up to the individual provider to determine how long that information is kept (Jansen & Ayers, 2007).

It's important to note that your cell phone is regularly communicating with the nearest cellular antennae, even if you're not talking on it. When you turn on your cell phone, it automatically begins searching for the nearest cell site. Once the antenna is found, the phone then transmits identification data so that the network can verify who you are and whether or not you have authorized access. This information would include things like the cell phone number along with the name of your service provider.

As you drive, your "connection" to the network must be transferred from cell tower to cell tower. This transfer is known as a **"handoff."** The handoff is made as the signal strength begins to fade. Not all handoffs are handled the same way. For instance, GSM (Global System for Mobile Communication) and Code Division Multiple Access (CDMA) for networks handle them differently. A **GSM** network uses what is known as a hard handoff. Here, the phone can only attach to one tower at a time. The conversation is separated from the current tower and passed to the new one. The phone will then switch to the new tower's frequency. In contrast, CDMA handoffs are considered "soft" handoffs. Here a phone can connect to multiple towers at once, utilizing the tower with the strongest signal.

Records showing when a certain phone is connected to a specific tower can be used to put someone (or more precisely their phone) in the vicinity of a crime or to establish an alibi.

Once your call hits the cell tower it's then transferred to the **Mobile Switching Center (MSC)**. If the call is destined for a phone that is out of the network, the MSC will pass the call to the **Public Switched Telephone Network (PSTN)**. The PSTN will then direct the call to its intended recipient.

We've all experienced dropped calls or a loss of signal at one time or another. One of the potential causes is dead spots. Dead spots can be caused by a gap in the cell coverage or obstructions to the signal. Cell phones are heavily dependent on having a clear and unobstructed (or very close to it) path to the cell tower. Obstructions can be tall buildings, mountains, and large trees.

Cell phones support two kinds of messaging services, **Short Message Service (SMS)** and **Multimedia Messaging Service (MMS)**. SMS are what we normally refer to as text messages. We get the name Short Message from the limitation of the maximum size of each message. SMS messages have a maximum length of 160 characters. MMS offers improved functionality over SMS. MMS messages aren't limited to 160 characters.

Types of Cellular Networks

Cellular networks can be differentiated or defined in how they transmit data. These transmission schemes include **Code Division Multiple Access (CDMA)**, **Global System for Mobile Communications (GSM)**, and **Integrated Digitally Enhanced Network (iDEN)**.

CODE DIVISION MULTIPLE ACCESS (CDMA)

CDMA was originally a military technology that was eventually released for use by the public. CDMA uses spread spectrum technology to transmit data. This technology permits several phones to send and receive through a single channel. Each part of these separate conversations is labeled with a specific digital code. The carriers that use CDMA technology include Sprint, Verizon, Alltel, and NEXTEL. CDMA phones typically do not utilize SIM cards. CDMA networks use an **Electronic Serial Number (ESN)** to identify individual handsets (Barbara, 2010).

GLOBAL SYSTEM FOR MOBILE COMMUNICATION (GSM)

As the name suggests, GSM phones can be used internationally. GSM uses **Time Division Multiple Access (TDMA)** technology. Worldwide, GSM is the most widely used transmission mode. Unlike CDMA, GSM phones use SIM cards. GSM carriers include AT&T, Verizon, T-Mobile, and Cellular One. The **International Mobile Equipment Identity (IMEI)** is used to identify handsets (Barbara, 2011).

INTEGRATED DIGITALLY ENHANCED NETWORK (IDEN)

iDEN, or Integrated Digitally Enhanced Network, provides two-way radio-like functionality, also known as "Push to Talk." Like GSM phones, they also utilize SIM cards. iDEN carriers include NEXTEL, Sprint, and Boostmobile.

PREPAID CELL PHONES

At their core, prepaid phones operate like other cell phones in that they use radios to transmit data and must connect to a network. The difference with prepaid phones is that they create some significant investigative hurdles, particularly when trying to identify the subscriber. For one, they can be paid for completely with cash, essentially leaving little to nothing in the way of a paper trail. This makes identifying the purchaser much harder.

Like other cell phones, however, we can identify the area where the phone is being used as well as the calls that are sent and received. With prepaid phones, the information we're looking for will be held by two entities. The phone provider will hold any subscriber information, and the network provider will maintain the call detail records.

OPERATING SYSTEMS

A phone's operating system (OS) has a significant impact on any forensic examination. The OS determines what artifacts are created and how they are stored. Modern cell phone operating systems include Symbian, Apple iOS, Windows CE and Windows Mobile, Google's Android, and Blackberry OS.

Originally, the Symbian OS was a product of a partnership between Nokia, Ericsson, Motorola, and Psion. Sony Ericsson rolled out the first Symbian-run phone in 2000. In 2008, Nokia bought the rights to the OS. Nokia recently made

Symbian open source. It's used today in Nokia and Sony Ericsson handsets (Barbara, 2010b).

Blackberrys were first introduced in 1999 by the Canadian company Research In Motion (RIM). Businesses and governmental entities are heavy Blackberry users. Blackberry phones synchronize with Novel's GroupWise and Microsoft's Exchange. As such, they are quite proficient in handling e-mail, calendars, and the like. The Blackberry OS supports multitasking as well as a variety of applications. This operating system is proprietary, and versions are specific to each carrier. That means that the Verizon version of a specific phone would be different than the AT&T edition (Barbara, 2010b).

Android is an open-source OS that is currently developed by Open Handset Alliance. In 2005, Google acquired the Android OS from Android, Inc. In 2007, the Open Handset Alliance was formed and has been developing the OS ever since. The Open Handset Alliance "is a group of 84 technology and mobile companies who have come together to accelerate innovation in mobile and offer consumers a richer, less expensive, and better mobile experience" (Open Handset Alliance, 2007). Some of the members include Sprint, T-Mobile, LG Electronics, Inc., Kyocera, Motorola, Google, and eBay. Thousands of third-party apps are available to augment Android's core functionality. Android is found on handsets produced by Motorola, Sony Ericsson, and HTC (Barbara, 2010b).

Apple's popular **iOS** can be found not only on the iPhone but also on other mobile devices such as the iPad and the iPod touch. iOS is based on Apple's Mac OS X, which is used on their laptops and desktops. iPhones make heavy use of third-party apps that are purchased/downloaded from the Apple App Store.

Windows Mobile is Microsoft's OS developed for the smart phone and mobile device market. Like its competitors, Windows Mobile also supports a huge array of apps.

CELL PHONE EVIDENCE

Now that we've looked at how cell phones and networks function, we can look at some of the information they hold that may qualify as evidence. It's important not to focus on one source, as relevant evidence can be found in multiple locations within the handset and the network.

Table 10.1 lists some of the potential evidentiary items found in modern smartphones.

Table 10.1 Potential Smart Phone Evidence

Call History	Text Messages	E-mail
Pictures & Video	Deleted Text Messages	Browser History
Contacts	Location Information GPS	Chat Sessions
Calendar	Voice Memo	Documents

The **Personal Identification Number (PIN)** is used to secure the handset. Three consecutive, unsuccessful attempts to enter the correct PIN will result in the user being locked out. The **Personal Unlock Key (PUK)** will be needed to unlock the SIM after this lockout has occurred. Typically, a PUK can only be supplied by the provider of the SIM card (Barbara, 2010).

You have probably noticed when typing an e-mail or text on your phone that many times the phone will complete words for you. This is called **predictive text.** Predictive text was developed to make texting easier on phones that lacked a full QWERTY keyboard. Those phones use three letters per key, forcing the user to "scroll" through the multiple letter options before selecting one. With predictive texting technology, the device attempts to predict the word most likely intended by the user. These guesses are based on a database dictionary containing thousands of words, names, abbreviations, slang, and so on (Mobile-phone-directory.org, 2009).

What is most interesting, from a forensic perspective is that these systems are capable of learning. Words, abbreviations, slang, and the like entered by the user is assimilated into the database. E-mail addresses and URLs can also be stored. If this database is recovered, it can produce some interesting evidence. For example, pedophiles could have routinely entered common abbreviations for child pornography (CP). A drug trafficker could routinely enter slang or a code word for their product when texting a buyer.

Several companies produce this technology. Some examples are Tegic Communication's, T9 (www.T9.com), Motorola's iTap, and ZiCorp's eZiText (Kessler, 2011).

Call Detail Records

Call detail records (CDR) are normally used by the provider to troubleshoot and improve the networks performance. The CDR is also valuable to examiners. They can show us:

- Date/time the call started and ended.
- Who made the call and who was called.
- How long the call lasted.
- Whether the call was incoming or outgoing.
- The originating and terminating towers.

Although the CDRs can tell you a lot, what they cannot tell you is who actually made the call.

You get what you ask for; therefore it is important to understand the difference between the CDR and the subscriber information. Subscriber information and the call detail records are not the same. Typical subscriber information would include things such as the name, address, and telephone. Other items included with subscriber information are account numbers, e-mail addresses, services, payment mechanisms, and so on.

Every service provider keeps all of these records for a predetermined period of time. The time period is spelled out in their data retention policies.

The retention period is also not uniform across all of the data types. For example, some carriers may keep SMS data for only seven to fourteen days. By contrast, cell sector information could be kept a year or longer. The takeaway here is that you don't have an unlimited amount of time to file the necessary paperwork to ensure that the records you seek won't get purged.

Carriers generally maintain meticulous records of subscribers and their activities for billing and other purposes. This stockpile of information can be enormously helpful during an investigation. These carrier records can tell us the subscriber's name, address, additional phone numbers, Social Security number, and so on. The credit information on file can give investigators billing addresses, credit card numbers, and more.

The **call detail records** describe the specifics of each incoming and outgoing call. These should not be confused with toll records. Toll records refer to land-line information rather than mobile phones. When asking for the call detail records, you must specify a date range. It's a wise practice to pad your request with a day or two on both ends.

The call detail records, when combined with the physical addresses of the towers, can show us the call's origination and termination locations. These records also show the cell sites that were used, the length of the call, the time the call began, the numbers dialed by the target phone, and so on (Jansens & Ayers, 2007).

The billing records do not represent a complete list of the inbound and outbound calls. The call logs will include data that have not yet made it into the billing system.

Information kept by the carriers will likely have a short, predetermined shelf life. Each carrier has some discretion on how these data are preserved and how long they're stored. This is usually described in the company's retention policies. In light of this practice, the legal paperwork should be generated and served sooner rather than later. This will help to ensure that your evidence won't get purged before it can be preserved and collected.

Cell phones can be located (with varying degrees of accuracy) by a few different means. **Triangulation** is one of the better-known methods. In triangulation, the phone's approximate location is determined using its distance from three different towers. The distance is calculated by determining the signal delay from the phone (or handset) to the three towers. A **directional antenna** can also be used for this purpose. Again, the signal delay is used to determine the distance, but this time only two towers are needed since they are able to also determine the direction. Finally, the location can be determined via GPS using latitude and longitude.

Collecting and Handling Cell Phone Evidence

Because cell phone data are not unlike other forms of digital evidence, the fundamental principles in handling digital evidence apply to cell phones as well. Job one when dealing with cell phones is isolating it from the network. Isolating

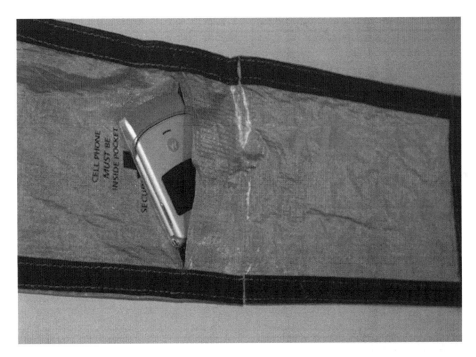

FIGURE 10.2
A Faraday bag and cell phone.

the phone is imperative. Aside from the danger of being remotely wiped (by the suspect or carrier), any inbound calls, messages, or e-mails could overwrite any potential evidence. We can effectively isolate the phone using a Faraday or arson can. A Faraday bag, shown in Figure 10.2, is a special container constructed with conductive material that effectively blocks radio signals. An arson can is really nothing more than a clean, empty paint can. These containers can be found in hardware or home improvement stores.

If the phone is on when you recover it, leave it on. If there will be a significant delay in getting the phone to the lab, then you may want to consider turning it off. This is done to ensure that the battery doesn't completely drain. If it does, you run the risk of locking the phone. If the phone is protected with a PIN, turning the phone off will result in the phone being locked when it's turned back on.

Isolating the phone with the power on creates some concerns regarding the battery life. Remember, while the phone is on it will continually attempt to connect to the network, further draining the battery. A dead battery could also trigger the security function, locking up the phone.

If the phone is off, we can remove the battery as well as remove and initial the SIM card. We'll also want to photograph the phone, front and back. During this process, we'll want to pay particular attention to the identifying numbers underneath the battery (the **IMEI, ESN/MEID**). We'll also want to isolate the phone from the network, just like a powered on phone.

Before conducting a forensic exam, it's important to identify the make and model of the handset you're dealing with. This information can help you get a full understanding of the phone's functions, features, and capabilities. The make and model of the phone can be typically found under the phone's battery. This same information can also be found in the phone's file system.

Like computers, we only want to access or examine the original evidence as an absolute last resort. Ideally, a forensic tool should be used to first acquire the data, giving the examiner a copy to work with. In the end however, a manual examination may be the only alternative. Should this be necessary, you will have to articulate your reasoning behind taking this course of action. Detailed documentation will be very helpful in accounting for your interaction with the device and establishing the integrity of any evidence that was recovered. Documenting a manual examination typically relies heavily on photographs as opposed to the digital evidence itself. In this instance, the examiner painstakingly navigates through the phone, taking photographs of the screens as he or she goes.

Voicemail is another potential source of evidence that shouldn't be overlooked. Typically, in order to access the voicemail, you will need the password-reset code from the carrier. When collecting voicemail evidence, there are a couple of options. The carrier can simply provide you with an access code or they can deliver you a copy of the data itself. This detail should be worked out early on with the provider, especially if you prefer one method or format to another.

At the scene, you should be on the lookout for additional handsets, SIM cards, and the related power and data cables. The power cable will help the lab ensure that the volatile memory is left intact until it can be properly collected and examined. Don't forget, while the phone is on, it will continually seek to connect with the network, rapidly draining the battery.

Subscriber Identity Modules

Subscriber Identity Modules (SIMs) can be valuable evidence all by themselves. They store a vast amount of information and should be collected and analyzed.

The SIM contains a couple of numbers that will be of particular interest. The first is the **International Mobile Subscriber Identity (IMSI)**. The second is the **Integrated Circuit Card Identifier (ICC-ID)**. The IMSI is used to identify the subscriber's account information and services. The ICC-ID is the serial number of the SIM card itself. The SIM can contain:

- Subscriber Identification (IMSI)
- Service Provider
- Card Identity (ICC-ID)

- Language Preferences
- Phone Location When Powered Off
- User Stored Phone Numbers
- Numbers Dialed by the User
- SMS Text Messages (Potentially)
- Deleted SMS Text Messages (Potentially)

The SIM cards contain several individual components including a processor (CPU), RAM, Flash-based non-volatile memory, and a crypto-chip. They are used in all phones but are present in GSM, iDEN, and Blackberry handsets.

A **Personal Identification Number (PIN)** may be in place to protect the SIM data. PINs are four to eight digits in length. As an added layer of security, only three attempts may be made to enter the correct PIN. After the third unsuccessful attempt, the data can only be accessed with an eight-digit Pin Unblocking Key (PUK) along with a new PIN. Attempts to enter the PUK are also limited. After 10 failed attempts, many SIM cards will permanently deny access with a PUK.

Cell Phone Acquisition: Physical and Logical

The data on a cell phone can be acquired in one of two ways: physically or logically. A physical acquisition captures all of the data on a physical piece of storage media. This is a bit-for-bit copy, like the clone of a hard drive. This acquisition method captures the deleted information as well. In contrast, a logical acquisition captures only the files and folders without any of the deleted data. Data can be collected using nonforensic tools such as those used to synchronize or back up the data on the cell phone (Jansen & Ayers, 2007). While this process is similar to the one used to acquire a hard drive, there is one important difference. In this instance no write blocking device is used. The phone must be able to interact with the phone's hardware and software.

A manual examination entails interacting with the device via the keypad or touch screen. Although examining or interacting with the original evidence is never our first choice, sometimes it may be the only option. For example, in cases where time is of the essence, it may be necessary to forgo proper forensic procedures. Those situations may include locating a missing child or preventing an imminent violent act of some sort. In other situations, it may not be possible to even mine the data or extract them in a way that would preserve their integrity. This could happen in cases where forensic tools and techniques hadn't caught up with the latest technology.

CELL PHONE FORENSIC TOOLS

As you might suspect, there are many, many different tools available to forensically examine a phone. These tools can come in the form of hardware or software. One of the realties is that not all of these tools support all cell phones. To further complicate matters, two tools that actually support a given phone may not read and recover the same information.

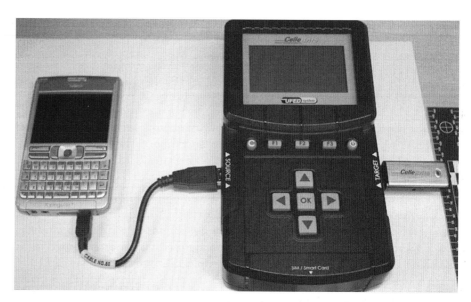

FIGURE 10.3
A Cellebrite UFED.

What follows is a sampling of the available tools for cell phone forensics. A close examination of the function and features shows that no single tool does it all. One glaring difference is the number of phones that are supported. Budget permitting, most labs will have multiple tools available to increase their capabilities. Figure 10.3 shows a Cellebrite UFED device.

BitPim is a robust open-source application that was not built for forensic purposes. BitPim is designed to work with CDMA phones that are produced by several vendors, including LG and Samsung among others. BitPim can recover data such as the phonebook, calendar, wallpapers, ring tones, and file system (http://www.bitpim.org/).

Oxygen Forensic Suite is a forensic program specifically designed for cell phones. It's a tool that supports more than twenty-three hundred devices. It extracts data such as phonebook, SIM card data, contact lists, caller groups, call logs, standard and custom SMS/MMS/e-mail folders, deleted SMS messages, calendars, photos, videos, JAVA applications, and GPS locations (http://www .oxygen-forensic.com/en/).

Paraben Corporation offers several hardware and software products targeted to mobile device forensics. In addition to cell phones, their tools also support GPS devices such as those from Garmin (http://www.paraben.com/handheld-forensics.html).

AccessData's MPE+ supports over thirty-five hundred phones. It's an on-scene, mobile forensic recovery tool that can collect call history, messages, photos, voicemail, videos, calendars, and events. It can analyze and correlate multiple phones and computers using the same interface. (http://accessdata.com/products/computer-forensics/mobile-phone-examiner).

The **Cellebrite UFED** (Universal Forensic Extraction Device) is a stand-alone, self-contained hardware device used to extract Phonebook, images, videos, SMS, MMS, call history, and much more. It supports over twenty-five hundred phones and is designed to extract information on scene. It also has a SIM card reader and cloner. As an interesting aside, Cellebrite devices (the nonforensic version) can be found in many cell phones stores. They're used to transfer a customer's data from one device to another. (http://www.cellebrite.com/forensic-products/forensic-products.html?loc=seg).

EnCase Smartphone Examiner is an EnCase tool designed to review and collect data from smartphones and tablet devices. It collects data from Blackberries, iTune backups, and SD cards. Once the information is collected, it is easily imported into the EnCase Forensic suite for continued investigation (http://www.guidancesoftware.com/encase-smartphone-examiner.htm).

So, what do you do if none of these tools will retrieve the information you're looking for? If that's the case, it's time to consider going "old school" and simply using a still or video camera. Although this would not be the first choice, it's better than coming away empty-handed.

GLOBAL POSITIONING SYSTEMS (GPS)

Like cell phones, **Global Positioning Systems (GPS)** can be a tremendous source of evidence. They can be used to pinpoint the location of suspects as well as the criminal acts themselves (if the device was active and in their possession at the time the crime was committed). They can also be used to show where suspects intended to go. Some GPS units can provide a great deal more evidence, including mobile phone logs, SMS messages, and images. Given these capabilities along with large storage capacities, examining these devices is well worth the time.

The GPS was originally produced for military use but was eventually shared with everyone. There are twenty-seven GPS satellites in the GPS system. Only twenty-four are in use at a time. The remaining three are held in reserve in case one of the primary satellites goes down. A GPS receiver calculates its position through a mathematical process known as trilateration (Brian & Harris, 2011).

Not all GPS units are the same. Some are feature rich, whereas others are pretty basic. We can separate GPS devices into four categories: simple, smart, hybrid, and connected. Simple units are designed to get users from one point to another. Most simple units can store **trackpoints**, waypoints, and **track logs**. Other features may be present depending on the make and model (LeMere, 2011).

Smart units can be broken down into automotive and USB mass storage devices. These units typically have 2GB of storage at a minimum along with an SD card. They provide the same base functionality as the simple systems. In addition, they can play MP3s, view pictures, and save favorite places.

Hybrid GPS units are feature rich and can provide a great deal of evidence. Hybrid devices possess the same features as smart devices plus some. Most notably, these devices provide hands-free access to your mobile phones via Bluetooth. This ability to interact with the cell phone can provide a secondary source of much of the data found on the phone. This would include call logs, an address book, as well as the MAC address of up to ten of the last phones that have connected to the unit. Finally, SMS messages can also be recovered (LeMere, 2011).

A connected unit provides hybrid features and the ability to get real-time information including Google searches and traffic information. These units have GSM radios along with SIM cards. This functionality is subscription based and as such, we may be able to obtain the subscriber information associated with the account.

GPS data can be grouped into two categories: system data and user data. System data will provide us with trackpoints and a track log. Track points are a record of where the unit has been. They are automatically created by the system. Trackpoints can't be altered by the user. By default, the system determines the interval at which they are recorded. Users can however modify this setting, changing the time or distance interval. The **track log** is a comprehensive list of all trackpoints. This list is intended to help users retrace their path (LeMere, 2011).

Waypoints are part of the user-created data. When interpreting a waypoint, you need to keep in mind what they represent. Unlike a trackpoint, waypoints don't always indicate the physical locations where the unit has been. They can be places the user intends to visit. The user can enter these locations based on the address, the actual coordinates, or from a list of Points of Interest (POI) supplied by the GPS unit manufacturer.

GPS devices are similar in many respects to cellular phones and are handled in much the same way. They can have volatile memory that may need to be preserved. When powered on, these units are constantly interacting with the satellites above. This interaction can cause complications from a forensic perspective, potentially causing relevant evidence to be overwritten or compromising its integrity.

GPS devices are cropping up in many different places. Taxi cabs, delivery trucks, and more are frequently being outfitted with GPS units. One such example of a GPS unit assisting investigators is the case of Las Vegas dancer Debbie Flores-Narvaez. The brutal December 2010 murder showed the value of GPS evidence. Police were able to locate her dismembered remains using GPS data from a U-Haul truck. The suspect, Jason "Blu" Griffith, apparently transported her remains in the truck and was unaware that the truck was equipped with GPS. Police obtained the GPS data and used them to retrace Griffith's movements, leading to her body.

Evidence in the case also included text messages. The victim's mother, Elise Narvaez, said that her daughter sent her this text message on December 1, 2010: "In case there is ever an emergency with me, contact Blu Griffith in Vegas. My ex-boyfriend. Not my best friend" (Hartenstein & Sheridan, 2010).

Q&A with Christopher Vance

Christopher Vance is a Digital Forensic Specialist assisting the West Virginia State Police Digital Forensics Unit. In the Q&A here, he shares some of his insights from the trenches.

[Q] What do you see as the biggest forensic challenges when dealing with cell phones?

[A] Vance: The single biggest challenge when dealing with cell phone forensics is that there are thousands of phones, each with different operating systems. There is such a wide variety when dealing with mobile devices it is impossible to be well versed in every single operating structure. It is a constant learning process by trial and error and validation.

[Q] What advice would you give a new examiner wanting to learn more about cell phones?

[A] Vance: There's a lot of training opportunities out there, especially for law enforcement. However, even with the best of trainings, it's absolutely key to get your hands on some devices and try it for yourself.

[Q] How important is continuing education?

[A] Vance: In this field, it's probably the most important thing there is.

[Q] How are you seeing cell phones used in the commission of crimes?

[A] Vance: Depending on the type of case, there's a variety of ways they're being used. However, the biggest pieces of evidence usually trace back to the SMS/MMS messages, stored images, and Call Logs. From drug trafficking, to solicitation, to murder, these always seem to be the biggest key to the case if the evidence exists on the handset.

[Q] Can you talk a little about the general process you follow when conducting an examination?

[A] Vance: The two largest keys are Isolation and Validation. The first step is always to isolate your device from its network and keep it that way until the case is completed. Then using a variety of tools and processes (as there is no "super tool" that works on every device) I will collect the data. After the data are collected, I attempt to validate the data either by using multiple tools, hash values, or even visual validation while checking the data against what the phone is saying.

[Q] What other mobile devices are you seeing brought to the lab? What kind of evidence are you recovering from those?

[A] Vance: The two biggest mobile devices outside of cell phones are iPod Touch devices and Tablets. Seeing as these devices can run the same operating systems as their cell phone counterparts, we can usually pull about the same. In most cases, it's usually chat logs from third-party applications installed on the devices, i.e., Skype, TextNow, Yahoo!, etc.

[Q] From your perspective, what does the future hold for cell phone forensics?

[A] Vance: Hopefully the "dumb-phone" will either die or become assimilated. If the major **smartphone** operating systems can take over the forefront and standardize the market a little, it will make analysts' and engineers' jobs much easier. It's my opinion that one day we'll talk about mobile device operating systems the same way we mention the "big three" of Mac, Windows, and Linux.

[Q] Can you talk a little about the tools you use?

[A] Vance: I use a lot of tools to get the job done. There's not one tool that will hit every phone every time and pull all the data. It just does not exist. In our lab we use the Cellebrite UFED Physical Pro, AccessData's Mobile Phone Examiner+, Paraben Corporations's Device Seizure, viaForensic's viaExtract, LogicCube's CellDek, Flasher Boxes, and a handful of other niche tools that are used from time to time.

[Q] Do you have a couple of "war stories" you can share?

[A] Vance: There have been a couple of cases I've worked where mobile device evidence has proven to be the smoking gun. Recently, in a murder investigation, there were multiple messages on a phone from the suspect to victim not only informing the victim the suspect was planning on murdering her but even saying when and how the crime would take place.

After the crime, the suspect even used the victim's phone to send out messages to other individuals confessing his guilt. In a solicitation case, we had a single iPod Touch, which we found evidence of not just one crime in the chat logs, but several victims of the same crime all by a single individual. I've even had cases where the individuals will store their entire Child Pornography libraries on the memory in their phones.

[Q] Are there misconceptions you would like to shoot down?

[A] Vance: Mainly what we refer to as the "CSI Effect." The job is never as fast or as glamorous as the TV shows make it out to be. In many cases, our job is sometimes as much an art as a science. When dealing with mobile devices, the memory that we have to analyze is so small and dynamic that it is much harder for us to recover deleted data in many cases. However, it's not impossible.

[Q] How would you compare and contrast the evidence you're finding on phones to that which is typically found on computers?

[A] Vance: The data actually play hand in hand. There have been many cases where we can see a chat log start on a computer and then carry over to a mobile device. A lot of times we still see the same types of data, mainly communications and user generated media. It is a lot easier to recover deleted information from a computer than it is a cell phone, however.

[Q] How big a role has geolocation data played in your investigations?

[A] Vance: There are so many issues with geolocation data that they haven't played a huge role to date. There have been investigations where we have found images with GPS data embedded to assist the investigators. The GPS "tracking" debates[1] of earlier this year were by and large unnecessary. While the GPS data can assist a case, it would take serious validation to make sure that the records you had were exactly what you were looking for. Just because you have geolocation points is not a 100 percent indicator your individual is in that exact point and location.

[Q] Anything else you would like to add?

[A] Vance: Cell Phone or Mobile Forensics is becoming its own specialization within the digital forensics field. I can easily see that this new wave of technology will one day replace our older machines in the same way the "Cloud" threatens to do.

---

[1] Researchers discovered that the iPhone or 3G iPad—anything with 3G data access—are logging location data to a file called consolidated.db with latitude and longitude coordinates and a timestamp.

SUMMARY

Our mobile technology allows us to check e-mail, browse the Internet, plot out a road trip, and instantly access other people in our lives. Many people can't remember when or even imagine how they made it through the day without their smartphone. The advent of this technology has created both sources of evidence and challenges for forensic examiners.

In Chapter 10, we covered a wide range of topics on mobile devices, particularly cellular phones and GPS units. Cell networks are comprised of several components including base stations, Mobile Switching Centers, Visitor Location Registers, and others. There are different types of cell networks, each with their own unique characteristics. Code Division Multiple Access (CDMA), Global System for Mobile Communications (GSM), and Integrated Digitally Enhanced Network (iDEN) are the most common.

Like computers, there is more than one operating system used by cell phones. Windows Mobile, iOS, Android, and Symbian were covered in Chapter 10. Cell phones can contain vast amounts of digital evidence including e-mail, call logs, text messages, images, videos, and more.

Records maintained by the carrier can also be valuable during an investigation particularly the Call Detail Records. These records can provide us with dates, times, phone numbers, as well as the originating and terminating towers used during a call. The tower information can help us determine the general vicinity in which the phone has been used.

How cell phone evidence is collected and preserved is critically important. The first priority in dealing with any mobile device is to isolate it from the network. A powered on device that isn't isolated is a major problem. In this state, evidence can be changed, overwritten, or destroyed. Keep in mind that certain cell phones can be wiped remotely by the suspect or the carrier. Isolating a cell phone can be done using a Faraday bag or an arson can. While Subscriber Identity Modules or SIM cards contain data worth examining, it's important to remember that not all phones will have them.

GPS or Global Positioning Systems are in wide use today and function as another source of digital evidence. There are different types of GPS units including simple, smart, hybrid, and connected. Waypoints, trackpoints, and track logs are some of the data recorded by the units that we can use. These artifacts can tell us where the unit has been and where a user intended to go.

References

Barbara, J. J. (2010, October 17). *Understanding the World of Cellular Telephones: Part 1*. Retrieved November 13, 2011, from Forensicmag.com: http://www.forensicmag.com/article/understanding-world-cellular-telephones-part-1?page=0,1

Barbara, J. J. (n.d.). *SIM Forensics: Part 1*. Retrieved September 19, 2011, from: http://www.forensicmag.com/article/sim-forensics-part-1

Barbara, J. J. (n.d.). *Sim Forensics: Part 2*. Retrieved September 19, 2011, from: http://www.forensicmag .com/article/sim-forensics-part-2

Barbara, J. J. (n.d.). *SIM Forensics: Part 3*. Retrieved September 18, 2011, from: http://www.forensicmag .com/article/sim-forensics-part-3

Barbara, J. J. (n.d.). *Understanding the World of Cellular Telephones: Part 1*. Retrieved September 21, 2011, from: http://www.forensicmag.com/article/understanding-world-cellular-telephones-part-1

Barbara, J. J. (n.d.). *Understanding the World of Cellular Telephones: Part 2*. Retrieved September 21, 2011, from: http://www.forensicmag.com/article/understanding-world-cellular-telephones-part-2

Barbara, J. J. (n.d.). *Understanding The World of Cellular Telephones: Part 3*. Retrieved September 21, 2011, from: http://www.forensicmag.com/article/understanding-world-cellular-telephones-part-3

BitPim. (n.d.). *BitPim*. Retrieved September 22, 2011, from: http://www.bitpim.org/

Brian, M., & Harris, T. (n.d.). *How GPS Receivers Work*. Retrieved September 14, 2011, from: http:// electronics.howstuffworks.com/gadgets/travel/gps.htm

Casey, E. (2009). *Handbook of Digital Forensics and Investigation*. Burlington, MA: Academic Press.

Casey, E. (2011). *Digital Evidence and Computer Crime: Forensic Science, Computers and the Internet*. Waltham, MA: Academic Press.

Hartenstein, M., & Sheridan, M. (2010, December 21). *Missing Vegas Showgirl Debbie Flores-Narvaez was Pregnant, Beaten by her ex, According to Police*. Retrieved September 25, 2011, from: http://articles .nydailynews.com/2010-12-21/news/27085062_1_license-plates-cell-phone-police

Hoog, A. (2010, April 30). *An Introduction to Android Forensics*. Retrieved September 2011, 2011, from: http://www.dfinews.com/article/introduction-android-forensics?page=0,0

Hoog, A. (2011). *Android forensics: Investigation, Analysis and Mobile Security for Google Android*. Waltham, MA: Elsevier.

Jansen, W., & Ayers, R. (2007). *Guidelines on Cell Phone Forensics*. Gaithersburg, TN: National Institute of Standards and Technology.

Kessler, G. C. (2011, June). *Cell Phone Analysis: Technology, Tools, and Processes*. Retrieved September 12, 2011, from: http://www.garykessler.net/presentations/CellPhone_201106_ICAC-sanitized.pdf

LeMere, B. (n.d.). *Enhancing Investigations with GPS Evidence*. Retrieved September 15, 2011, from: http://www.forensicmag.com/article/enhancing-investigations-gps-evidence

LeMere, B. (2011, April 25). *Enhancing Investigations with GPS Evidence*. Retrieved September 15, 2011, from: http://www.forensicmag.com/article/enhancing-investigations-gps-evidence

Mobile-phone-directory.org. (n.d.). *Predictive Text Input*. Retrieved September 17, 2011, from: http:// www.mobile-phone-directory.org/Glossary/P/Predictive_Text_Input.html

Morrissey, S. (2010). *iOS forensic analysis: for iPhone, iPad, and iPod Touch*. New York: Apress.

Open Handset Alliance. (2007, November). *FAQ*. Retrieved September 19, 2011, from: http://www .openhandsetalliance.com/oha_faq.html

Shachtman, N. (2006, May 3). *Fighting Crime With Cellphones' Clues*. Retrieved September 19, 2011, from: http://www.nytimes.com/2006/05/03/technology/techspecial3/03cops.html

CHAPTER 11

Looking Ahead: Challenges and Concerns

Information in This Chapter:

- Standards and Controls
- Cloud Forensics
- Solid State Drives
- Speed of Change

INTRODUCTION

Digital forensics is still in its infancy. It is very much a work in progress given its relatively short existence as well as the rapid rate of technological change. This work in progress status is likely to carry on for quite some time. This situation results in many challenges and controversies that the legal and forensic communities must wrestle with. The challenges are many. One such challenge is wrestling with emerging and potentially "game changing" technology. Another is reaching a consensus with the forensic science community at large, particularly when it comes to established best practices.

Digital forensics is causing a massive collision if you will, between two seemingly unyielding forces: the legal system and forensic communities that operate at a relatively slow and deliberate pace versus the blinding speed of technology. Neither is built for speed. There are good reasons for that. The stakes are far too high to admit forensic evidence that hasn't been proven reliable. This proven reliability takes time and can't be achieved over night.

Two technologies, cloud computing and solid state hard drives, present "game changing" challenges. As it stands, digital evidence in either of these environments could very well be unrecoverable for either technical or legal reasons (or both). These technologies are in use today and represent a problem to which there is no easy answer. How all of these challenges will be met has yet to be seen.

STANDARDS AND CONTROLS

Standards and controls are a fundamental part of scientific analysis, including forensic science. A **standard** is "a prepared sample that has known properties that is used as a control during forensic analyses" (Barbara, 2007).

A **control** is defined as "a test performed in parallel with experimental samples that is designed to demonstrate that a procedure is working correctly and the results are valid" (Barbara, 2007). In essence, a control is simply a sample that provides a known result.

That may hold true for serology, chemistry, toxicology, and the like, but its relevance to digital forensics is a matter of dispute. More traditional forensic scientists are taking the stance that standards and controls are essential for all forensic disciplines, including digital and multimedia forensics. One of the major digital forensic bodies, the Scientific Working Group on Digital Evidence (SWGDE), is taking the exact opposite position. The controversy began with an article on Forensicmag.com in 2007 by John Barbara. In the article, Barbara raised the issue of standards and controls in digital forensics. He is a Crime Laboratory Analyst Supervisor with the Florida Department of Law Enforcement (FDLE). He is also an ASCLD/LAB inspector and has been since 1993. In the article he laid out his case citing the mandatory use of standards and controls in every other forensic discipline. He argued that the use of standards and controls is necessary to prove that the tests were performed in a scientific manner and that quality assurance measures were followed.

In the end, closely following these established scientific practices ensures that any results gained are accurate, reliable, and repeatable. He further argued that without the use of standards and controls, it would be "extremely difficult or impossible to scientifically assess the validity of the results obtained from the analysis of the physical evidence" (Barbara, 2007). Finally, he raised the admissibility standards required by the *Daubert* case.

In *Daubert*, the court said that when considering the admissibility of any scientific evidence, the focus should be on the principles and methodology and not on the conclusions that they generate.

The Scientific Working Group on Digital Evidence (SWGDE) doesn't agree. Their position is that standards are being used in digital forensics, but controls are "not applicable in the computer forensics sub-discipline" (Scientific Working Group on Digital Evidence, 2008).

SWGDE's position centers on false positives. They say that false positives do not exist in computer forensics. Tools and processes may miss evidence, but they will never find evidence that doesn't exist. The main objective of any digital forensic examination, says SWGDE, is to find data relating to criminal activity that already exists. Therefore, there is no real value to the analysis or the results.

They conclude by saying that "validation, data integrity (through hashing), and performance verification" are a more appropriate solution than the traditional use of standards and controls (Scientific Working Group on Digital Evidence, 2008).

SWGDE agrees, saying "New technology, typically proprietary in nature, emerges daily. As these new technologies emerge, new solutions and techniques are needed to understand and examine evidence. Comprehensive understanding and validated techniques need to move swiftly from the research community to the examiner community" (Scientific Working Group on Digital Evidence, 2008).

CLOUD FORENSICS (FINDING/IDENTIFYING POTENTIAL EVIDENCE STORED IN THE CLOUD)

Cloud computing is a hot topic in information technology. The many benefits it brings are undeniable and not lost on organizations across the globe. As such, it's being widely adopted. The cloud, however, is a double-edged sword, and a sharp one at that. With its many benefits come major challenges from both forensic and legal perspectives.

What Is Cloud Computing?

There are many definitions of **cloud computing** from which to choose. Tech-Target describes cloud computing as "a general term for anything that involves delivering hosted services over the Internet" (TechTarget, 2007). These hosted services generally fall into a few different categories including:

- Infrastructure as a Service (IaaS).
- Software as a Service (SaaS).
- Platform as a Service (Paas).

The term "cloud computing" is derived from the "cloud" symbol that is normally used in network diagrams to represent the Internet.

The National Institute of Standards and Technology (NIST) provides a more complex definition. They define the cloud this way: "Cloud computing is a model for enabling ubiquitous, convenient, on-demand network access to a shared pool of configurable computing resources (e.g., networks, servers, storage, applications, and services) that can be rapidly provisioned and released with minimal management effort or service provider interaction" (Mell & Grance, 2011).

Not all clouds are the same. There are **private clouds** and public clouds. **Public clouds** sell services on the open market. Technology behemoths such as Microsoft (Azure), Amazon (Amazon Web Services), Rackspace, and Google are just some of the major players in the cloud market. These **Cloud Service Providers,** or **CSPs,** can have data centers scattered around the world.

The cloud model relies heavily on virtualization and redundancy. TechTarget defines virtualization this way: "**Virtualization** is the creation of a virtual (rather than actual) version of something, such as an operating system, a server, a storage device or network resources" (TechTarget, 2000).

The Benefits of the Cloud

Recognizing the many benefits of the cloud, companies and other organizations are flocking there in droves. They are seeking both the convenience and cost savings this computing model offers. The ability to essentially "dial-up" computing resources as needed is hard not to like. With the cloud, an organization's infrastructure can expand and contract as needed. From a cost perspective, this approach can save a significant amount of money. Companies can save on much of the initial investment for network hardware and software.

Having the data or services replicated in more than one data center provides redundancy. The redundant nature of the cloud ensures that the user's files and/or applications are safe and available whenever they need them. Should one center or its connectivity go down, the second should be able to respond.

Cloud Forensics and Legal Concerns

The cloud may be a dream come true for those in business and information technology, but it represents a nightmare for those who deal with digital evidence. The primary challenges are twofold, one technical and the other legal. Technically, the cloud is without question not a forensically friendly environment, especially when compared to the relatively cozy confines of magnetic drives. Pulling deleted data from traditional drives has long been a staple of digital forensics. The cloud will likely be putting that to an end. Deleted files on a magnetic drive remain on the disk until they are overwritten. In the cloud, when a file is deleted the mapping is removed immediately, usually within a matter of seconds. This means that there is no remote access to the deleted data. As is the case with magnetic drives, that space is now available and will likely be overwritten in the cloud (Ruan, Carthy, Kechadi, & Crosbie, 2011).

There is an alarming lack of established forensic tools and procedures for acquiring and analyzing digital evidence in the cloud. Current tools and methodologies are largely ineffective in this environment. Much more research needs to be done.

> **ALERT!**
>
> **Cloud Persistence—Dropbox**
> As many challenges as cloud functionality presents, in certain instances it can work in our favor. For example, Dropbox saves all deleted files (by default) for thirty days.
>
> Dropbox's "Pack-Rat" service can keep data indefinitely (with the Pack-Rat add on). Granted, you will need a subpoena or search warrant to get to it, but the fact that it could be available is nice to know (Dropbox, 2011).

Legally, dealing with multiple jurisdictions can significantly frustrate efforts to get to the relevant data in the first place. As we've seen, CSPs can have their data centers located almost anywhere in the world. Legal requirements and procedures can vary, and vary considerably from country to country, and from jurisdiction to jurisdiction. This problem compounds exponentially if the data have crossed international boundaries.

Regulation could assist in mitigating this issue. It could help by mandating that CSPs operate in such a way that facilitates the preservation and recovery of potentially relevant data. Service Level Agreements, or SLAs, can also make a difference. An SLA is a written agreement between a customer and a provider. The SLA spells out in great detail what support and services the customer will get from the provider. As part of that agreement, the customer can require certain assurances regarding information security and how digital evidence will be preserved and collected should that ever become necessary. From a customer's perspective, this is an important detail that shouldn't be overlooked. This is particularly true in organizations where litigation is likely. Having this arrangement in place can be very beneficial to the forensic examiner, especially as opposed to starting from scratch with no protocols, procedures, or relationships in place.

SOLID STATE DRIVES (SSD)

Magnetic drives have been a mainstay in personal computers for years. Forensically, they afford examiners the ability to recover significant amounts of user-deleted data. Those days, it appears, may very well be coming to an end. These traditional magnetic drives are being replaced more and more. Welcome to the era of solid state hard drives (SSD).

How Solid State Drives Store Data

Traditional magnetic drives have multiple moving parts including the platters and the actuator arm (that moves the read/write head). As the name implies, solid state drives do not. SSDs are somewhat similar to RAM and USB thumb drives, storing data in tiny transistors. Unlike RAM, SSDs are nonvolatile and can store data even without power. In order to keep the charge over long periods of time, without power, SSD transistors employ an additional gate (called a floating gate), which is used to contain the charge (Bell & Boddington, 2010).

If you recall from Chapter 2, magnetic drives break the storage space up into smaller units. These units include sectors, clusters, and tracks. SSDs also separate the storage space into smaller units. The base units are called blocks and are normally 512 KB in size. Blocks are then subdivided into even smaller units called pages. Each page is typically 4 KB in size.

Wear is a concern with SSDs. Each block can only withstand a certain number of writes. Some estimates put that number somewhere between one thousand and ten thousand times. Given this limitation, you would want the drive to avoid writing to the same block over and over. Writing to the same space repeatedly will cause it to wear out faster than others. Manufacturers solved the issue by instituting a **wear leveling** process performed by the SSD.

MORE ADVANCED

File Translation Layer

On a solid state drive, the computer thinks the data are stored in one location, while in reality they are physically located in another. An SSD drive uses a File Translation Layer to ensure that the computer isn't writing to the same block over and over. If the SSD detects this is occurring, it will "translate" the new writes to a less used location (Bell & Boddington, 2010).

Magnetic drives have the ability to instantly overwrite data to any sector that's labeled as unallocated. SSDs do not. Each transistor must be "reset" (erased) before it can be reused. This reset process slows down the drive. To speed things up, SSD manufacturers have configured the drive's controller to automatically reset unused portions of the drive. This process is known as **Garbage Collection.**

The Problem: Taking out the Trash

Solid state drives have a mind of their own. Many drives initiate the Garbage Collection routine completely on their own, without any prompting by the computer at all.

This is both problematic and troubling from the perspective of the forensic analyst. First, verifying the integrity of the evidence becomes extremely difficult and jeopardizes its admissibility in court. Second, there is the automated destruction of potentially relevant data on the drive. If the Garbage Collection routine is run during or after its acquisition, validation becomes exponentially more difficult because the hash values won't match.

Today, we routinely use cryptographic hashing algorithms, such as MD5 or SHA1, to take the "digital finger print" or "digital DNA" of a hard drive. We can then retake the "fingerprint" of our clone at any time and compare it with the "fingerprint" of the original. They should match exactly, verifying the integrity of the evidence (Bell & Boddington, 2010).

SPEED OF CHANGE

You may have noticed that the speed of technological change is a recurring theme throughout this book. Its impact is truly significant and felt across both the digital forensics and legal communities. It also impacts the organizations that rely on the results such as law enforcement and private companies. Take case backlogs, for example. In most if not all laboratories there is a significant backlog of cases including those involving digital evidence. Change contributes to this backlog by slowing down the examination process. Take an updated application such as a chat client. There can be major differences in where and how the software stores the artifacts examiners need to locate and analyze. Artifacts that may have been written to the registry in a previous version are now held exclusively in RAM and disappear when the machine is powered down.

Examiners presented with this situation will have to attempt to find a proven solution from others in the digital forensics community. Failing that, the examiner may have to conduct the research on their own and validate the results. This takes time. Message boards (such as the one for HTCIA members) and e-mail lists are worth their weight in gold in these circumstances. They provide a ready channel for communication and problem solving.

ADDITIONAL RESOURCES

Twitter

Twitter can be a great resource for digital forensic professionals. It can alert you to new techniques, research articles, court decisions, news, and more. There are many individuals and companies that share a great deal of news and information pertaining directly to digital forensics. Today we are bombarded with information, some good and some bad. Following well known, established entities on Twitter can help reduce the "noise" and help keep you current. This is one tool that can help you deal with the speed of change. These are just a sampling of the people and companies worth following.

Digital Forensics

Vendors/Organizations	Individuals
@AccessDataGroup	@robtlee
@EnCase	@jtrajewski
@sansforensics	@girlunallocated
@DFMag	@keydet89
@HTCIA	@codeslack
@MFITraining	@4n6woman
@cellebrite USA	@AppleExaminer
@syngress	@chadtilbury
	@hal_pomeranz
	@4cast
	@CyberCrime101

(Continued)

(Continued)

Electronic Discovery

Vendors/Organizations	Individuals
@DiscoverTERIS	@sharonnelsonesq
@EDDUpdate	@RalphLosey
@e_discoverynews@KrollOntrack	@EUdiscovery@InfoGovernance
@Clearwell	@ComplexD
@PosseList	

SUMMARY

Digital forensics faces many tests on the road ahead. The blinding speed of technology, new game-changing technologies such as cloud computing and solid state hard drives, and disagreements with established forensic disciplines, just to name a few. The constant, relenting pace of technology hits the DF community hard as it fights to keep pace. The speed of change affects the legal system as well. The system itself is not "built for speed" in general and certainly not for the speed of technology. The end result is that in certain situations, previously tried-and-tested tools and protocols will be ineffective. The research, development, and testing needed to solve the problem takes time.

Delivering services over the Web, cloud computing's bread and butter, represents a major shift away from the computing model that the world has grown accustomed to. Remote applications, hardware, platforms, and infrastructure have a great many benefits; reduced costs and elasticity are just two. Behind the scenes, the cloud relies heavily on virtualization and redundancy. The massive data centers used to deliver public cloud services are likely to be widely dispersed, residing in multiple states or even different countries. Meeting the legal requirements to gain access to this data can take an astronomical amount of time. It's entirely possible that by the time the legal burden is met, the evidence in question may no longer exist.

Solid state hard drives are another game-changing technology that must be addressed. These devices may serve the same function as our familiar magnetic drives, but they certainly don't act like them. The storage method they use, tiny charged transistors, must be "reset" before being written to. This process slows down the drive, impacting performance. To mitigate the slowdown, drive makers have built in a process known as Garbage Collection. This process begins this reset process in only minutes. This procedure destroys data on the drive in such a way that current tools and techniques cannot recover it.

Digital evidence and its associated forensic processes are sometimes radically different from other, established disciplines. Bedrock forensic practices such as the use of standards and controls are found to be meaningless to some in the digital forensics community. Those opposed say that unlike serology and toxicology, it simply isn't possible to get a false positive result from a digital forensic examination. The tool, they say, may miss some evidence, but it will never find evidence that wasn't already there.

These are just a few of the significant challenges faced by front-line practitioners. There is much work to be done if these challenges will be met.

References

Bell, Graeme B., Boddington, Richard (December 2010). *Solid State Drives: The Beginning of the End for Current Practice in Digital Forensic Recovery?* Journal of Digital Forensics, Security and Law.

Mell, P., & Grance, T. (2011, January). *The NIST Definition of Cloud Computing.* Retrieved October 9, 2011, from: http://csrc.nist.gov/publications/drafts/800-145/Draft-SP-800-145_cloud-definition.pdf

Microsoft Corporation. (n.d.). *IPv6.* Retrieved September 17, 2011, from: http://technet.microsoft.com/en-us/network/bb530961.aspx

Ruan, K., Baggili, I., Carthy, J., & Kechadi, T. (n.d.). *Survey on Cloud Forensics and Critical Criteria for Cloud Forensic Capability: A Preliminary Analysis.* Dublin, Ireland: University College Dublin.

Ruan, K., Carthy, J., Kechadi, T., & Crosbie, M. (2011). *Cloud Forensics: An Overview.* Dublin, Ireland: IBM Ireland Ltd.

TechTarget. (2007, December). *Cloud Computing.* Retrieved October 11, 2011, from: http://searchcloudcomputing.techtarget.com/definition/cloud-computing

Index

Page numbers in *italics* indicate figures and tables